ENDORSEN

Marty Akins is an extraordinary man,
remarkably accomplished in a number of ways.
Very few people reach such pinnacles of success
on the football field, in the courtroom and,
more importantly, as a citizen, and as a family member.
His book reveals something vital about being human and
having a relationship with God. Marty's beautiful experience
was transformative to him and coming from Marty, that means
a lot. The book is an inspirational story of a man who is so
accomplished that we might expect him to be self-satisfied
or even jaded with life. Instead, Marty is overwhelmed,
as he is touched by God.

ALFREDO A. SADUN, MD, PHD
Thornton Professor
and Vice-Chair, Ophthalmology, UCLA

Believe in Miracles will strengthen your trust and faith that God is Alive and Well. Hunting and the outdoors has always brought us closer to nature and God. This compelling true story about a bow hunt and a miracle from God is a MUST READ for everyone. This powerful book is one for the ages.

GLENN HALLE
Safari Club International, Dallas Safari Club

This is a book to be read and savored.
A gripping story of one man's personal miracle from God.
It offers us all a great reassurance that God is Alive and Well.
Believe in Miracles will change your life.
It is an absolute MUST READ for everyone.

SCOTT FRANKLIN SPEARS
Attorney at Law, Austin, Texas

Believe in Miracles is a chilling account of God's presence.
The book shows the value in trusting in the Lord with all our hearts as mentioned in Proverbs.

QUAN COSBY
Professional Athlete, Austin, Texas

Believe in Miracles is a great testament that our Lord is Alive and Well. He is active in our lives and in our obedience, and in this book we can clearly see it.
You will enjoy this personal account of God's presence.

COREY MASON
Dallas Safari Club, Executive Director
Certified Wildlife Biologist

This book needs to be read and re-read.
Believe in Miracles is an amazing true story,
written by an incredibly accomplished man who was touched
by the grace of God when he least expected it.
This is yet another example that God is ever present in our
lives, and during these especially trying times our faith should
continue to grow stronger.

JUAN D. ARENAS, MD
Transplant Surgeon
Hollywood, Florida

BELIEVE

in

MIRACLES

*An inspirational and gripping true story that brings
one man face to face with the awesome power of God.*

MARTY AKINS

Believe in Miracles

Trilogy Christian Publishers
A Wholly Owned Subsidary of Trinity Broadcasting Network
2442 Michelle Drive, Tustin, CA 92780

Cover design by: Akins & Jackson

For information about special discounts for bulk purchases, please contact Trilogy Christian Publishing.

Manufactured in the United States of America
10 9 8 7 6 5 4 3 2 1
Library of Congress Cataloging-in-Publication Data is available.

ISBN: 978-1-63769-572-2
E-ISBN: 978-1-63769-573-9

DISCLAIMER

This story is true, but any reference to names, characters, and places are either the product of the author's imagination or are used fictitiously. Any reference to real locales, businesses, organizations, and resemblance to actual persons, living or dead, is entirely coincidental.

DEDICATION

Dedicated to God.

Dedicated to my amazing, wonderful family.
To my wife, Pamela, my daughters, Tara and Angela;
my grandkids, Vivienne, Cinco, Azalea, and Enzo;
my sons-in-law, Sergio and French;
my mother and father, Dorothy Virginia Schultz Akins and Robert Ray
Akins. I love all of you. Thanks to each of you for always being there for me.

Recognition: to my great friend and brother, Dale Jackson,
who tirelessly assisted and helped me edit and put this book together.
It was a labor of love and a mission from God.
You're the absolute greatest. Thank you for all you have done.

———————

"Nothing is impossible if you believe it."
MARTY AKINS

"I believe we all pray to the same God."
MARTY AKINS

TABLE OF CONTENTS

Disclaimer vii
Dedication ix

Prologue 13
Chapter One 15
Chapter Two 25
Chapter Three 33
Chapter Four 45
Chapter Five 59
Chapter Six 69
Chapter Seven 77
Chapter Eight 83
Chapter Nine 95
Chapter Ten 107
Chapter Eleven 117
Chapter Twelve 129
Chapter Thirteen 141
Chapter Fourteen 153
Chapter Fifteen 163
Chapter Sixteen 169
Chapter Seventeen 181
Chapter Eighteen 191
Chapter Nineteen 201
Chapter Twenty 213

Chapter Twenty-One 219

Chapter Twenty-Two. 231

Chapter Twenty-Three 241

Chapter Twenty-Four 251

Chapter Twenty-Five 263

Chapter Twenty-Six 271

Chapter Twenty-Seven. 283

PROLOGUE

Four things I learned growing up in the Akins family—

- Believe in God.
- Never let anything go unresolved.
- Do your very best.
- Never quit.

My father, Robert Ray Akins, joined the United States Marine Corps right out of high school. He was a teenager in the 1st Marine Division when they dropped the ramp on the amphibious landing craft he was in, and he waded ashore with thousands of other young boys directly into the face of enemy machine gun fire.

That was day one in what was to become the most horrific battle of the Pacific theater in World War II—the Battle of Okinawa. It was an eighty-one-day-long nightmare that claimed the lives of 160,000 American and Japanese soldiers and countless innocent Okinawans caught in the middle of it all.

My mother, Dorothy Virginia Schultz Akins, among her other accomplishments, was a stalwart Sunday school teacher and the religious beacon for our family. While Pop was determined through hard work and strict discipline to prepare us for life here on earth, my mother, with her longer range spiritual vision and her love of God, worked hard to prepare us for the afterlife in heaven.

Of the two, I'm not sure who was the most unyielding, but their dedication was equally steadfast and resolute. For a tough, headstrong young boy like I was growing up, the strict guidelines under which I was raised was a burden almost too heavy to bear. But, like my father before me, it was never in my nature to do anything halfway. Giving 100 percent and striving for perfection was in my DNA. I was never sure if that trait was a blessing or a curse, but it did end up playing an important part in what I am about to tell you.

CHAPTER ONE

This story is true. It changed my life. It may change your life too. This story is about a miracle—an intervention by God.

My life has been filled with highs and a few lows. I have had mostly favorable thoughts, worked hard, and had good luck. I have had an abundance of fulfilled dreams, encouraging words, great successes, and only a handful of failures. Whatever I have done, I have given it my all—my whole body and mind, my entire spirit and soul.

I believe we awaken each morning with choices. We can choose to be happy or sad, friendly or a bully, loving or mean, a helper or a user, to be positive or negative. I have tried each day to be a happy, friendly, loving person with positive thoughts.

Starting as a young boy, I was trained to prepare, practice, play, and compete like there was no tomorrow. I was instructed that making mistakes was the difference between winning and losing. I was taught there was nothing I couldn't tackle or handle. And with a strong, tough mind, I could direct and control everything in my life.

My father, the World War II Marine and a legendary head football coach, was my hero. He was the leading force in my life. He demanded positive thinking, common sense, and good values.

His words resonate in my mind every day.

"Do it right, or don't do it at all. Do your very best and never quit. What you think and what you believe is who you are."

I learned from him that I had to be mentally and physically tough, supremely confident, and, above all else, to walk with God.

"All of these things are the keys to being successful and having a great life," he told me.

Those many years of strict discipline, hard work, dedication, and sacrifice under my father's watchful eye were how I was raised. And whether in a classroom, on a football field, litigating lawsuits in a courtroom, or doing anything in life, I have always endeavored to be the very best at everything I did.

My father, my best friend, died on December 26, 2017. I will never forget the strict discipline, daily encouragement, and love my father gave me. *Coach Robert Ray Akins, you made me who I am today. You are the greatest father of all time.*

My mother, Dorothy Virginia Schultz Akins, a dedicated junior high school teacher and inspirational Sunday school teacher, advocated reading a new book weekly. She believed in completing crossword puzzles, expanding the mind, being kind and generous, doing good deeds, loving your family, and reading the Bible with a daily dose of prayer as the perfect recipe for having a successful life.

She is the reason I grew up striving to read more books and learn new things. Her influence drove me to try to be a kind and morally good person. She enlisted me as a church altar boy, encouraged me as a Boy Scout, and guided me as a member of the children's choir in church.

Thank you for being a wonderful, loving, dedicated mother. You are the best.

As much as I have always tried to live up to the expectations of my parents, to be the very best at whatever I did and to never quit, my mother, in her infinite wisdom, must have known I would need a way to deal with those times I felt like I had failed. And to this day, every time I feel like I have fallen short, I go back to those Bible verses she gave me to read.

"I can do all things through Christ
who strengthens me."

PHILIPPIANS 4:13

"The Lord upholds all who fall."

PSALM 145:14

"Trust in the Lord with all your heart."

PROVERBS 3:5

"For all have sinned and fall short
of the glory of God."

ROMANS 3:23

I learned that falling short isn't the problem—we are all going to stumble at some point in our lives. The challenge is to do our very best and never quit. And it's a blessing to know that God is always waiting for us with open arms when we do.

My parents constantly reminded me: "Life is short, and you have a lot of things to do."

Growing up, deep down in my gut, I knew my mother and father had lofty goals and dreamed big dreams for me. They consistently molded me and guided me, giving me the motivation to excel as a student, an athlete, and a trial lawyer—my father with his firm hand, my mother with her gentle touch.

My friends say I'm lucky. My University of Texas football coach, the legendary Darrell K. Royal, put it this way.

"All people are created equal, but some people just work harder than others. The harder you work, the luckier you become."

I agreed with him and strived to outwork my competitors, a discipline that has followed me throughout my life. With hard work, I have found there are no limits.

Coach Royal was a motivator, and his words became forever etched into my memory.

"The more confident you are in yourself, the more confident people around you will become," he told me. And then he added, "You can never lose if you never quit. The bigger your dreams, the greater your success. If you choose to be the greatest, you will be the greatest. Nothing is impossible if you do it."

During my college days, Coach Royal and I were together almost every day from the summer of 1972 until the spring of 1976. As a coach and his All-American quarterback, we dreamed, talked, and lived football daily. During the off-season, we played a lot of golf together but mostly talked football. We stayed great friends until his death on November 7, 2012. I will never forget the inspirational talks and fatherly advice Coach Darrell K. Royal gave me. I loved the man.

I cannot say my life has been perfect. Everyone faces hurdles or stumbling blocks along life's journey. I admit I have experienced a few bumps in the road, but nothing I couldn't fix or handle. Early on, I learned at a young age there are really never any do-overs or second chances in life. Therefore, get it right the first time. Mistakes are not acceptable.

Luckily, I can state, life has been good.

I have been married for forty-three years to my beautiful wife and soul mate, Pam. We have two wonderful daughters and four terrific grandchildren that light up our lives.

Thus far, bad days on earth have been few and far between. Using a football analogy, I can report I have won a tremendous number of games and scored a lot of touchdowns in my life. Only on a few rare occasions have I thrown an interception or fumbled, producing a mental hurdle for me to get over.

Doctors routinely diagnose psychological or behavioral problems in people with distinctive mental sufferings such as anxiety, depression, stress, anger, and frustration. I presume all of us might possibly fit into one or more of these diagnoses at some point in our lives. I experienced a stretch of anxiety, stress, and depression when my father died. But because of my strict upbringing, my good spiritual foundation, and my strong belief in God, I was able to overcome any mental suffering I might have had in the past.

I can state unequivocally; God has been in my life from the very beginning.

I recall praying to God when I was five years old. Through my parents, I learned it was important and necessary to find time each day to have a personal relationship with God. Normally, I located a quiet place and spoke to God like He was sitting next to me. Usually, I would begin my prayers by saying the Lord's Prayer or the Psalm 23, or the Apostles' Creed. Then, I would thank God for my many blessings and good fortune. I consistently repeated my devotion to Jesus Christ as my Lord and Savior. And lastly, I talked to God about forgiving me of my sins, strengthening my deep Christian faith, my hopes and dreams for a better world, and how much I appreciated His love.

Looking back through the years, I believed praying to God was primarily for thanking Him, praising Him, and exalting Him. I did ask God to help me with my mental suffering when my father died. And I had routinely asked God to keep me and my family safe and in good health. But I never asked God to help me win something, achieve something, or attain something. In other words, I never asked God to help me win a football game, or make All-American, or win a lawsuit, or make enough money to buy a ranch, or help me with my drawings and paintings. I never thought God got involved in minor things like that. I believed God left those kinds of things to us and was busy doing bigger and better things.

I believed in thinking out loud, having positive self-talks where I kept telling myself what I needed to do to be successful over and over until I believed it and did it. This made me strong and happy.

Epictetus, the Greek philosopher, said it best, "It's not what happens to you, but how you react to it that matters."

Life really does test our faith on a daily basis. It's crazy how our faith in God goes up and down like a roller coaster. When our lives are filled with success and ease, God is great, and we praise Him. When we hit the wall, crash and burn, and our luck runs out, God is nowhere to be found in our lives, but we blame Him anyway for our failures. There is no question in my mind; my faith in God and Jesus Christ has held my life together.

I know this may sound strange coming from a life-long Christian, but in the last five months, I have discovered the best way for me to cope with everything in my life is to ask God to *please help me.*

And, although it is not new to most Christians, asking God to help me was new to me. Prior to this time, the old saying "If it is to be, it is up to me" fit me perfectly.

But, now I can say my life has changed. I discovered asking God to help me with all of my problems makes everything work out better for me. That, when God is in complete control of my entire life, things are much easier for me. That, with God's guidance, I function better, and all my hopes and dreams are alive. That, when God is directing me, my mental happiness and daily successes are enhanced.

I now realize the hardest part of praying is listening for God's answers. In the past, I never stopped to listen for His responses because I wasn't asking Him for anything. But now, I have learned to stop talking and to listen for God's answers. To hear His voice and digest what He is saying. From my personal experience in the past five months, I can state explicitly praying for God's help and listening for God's answers has changed my life forever.

The story I want to tell you about concerns a miracle that happened while I was hunting. Hunting has consistently signified friendship and fellowship to me. It has meant bridging the gap between genders and generations. To me, hunting is not about the killing of animals; it is about enjoying life in the outdoors. It is the thrill of being in the wilderness, the camaraderie with fellow hunters, and the lifetime of memories and stories exchanged between friends while sitting around a campfire.

In order to understand the foundation upon why I am an outdoorsman and why hunting and fishing are part of my life, it is essential to understand the man who helped shape my father into the man he was and who, along with my father, was a major influence on shaping me into the man I became.

My grandfather, Lester Thomas Akins (Grandpa Akins), was an orphan. He never spent a day in school. He couldn't read. He couldn't write. His signature was a poorly scribbled X.

Early on in my childhood, he taught me how to ride a horse and rope and how to work cattle. He had me wrestling calves at brandings, dehorning, and castrating. Grandpa Akins was the classic image and the quintessential definition of the early-day American cowboy.

The few times I stayed with him, we slept outside in our blankets on the ground under the moon and the stars. When it rained, we slept inside on the dirt floor of his plank lumber lean-to.

What little money he earned, he did so from breaking horses, day working cattle, and as a rough stock rider in many of the local rodeos—a lifestyle from which he never deviated until he died at the age of sixty-nine.

In my mind, I carry the indelible image of the man the only way I ever saw him—wearing a battered old cowboy hat, blood-stained chaps, and boots with spurs he never took off.

He lived off the land, feeding himself by eating wild plants, fruits, and animals. He ate wild berries and grapes, as well as wild onions, mushrooms, cactus apples, and pecans. He hunted rabbits, squirrels, deer, turkey, quail, doves, prairie chickens, ducks, and geese. And he showed me how to noodle (hand-catching) catfish in the rivers and streams that flowed through that part of central Texas where my father and I were born.

My Grandpa Akins lived an outdoor lifestyle every day of his life. The little time I spent with him, he made it his mission to mold me into an outdoorsman, and to help me appreciate the necessity and value of eating wild plants and fruits as well as hunting and fishing to provide food for the table.

"Everything we need to live and survive is right here on this land," he told me.

At the time, I did not fully appreciate the wisdom of all he taught me, but looking back on it now, I can see his lessons were the backbone of what I know and believe today about hunting and fishing.

The one thing he told me that sticks in my mind on every hunt I've ever been on is: "Only take a good clean, ethical shot or don't shoot at all."

He was a man of few words, but he made me understand the importance of what he was trying to teach me. I will always remember his words and his big smile. "These native plants and fruits, and wild animals and fish are our food supply. We only take what we need. We take the old to make room for the new offspring."

I don't ever recall my Grandpa Akins going to a grocery store for food. And, at the time, I wasn't aware that he was probably one of our early day ecologists in some sense.

Today, people would say he lived an eco-friendly, renewable, healthy lifestyle. And they would call the food he ate from hunting and fishing organic, natural, and environmentally sustainable. I never heard him use any of those terms, but I'd like to think my Grandpa Akins was simply sixty years ahead of his time.

And for those things he taught me as an outdoorsman—hunting and fishing and living off the land—I am greatly appreciative.

I realize hunting is a controversial subject in this day and time. I know there are people and organizations expressly against any kind of hunting. Some people have devoted their entire lives to protesting and banning the right of humans to hunt. This story in no way challenges the rights and freedom of those who choose to be opposed to hunting.

The ecosystems of all animal species and subspecies have thrived for many centuries without much interruption or harm in numbers from humans. But yes, in recent years, some animals have become near extinction and have required the help of humans to intervene on their behalf in order to stay alive. For these logical and heroic efforts of keeping certain animal species and subspecies from extinction, we are all thankful and grateful to those who have fought to preserve these animals. Of course, the right of animals to hunt and kill each other has not yet been challenged by hunters or non-hunters.

This story is not about debating the rights and wrongs or good and evil between hunters and non-hunters. This story is about God. I make no apologies for the fact the miracle I want to tell you about arises out of a hunt. It doesn't matter whether you hunt or don't hunt; I believe this story and miracle will change your life.

I'm asking you to put aside your love or hate of hunting. I'm asking you to put on your outdoor pants and shirt, your warm coat, your hiking boots, and your favorite cap. I am asking you to walk with me through the steep hills, mountains, and wilderness. I want you to bear down and walk side by side with me through the brutal, thick brush, the cactus and trees, and the native grasses. I believe you will feel God's spirit and presence during our walk. And I believe at the end of our journey together, you will find in your heart and in your mind that *God is alive and well.*

CHAPTER TWO

The big day had finally arrived. Monday, October 21, 2019. I had no legal business or pro bono work to handle, and I had no ranch work scheduled for the next few days. It was time for me to have some fun in the wilderness. I was ready to travel to southwest Texas to bow-hunt a trophy aoudad.

The aoudad, also known as the Barbary sheep, is from the Barbary Coast of Africa and is native to the rocky mountains of northern Africa, where it thrives in the dry, barren, and waterless habitat. We were going to be hunting in rough country, exactly like that of the rough mountainous terrain to which the aoudad is so well adapted. Experienced hunters know hunting the male species is difficult and complicated since the aoudad mostly restricts his movement to dusk and after dark. I knew this bow-hunt would be a challenging and grueling undertaking. The pre-hunt anticipation and uncertainty I was feeling, as usual, created a thrill for me.

The Champion Exotic Trophy Ranch, where I am traveling this day, has built a fine reputation for raising big trophy aoudads. But, more importantly, it has supported a long-running conservation program that provides a place for a hundred different species of exotic animals to reproduce and flourish.

I have hunted this ranch several times before, and I am familiar with its hunting practices, brush-studded terrain, and large variety of animals. The ranch provides an ideal habitat for its resident wild stock with abundant feed, water, and shelter. Their carefully planned harvest program ensures a balanced population of males to females and a concentration of livestock commensurate with good land management practices that are sustainable for the long term and guarantee longevity for the species fortunate enough to be housed here.

Most geographers call the area where this legendary exotic hunting ranch is located the Hill Country portal. This southwest Texas hilly-mountainous region sits between the Texas Hill Country and the South Texas Plains.

Hunters from all over the world come to this impressive ranch. And like the large concessions in Africa, Europe, and South America, this ranch provides professional hunters/guides for all its clientele.

It requires immediate payment for trophy fees, daily rates, tipping, and lodging. Commercial processors are employed by the ranch to cut and wrap the meat. The trophy animal's hide and horns are shipped to a professional taxidermist to be mounted if desired. And lastly, there are two highly-rated chefs and a professional support staff residing on the premises that make dining and lodging at this ranch a five-star experience.

The cold air that autumn morning when I stepped outside my house in Austin was exhilarating. Perfect bow-hunting weather.

7:28 a.m. The sun was beginning to color the horizon a fiery red, pink, and yellow. A beautiful fall sunrise only God could paint. The sunrise, combined with the anticipation of the hunt that lay before me on one of the most prestigious ranches in Texas, was invigorating.

My mind was racing as I stepped into the shower, now fully focused on the tough terrain and the challenges of navigating that forbidding environment stalking big game with nothing but a bow. The statistical odds of the average hunter bringing down the rugged and wily aoudad with an arrow at fifty to seventy yards on a spot-and-stalk hunt was probably less than 5 percent. I figured that, with my years of experience, my chances of success were much better than most.

This outing was going to be what seasoned hunters call "real hunting." In any case, it didn't matter if I shot anything or not. It was going to be another great adventure for me because I have always measured the success of any hunt by how much excitement, challenge, and memories I brought back with me to enjoy.

On most of my hunting adventures as a young boy, I used a rifle. But, for the past five decades, I have mostly employed the use of a bow and arrow. Bow-hunting is more challenging and difficult than hunting with a rifle, and it requires more practice and focus. It also requires more skill. Bow-hunting levels the playing field between the hunter and the hunted. It is about playing fair between man and beast.

There are two strategies to bow-hunting—ambush or spot-and-stalk. Under either approach, the hunter must remain undetected and control his or her human scent in the hunting area. The terrain or species of animal being hunted normally dictates the strategy for bow-hunting. Most bow-hunters prefer the ambush strategy—sitting in a hidden ground blind or a tree stand to harvest an animal.

To me, the key ingredients to ambush are proper scouting, locating, selecting, and then meticulously preparing the perfect hunting site. Under the ambush strategy, the hunter waits patiently and quietly in an unnoticed, camouflaged hideout. The long periods of sitting and waiting in the hideout sometimes take several hours with the hunter mostly in a fixed, motionless position before the animal approaches into range, allowing the hunter an opportunity to take a shot.

My favorite strategy is spot-and-stalk. In other words, who can outwit and outsmart whom? Under the spot-and-stalk strategy, the hunter mostly walks for miles trying to locate his quarry. When the animal is finally seen, the hunter approaches and pursues the animal quietly and slowly. During this stealth mode, sometimes for hours, the hunter must constantly remain undetected by the animal as the hunter moves slowly, quietly, and patiently—walking or crawling—until he or she sneaks close enough for a good, lethal shot.

The thrill of bow-hunting in the great outdoors is the challenge. There are no guarantees of success. Trying to bring down a large, thick-skinned, heavy-boned animal with an arrow is extremely difficult. It takes a tremendous amount of discipline, concentration, and skill, plus a strict daily routine of practice. Making the perfect bow shot under pressure at any big game animal is a formidable task.

I've learned bow-hunting continually finds a way to test our strength of mind, body, and soul. And, I can say from a half-century of experience, when a person tries to hunt an animal with a bow and arrow, it makes all the difference in the world. Bow-hunting consistently tests your mettle.

In my mind, hunting is about living the dream and walking the same paths in the wilderness as our ancestors. It's about the old settled ways of life. It's about the Native Americans and the old southwestern traditions. It's about the old Mexican ways and the old cowboy ways living in Texas. It's about the folklore of nature, animals, and those who came before us. It's about the allure, magic, and fascination of the outdoors. And lastly, what I love most about bow-hunting, it allows me the opportunity to walk with God, relax, and free the stress in my body and mind that accumulates over time.

This exotic game ranch where I am going today occupies approximately 35,000 acres of brush, live oaks, cedar, mesquites, cactus, native grasses, and steep rocky hills with deep ravines and valleys. It also sports a majority of its animals from Africa, Europe, Asia, and New Zealand.

Anyone familiar with this type of terrain knows that carrying a rifle in this concentrated brush is considerably easier than trying to traverse it with a bow and quiver of arrows. I knew this hunt would require several miles of stealth walking, possibly some crawling, being absolutely motionless for minutes at a time, and then, if lucky, a long-range perfect bow shot.

I finished my long hot shower with a shave, toweled off, dressed, and then brushed my teeth and exited the bathroom.

I knew this was going to be a tough hunt from what my friend Josh Morris, the ranch foreman, told me when I called the ranch in early May 2019 to set up the aoudad hunt.

"These aoudad hunts on this ranch are a real booger," Josh warned me. "You're going to need at least five days to hunt the aoudad, probably more."

"How about I come to hunt in the middle of October?" I asked.

I could hear Josh flipping through the pages of his calendar.

"That sounds good," he said. "I've got an opening on Monday the 21st through the evening of Friday the 25th. No other hunters on my schedule. Come stay at the ranch for five days or as long as you need."

I wrote the dates on my calendar.

"All right, I'll get there around noon on the 21st."

"Perfect," he said. "Looking forward to it."

"Hopefully, we can start hunting that afternoon, if possible."

"No problem," Josh hesitated for few seconds. "It looks to me like the sun won't set until around 7:00 in the evening, so an afternoon hunt on the 21st will be okay."

I stared at my calendar. I saw that I needed to be back in Austin on Wednesday night because of an early Thursday morning appointment. I knew if I told Josh I only had two and a half days to hunt the aoudad, he would veto my plans and suggest I come another date when I had more time.

In my mind, it wasn't about shooting the aoudad; it was about getting out of the city and enjoying the outdoors with my great friend.

"It all sounds perfect," I told Josh. "Plan on picking me up around two o'clock in the afternoon at the lodge. I'll be ready to hunt."

"Got it. I'll meet you there." After a few seconds, Josh continued. "We're going to be hunting a much different part of the ranch for the aoudad."

"I understand."

"And brother, it's going to be a real butt-kicker. Much tougher terrain than what we've been hunting in the past," Josh warned.

"I guess we'll be hunting those rugged hills on the ranch."

In my mind, the hills on this ranch were really mountains.

"Yes, sir. There's a heck of a lot of jagged rocks, ledges, and a treacherous ravine up in those steep hills and mountains. And pretty much impenetrable brush."

I heard Josh take a deep breath.

"There's just no telling how many mesquite thorns or cactus thorns you're going to find in your butt when this hunt is over." I could hear Josh laughing into the phone.

"Sounds like another grand adventure for us."

"Copy that."

"I'm looking forward to it."

"Right on. It's right up our alley," Josh said.

"Okay then, I'll be there on the 21st, ready to hunt."

"You got it." I could hear him breathe deeply. "And oh yeah, you're going to get a lot of scrapes and bruises too."

"Just like every other bow-hunt you and I have enjoyed on that ranch."

Josh laughed. "Yes, sir, that's just part of the thrills you're paying for out here. And there's no extra charge for all of that either."

"Yeah. Yeah. I know all about that, brother Josh."

"Come prepared for some difficult hunting. Those jagged rocks and mountains are a real workout."

"I'll be ready. You know, we always have fun."

"Always," Josh replied. "All the animals should be in the rut around that time. It should be a great hunt."

"I have no doubt. God always blesses us."

"Yes, sir. I can't wait to see you, my friend."

"Ditto, man. Okay, I'll see you on the 21st. Take care," I said and then hung up.

I love challenges, rough terrain, and clever animals that try to outwit me. Scratches and thorns and a good test of strength and endurance have always been a large part of my lust for the outdoors. Every hunt is new, and every hunt is different—that's the ultimate thrill that drives all hunters. Getting close to wildlife and competing in a game of wits with these intelligent creatures is an extraordinary experience. As a seasoned bow-hunter, I knew what to expect on this unusual hunting ranch. Sometimes the unforgiving and seemingly impossible landscape is such a strong deterrent to spotting-and-stalking that guides refuse to even consider it as an option for hunters. I recollect a handful of times I've been told by my professional guide that a certain area I wanted to hunt was an impossible place to spot-and-stalk with my bow. Frankly, I have never allowed anyone to tell me I couldn't do something. That's never been a part of my playbook.

Mostly, my trip down south was for me to relax and spend some quality time hunting with my friend and professional hunting guide Josh Morris. He was like a brother to me. For years, we had shared many happy memories of hunting together. My plan was to drive four hours to southwest Texas, hunt the aoudad with him until Wednesday evening, and then drive back to Austin the night of October 23rd, so I would be available to see clients on Thursday. I had a two-and-a-half-day window of time and opportunity to make things happen.

It didn't matter to me that Josh thought I needed at least five days or more to successfully hunt the aoudad. If I didn't take the animal in the two and a half days, I'd still leave the Champion Exotic Trophy Ranch a happy man.

The night before I departed, I packed my red pick-up with my hunting gear—camouflage clothes, caps, coats, gloves, boots, bow and arrows, and most importantly, my hunting license. I also loaded a couple of archery practice targets in the back bed of the truck.

In all my years of bow-hunting, I routinely took a few practice shots before heading out in the wild to hunt. Because, just like every other venture in life, confidence and believing you can make the shot at the right moment is vital to being a good bow-hunter.

For five minutes, I sat in my living room sipping coffee and talking with my wife. I also ate two waffles with maple syrup. When the grandfather clock in the hallway chimed eight o'clock in the morning, I rose to my feet. I was ready and focused on the upcoming hunting adventure.

By the time I kissed and hugged my wife goodbye, told her I loved her, and made sure I had everything in my truck, it was 8:20 a.m. When I finally departed the Spanish Oaks subdivision in Austin, cruising toward southwest Texas, I felt on top of the world.

CHAPTER THREE

As a young boy, I grew up in Duval County, Texas. It's a rugged brush-country section of land right smack in the middle of the South Texas Plains. I began shooting my BB gun at age four, honoring my hunting and shooting heritage. In those boundless, wide-open spaces around Freer, I fell in love with free-range hunting. My old stomping grounds were not far from the prestigious Champion Exotic Trophy Ranch, where I was journeying today. Indeed, because this ranch was very close to my childhood playground, it brought back good, warm-hearted memories.

I have routinely found traveling south to my country roots has consistently provided me with a good way of rejuvenating my youthful spirit. I knew this hunting trip to the hilly brush country was going to be another glorious chapter in my outdoor career. But mostly, I was looking forward to walking the outdoors, seeing the beautiful animals, and visiting with my good friend Josh.

I sang old hit songs playing on the truck radio for the majority of my drive down south. I rocked it. And when I arrived at the Champion Exotic Trophy Ranch at approximately 12:35 on Monday afternoon, October 21st, I felt energized.

As I entered the large, impressive lodge, I saw two professional guides sitting at the bar to my right, enjoying a soft drink and talking with their hunters. Then I glanced to my left and saw several excited hunters sitting around the crackling hot fireplace in the trophy room exchanging stories. They looked happy.

This new group of hunters had arrived at the ranch yesterday evening, supplanting the previous group from the week before. This group of twelve or more hunters was very animated, talking about their morning hunts as well as some of their past adventures.

Scanning the group, I noticed three of the hunters were women, which I loved to see. I didn't recognize any of the hunters specifically, but I nodded my head at several of them and exchanged pleasantries with even more. This was a friendly group. A couple of the older gentlemen in the crowd recognized me from my college football days and flashed me the *hook'em* horns sign. I smiled back at them and waved *hook'em* horns to the whole group.

After I spoke to most of these hunters for several minutes, we all shook hands. It was nice seeing these men and women having so much pleasure. Deep inside, I was smiling. This was exactly why I loved to hunt. The camaraderie and fellowship and strong friendships it developed. To have fun and excitement, living and enjoying life to its fullest in the outdoors.

Inside the expansive lodge, there was a well-designed trophy room connected to the dining room and an attached larger section of the building with at least ten sleeping quarters for guests. It was like a hotel. One of the ranch workers told me I was in room four. And, after three trips to my truck, I finally filled the room with all of my hunting gear and boots, my hunting box, a suitcase, a large bow case, and lots of arrows.

Not long after I arrived, my cell phone lit up with a text message from Josh.

I'll pick you up in front of the lodge at 2:00 p.m. Be ready, the text read.

I immediately fired back a text to Josh.

I'm always ready. And FYI—I've been practicing long-range bow shots— sixty and seventy yards—so I can't wait for us to hunt the aoudad.

Within five seconds, Josh replied with an emoji thumbs up. I placed my phone on the nightstand and laid back on the bed to relax from my four-hour drive.

I rested for twenty minutes before dressing in my camouflage clothes, hunting boots, coat, and cap. Then I grabbed my bow and quiver of arrows and headed out the door and through the lodge to my truck.

I placed the two archery practice targets approximately two hundred yards away from the lodge where it was safe to shoot. One of the targets rested sixty yards away, and the other was placed at seventy yards away from where I was standing.

My golf course range-finder came in handy setting the distances. The first practice arrow I shot at the sixty-yard target missed the bulls-eye by three inches to the left. I knew immediately I had jerked it a little.

Come on now; you've got to be smooth with the release, I told myself.

My second practice arrow hit dead in the bulls-eye of the sixty-yard target. Then the next two practice arrows I shot were both inside the bulls-eye at the seventy-yard target. Now, going into the woods, I felt good and very confident about making a perfect shot. I retrieved the targets, pulled the arrows, and then went back to the lodge to wait for Josh.

I knew when Josh showed up he would be full of information for the aoudad hunt. Like me, he always used trail cameras as well as spotting with binoculars to search wildlife areas to locate specific animals prior to hunting. This vital information would help us formulate a successful strategy before setting out to walk and stalk the many miles necessary to hunt the aoudad.

Sitting on the front porch, I began reciting my hunting rules in my head. Being a hunter since I was five years old, I recalled the three most important hunting commandments I learned as a young boy. I continued to utilize these rules to my current age of sixty-five.

The rules were simple.

- Rule 1. Safety is first and foremost. *Always be safe.*
- Rule 2. Take a deep breath—be completely calm and relaxed when shooting a gun or a bow at an animal. Never rush a shot and never shoot at an animal when excited or nervous. Rushing a shot or having a fast heart rate, a pounding pulse, or a high anxiety level usually brings about a bad shot that can only wound and inflict non-fatal pain and injuries to an animal.

  Through the years, I have discovered that weeks and months of practice—shooting a bow or a rifle—prior to a hunt makes me calm and relaxed when out in the field where I need to make a perfect shot.
- Rule 3. Never seek to recover a wounded animal if you believe your shot was not perfectly placed in the kill zone. Waiting for at least ten hours or until the following morning before you begin searching to locate and recover the animal is the best and safest method. Waiting these extra hours gives the animal an uninterrupted period of time to lay down and expire not far from where it was shot. This added time prevents the animal from being run and pushed to a much greater distance where there is a high risk of losing the animal forever.

I leaned back and smiled. These rules were as relevant today as they were sixty years ago when my grandfather, Hans Paul Schultz, handed them down to me. As a child, I enjoyed several memorable hunts with my Grandpa Schultz. He was a great man and hunter. I loved him.

2:12 p.m. When Josh arrived, I was relaxing in a rocking chair with my bow and quiver of arrows nearby. I waved at him, and he waved back. I rose to my feet and stepped off the porch toward him. Josh hustled out of his big hunting truck and walked at a speedy pace toward me. "Sorry I'm late, brother. I got hung up," he shouted.

"No problem."

As always, Josh had a big smile, and he greeted me with his tough-guy handshake and bear hug.

We shook hands firmly.

"It's so great to see you, my friend," Josh said.

"You're looking great, Josh."

Josh stepped back.

"I've got a great aoudad hunt planned for us," he said.

"I expected nothing less from you."

As usual, Josh was dressed in his khaki pants, a long-sleeved camo shirt, and dusty cap. I watched his eyes. He was staring straight at my bow.

"Are you gonna try to use that bow?"

"Of course, I am."

"Well, I can tell you right now, that bow isn't gonna work on this aoudad hunt," Josh said. "I just don't think you'll have a chance to get him."

I stepped closer, patting him on the shoulder.

"I know using my bow will make the hunt more difficult, but I'd like to give it a try and see what I can do."

"Okay, but, in my opinion, you'll be wasting our time."

I laughed. "I knew you'd say that."

"Well, it's true. You might as well throw a rock at him."

I laughed.

"You know me; I don't sugarcoat a thing when it comes to hunting," Josh said.

"That's why I love to hunt with you," I replied. "Just let me try using my bow for a day or two."

Josh shrugged his shoulders.

"You know bow-hunting is what I love to do," I said. "In all the years that we've hunted together, I've used a rifle… what, only a couple of times?

"Yes, sir. And this aoudad hunt is going to be your third time to use a rifle with me."

I looked over at Josh and laughed.

Josh smiled back at me. He put his left hand on my shoulder.

"I know you love to bow-hunt, brother, but on this rugged aoudad hunt in the mountains, it's going to be impossible."

"Nothing's impossible," I said.

"Look, I've been working and guiding on this ranch for almost twenty years. Spotting-and-stalking an aoudad in these steep hills and mountains on this ranch with a rifle is hard enough. But trying to hunt an aoudad with a bow up in that dense brush and butt-kicking hills—well, it's virtually impossible."

I stood silently, listening to him.

"I can tell you this right now; I can't recall anyone ever successfully bow-hunting an aoudad in these mountains on this ranch."

"Well, good. Then I'll be the first one to do it."

Josh shook his head at me.

"You always think you can do anything."

I didn't answer.

He paused, kicking the ground with his boot.

"You're just a hard-headed dude," he stated.

He stared at the ground for another moment, then looked up at me.

I stood there gripping my bow and didn't say a word.

"All right then, fine. If you want to use your bow on this aoudad hunt, then do it."

He turned and walked briskly toward his truck.

"Come on; we're wasting time arguing," he hollered back at me.

When we both arrived at Josh's truck, I opened the passenger front door and got into the seat with my bow and arrows. I watched Josh open the back-passenger door behind the driver's side and pull out a heavy rifle. He checked the gun's magazine to make sure it had bullets; then, he looked over at me.

"You know, brother, I've hunted with you for many years, and I know you're an expert shot with a bow. Maybe the best I've ever seen. But I'm going to bring along my 300-Win Mag rifle today just in case we see the aoudad, and you need a rifle to shoot him."

"I thought we were finished arguing about that," I shot back.

"We are finished."

Josh stared at me. "I was just trying one last time to talk some sense into you."

"Well, thanks, brother, for trying to talk some sense into me," I stated. "But I'm going to use my bow these first couple of days."

Josh was still looking at me, but he didn't answer.

"Look, I'll switch to your rifle Wednesday morning if we haven't shot the aoudad before then," I assured him.

Josh laid the rifle across the console of his truck and got in the driver's seat. There were several long moments of silence before he turned and looked at me.

"Do you really want to risk taking a long-range bow shot at this huge trophy aoudad through the impenetrable mountain brush?"

"Of course not. I can't believe you would even ask me such a ridiculous question."

I looked over at Josh. I was a little hot under the collar now.

"You know I would never take a risky shot under any circumstances at any animal."

Josh sat silent, staring out the front windshield.

"You haven't listened to a thing I've said to you," I snapped back at him.

Josh turned his eyes toward me, "I'm listening."

"I told you, I feel very confident and comfortable taking up to a seventy-yard bow shot. I've been practicing those shots for six months. I mean, if the aoudad is standing out in the wide-open at seventy yards or closer from us, then I know I can shoot him."

Josh was still listening as I continued. "I think you know I would never take a risky shot at any animal through the brush or otherwise where I might wound or hurt the animal where we couldn't recover him."

"You're right; I know that," Josh answered.

He tightened his grip around the steering wheel. "I just hate to see you try to shoot this monster, big-boned aoudad with your bow at such a long distance."

He looked down at the floorboard. "I just don't want you to shoot the aoudad, then lose him, and still have to pay the ranch for him."

"Brother, I don't want that to happen either. And that's not going to ever happen—I've never shot and lost an animal in my life."

"I know that."

Josh looked me in the eyes.

"And hopefully, this aoudad bow-hunt isn't going to be your first time to shoot and lose an animal," he said. "I don't think you realize how thick-skinned this animal is and how brutal this terrain is going to be."

"I understand all of that."

He was still staring me in the eyes. "As your good friend and as an experienced bow-hunter, I honestly do not think you can get this big trophy aoudad with your bow in these dense, rugged mountains."

"Well, I'm going to give it a try for a day or two."

Josh took a deep breath. "Okay. Fine. It's your choice. You know the rule."

"Of course, I know the rule. Every hunter knows the rule."

There was a long pause from Josh. "Then you know, if you shoot the aoudad and draw one drop of blood and we can't find him or he doesn't die, or no matter what happens to him, then you still have to pay the trophy fee to the ranch for the cost of the animal."

This prolonged discussion about me using my bow to hunt the aoudad was really starting to make me mad. "I understand all of that completely. This isn't my first rodeo Josh."

"Well, I know that. I'm just trying to help you," he said.

I knew this long-standing rule in hunting. This rule was used in Africa, South America, Europe, Canada, and everywhere else I had hunted. This was the same rule that applied to hunters universally all over the world. I had never in my life shot an animal I didn't immediately recover.

I knew the rule, but in my mind, it just didn't apply to me, I thought. Mainly because I was a very good shot with a bow, and I never tried risky shots.

I pointed for Josh to turn the key. "Come on, brother, let's stop arguing and go hunt."

I looked at my watch. It read 2:25 p.m.

"You got it," Josh said. And, within a split second, the truck was moving, and we were driving away from the lodge.

During the ride through the ranch, Josh talked to me about a huge aoudad he had seen spotting with binoculars and using trail cameras.

"That thing is a giant toad," he told me. "Both horns are very thick and at least thirty-five inches."

"Wow, I can't wait to see him."

I knew if Josh thought the aoudad was a giant, then he must be a giant.

"He might even be bigger than that," Josh said. "Nobody on this ranch knows about this monster but me, and I've saved him just for you."

Josh winked, then he shot me a big smile.

"I really want you to be the one who puts your hands around those heavy, massive horns."

"Thanks, brother," I answered. "You know how much I appreciate you."

Josh nodded. "I first got a glimpse of this giant aoudad two months ago in a valley between two mountains. I was darting elk in that valley and moving them to a different pasture on the ranch before the rut started."

I was listening.

"Then I saw the monster aoudad about four weeks ago. He was lying up in the shadows underneath a thick grove of cedar trees at the base of one of the mountains. He and another big aoudad laid perfectly still, all hunkered down, about forty yards away from me as I drove past them."

"So, you could see his horns clearly?"

"Absolutely."

"And you think his horns are the biggest you've ever seen?"

"Yes, sir. Probably at least thirty-five inches. I haven't said anything to anybody about him. I knew you were coming later on this month, so I saved him for you."

"You're the greatest. Thank you."

I smiled at Josh.

"And a couple of weeks back, I saw him resting in the sun on a ledge not far from one of the valley floors between the mountains."

Josh looked over at me then back at the road

"You know, the shrubs and native plants and grasses growing on these steep hillsides are a great natural food source for all the animals."

I nodded.

"And that's why the monster aoudad likes it there."

"I completely understand. Is that valley where you have seen him accessible by foot?"

"Yes, sir, but only if we try to enter it from the western boundary."

I nodded.

"So, our plan this afternoon is for us to make our way into these steep hills and then the mountains, checking out as many clearings and valleys as we possibly can before dark."

"That sounds perfect." I was getting excited.

Josh drove another quarter of a mile.

"There is one particular spot overlooking a beautiful little valley where we'll be on top of the highest ridge in the pasture."

"Wow. I can't wait to see that."

"Yeah, the views are incredible, and the aoudad likes it there," Josh said. "I think one can see for thirty miles standing at the peak."

My adrenaline was flowing. I was ready to hunt.

"But I'd say there's pretty much zero access to any of the valley floors we are going to see on the spot-and-stalk route we'll be taking today."

"No problem, as always, we'll figure something out if it becomes a problem," I said.

Josh nodded. "Right on."

After a few seconds, he glanced at me.

"I've spotted that monster aoudad twice in the past ten days on the trail cameras. Both times at some protein feeders in the mountains. The feeders rest on a northern hillside near an overlooking ledge not far from that highest peak."

"So, the big boy likes protein pellets?"

"Yes, sir, and if he's at those feeders, he just might give you a sixty-five to seventy-yard shot."

"I love it. Sounds good."

"I think we might have a good chance to get him if we can stay quiet during our walk to those feeders and keep the wind in our face."

"I like the plan," I said. "I can't wait to start the hunt."

Josh cut his eyes over at me and then back to the road. "I'm just glad to see you, my friend," he added. "We always hunt for the memories."

"Yes, we do."

I smiled, leaning back in my seat, clutching my bow as the truck flew down the caliche road leading us toward another memory.

CHAPTER FOUR

Through our many years of walking, stalking, and hunting in the outdoors together, I have consistently respected Josh's expertise and opinion on how to hunt. There is definitely a strong bond between us. He is one of my best-hunting friends. And what he thinks is extremely important to me. Sure, we argue like brothers, but I know Josh's experience and knowledge of hunting, especially bow-hunting, is as good as anyone in the world. I trusted this man with my life on many hunting adventures. He is a loyal friend and honest gentleman.

Josh's words were stuck in my brain. "As your good friend and as an experienced bow-hunter, I honestly do not think you can get this big trophy aoudad with your bow in these dense, rugged mountains."

I knew Josh was looking after my best interest. And mostly, I knew he was probably right. During the remainder of our ride, I tossed around the possibility of using Josh's heavy rifle and leaving my bow in the truck.

Finally, we came to a large iron gate. Josh handed me the key to the lock on the chain, and I got out of the truck to open it. I sat my bow gently in the seat, making sure my sights would not be compromised. I knew if the bow slipped and fell while the truck was moving, it might affect my yardage pins. I opened and closed the gate, locked it, and then re-entered the truck. It was 3:05 p.m.

"What's the name of this pasture?" I asked.

Josh was smiling. "Welcome to the 52-Pasture."

"I guess this place is 5,200 acres, am I right?

"Yes, sir. And in all our years of hunting together, we've never been on this part of the ranch," he told me.

I nodded.

"It's 5,200 acres of the most rugged, harsh landscape on this place."

I didn't say a word.

"The old-timers say the Comanche called this area *tseena soko*."

I was listening.

Josh turned to me. "That means coyote ground, and crazy enough, this place is still full of coyotes."

"Really."

"Yes, sir. They're bad in here."

The rough road bounced the truck sharply to the right, and Josh tightened his grip on the steering wheel.

"Even the animals have a hard time walking and surviving this terrain. It's a little over eight square miles of dense, brutal territory," he added.

I nodded toward Josh. But mostly, I was looking through the windshield, witnessing the beginning of the steep hills and mountains in the distance.

Josh quickly glanced over at me. "Thick cedar motts, massive amounts of cactus, horrible mesquite, and a good variety of dense brush make this pasture impossible to spot-and-stalk with a bow."

"It does look difficult," I said as I was staring at the heavy brush on both sides of the road. It appeared impenetrable.

"Plus, the rocks and the unstable conditions of the mountains with the steep elevations, the ups and downs, the ledges on tight, narrow trails with the small valleys down below make this place extremely dangerous to walk."

I clutched my bow as I listened.

"All of us guides say this 52-Pasture is the meanest, toughest, nastiest part of this whole cotton-picking ranch," he added.

As we drove, I was looking at the imposing terrain.

"It sounds and looks like our hunt is going to be a real challenge," I replied.

"Copy that, brother."

I didn't answer.

Josh glanced at me. "With the unexpected cliffs and sheer drop-offs that suddenly emerge along the trails, plus the sharp uneven rocks with the deep hillside erosion leading down into several wide gullies makes it exceedingly difficult and dangerous to traverse."

I looked over. "I understand."

"And finally, brother, there's what seems to be a bottomless, treacherous ravine that runs for a couple of miles along the southwest boundary in this pasture."

"It's way over there." Josh removed his right hand from the steering wheel and pointed to his left.

"It was called *kenatuka kooi*, deep canyon of death by the Indians."

I didn't answer. My eyes were focused intently on the brutal landscape all around us.

"Brother, are you listening to me?" Josh asked.

I turned toward Josh. "Sure, I'm listening."

"I'm very serious about this."

He was looking at me and trying to drive.

"No one—and I mean no one ever goes into that deep, hazardous ravine, not even the animals. You got it?"

"Yes, sir. I've got it," I replied.

"No exceptions."

"I understand."

Then Josh began talking strategy—how he wanted us to spot-and-stalk the aoudad, how we needed to constantly be aware of the wind and keep it in our face. Josh had a very good plan, but his plan had me using a rifle.

At the end of his plan, he stated, "The aoudad has a great sixth sense and a good nose. We absolutely need the element of surprise on our side to shoot him. That's why we need to stay a good distance away in order to take our shot. Under these brutal surroundings and circumstances, I believe a long-range rifle shot works best."

I didn't respond.

I also had a good plan. With my experience and five decades of bow-hunting, I knew getting close with a bow was absolutely necessary to take this elusive aoudad. But I also knew getting too close to the animal where it could smell me would definitely foil the hunt. That's why I had diligently practiced my long-range bow shots for six months. My plan was to outwit the aoudad, use the element of surprise to my advantage, sneak up quietly with the wind in my face, and then shoot this sturdy, muscular specimen from sixty to seventy yards with an arrow.

We drove slowly. The caliche road was becoming rougher, narrower, and winding. Josh finally brought the truck to a crawl, fifty more yards, and we stopped about five miles from where we left the iron gate. Josh parked the truck in a big mott of live oaks, hiding the vehicle about thirty yards off the main caliche road.

"We're here," he said, quietly putting his finger to his lips.

During the drive into the 52-Pasture, I was keeping a keen eye on the terrain and listening to Josh. The landscape appeared similar to a few places I had hunted around the world. Plus, in my opinion, there were a couple of areas on this ranch we had hunted years earlier that were comparable. But, for the most part, Josh was right; this terrain and hunt were going to be a genuine test of mental endurance and physical strength. More strenuous and difficult than normal.

"Maybe we'll get lucky and spot the trophy aoudad first thing," I said.

Josh stared at me.

"Maybe we'll catch him out in a clearing before he sees us, and I'll put the perfect bow shot on him," I added.

Josh leaned toward me and whispered, "Brother, you're going to need all the luck in the world that you can muster here in this 52-Pasture to get this aoudad."

With that, Josh opened his truck door, stepped out, and headed for the brush. It was 3:30 p.m. when we started our walk.

Grabbing my bow and arrows, I caught Josh within thirty yards. The hike was brisk and steady. And after a quarter-mile into the brush, we both stopped. He had the rifle and sling pulled over his shoulder, and I had my bow and quiver of arrows in hand.

The wind was blowing gently out of the north. It was cold, but the sun was still shining through the clouds. Josh held out a compass and found northeast. We were still on the flatland, several hundred yards from the base of the hills. We started walking, striding toward the northeast, when unexpectedly, a few large red stags and a dozen hinds came crashing through the trees thirty yards in front of us. It was a beautiful surprise.

"Everything is in full rut right now," he said.

"It's that time of year," I replied.

Josh led the way along the narrow, brushy trail. We stopped after another two hundred yards, and he checked his compass one more time. Then we turned slightly to our left, heading straight north about a half-mile through the thick cactus, mesquite and hackberry before we started our climb up the steep hills heading into the mountains.

The first part of the climb wasn't difficult, but then the terrain turned extremely steep, and we continued to feel the burn in our thighs and lower back for at least a mile. The sun stayed mostly behind us as we worked our way along a tight rocky ledge. Later, the ridge turned into a well-traveled game trail, two feet wide, and for the most part, provided us sufficient space to walk comfortably. The majority of the country to our left and our right was thick brush and cactus. In most places, we could only see twenty to thirty feet. Josh was right—it was primarily a wall of impenetrable foliage. We hiked northeast for five hundred more yards until we came to a drop-off, then we cut back to the north, where every once in a while, there were random areas where we could see slightly further. We found several red sheep, markhor, and dall, in the small clearings, and there were also a few feral hogs that cut across our path. But mostly, we saw small herds of the Barbary Sheep. Lots of female aoudad with young, feisty males.

Five and ten-mile views of the horizon began to spring up sporadically as we got higher elevation. These vistas were inspiring.

There were only a handful of open areas where we could see up to eighty yards. At each of these clearings, Josh and I crawled or crouched down, moving slowly and deliberately into each of them. There were a couple of clearings where we sat for long periods glassing and searching the areas with precision.

Hunkering down in the brush and cactus, we waited. "Be ready; that monster aoudad likes it up here. He won't be far from these herds of females," Josh whispered.

My eyes searched the field. "I'm ready."

"We might catch him in any one of these clearings."

I nodded at Josh.

If the giant aoudad showed himself and hesitated for a brief moment while out in the open, I was prepared to draw back my bow and quickly stick him with an arrow. But the old astute trophy aoudad we were looking for never revealed himself.

After another mile of walking fast, the path narrowed, and the conditions changed. To our left was an immense sixty-five-degree drop-off, and to our right, a steep climb. We walked stealthily—slowly and quietly—stopping every minute or so, attempting to locate the trophy aoudad in smaller clearings.

In the process, we spotted a lot of game. Sometimes we got down on our stomachs, looking under the brush for legs and any movement. Along the way, we saw mouflon, Corsican, urial, and more female aoudad. Later, we saw some Catalina, Nubian ibex, and Spanish goats, along with some mature male aoudad. And there was a large, rogue bull elk running crazy through these brushy mountains trying to find cows to mate.

It was non-stop action. Because it was during the rut, all of the male species were acting crazy. They had sex on their minds. All these beautiful animals were all around us in these mountains feeding, dashing, and flirting throughout the grass and thick foliage. It was like Jurassic Park. And strangely, none of these animals acted like they cared we were there.

For a flatlander, these steep hills and mountains in the 52-Pasture were a real workout. The different slopes and ridges coming together were definitely tricky. In some places, there were sharp jagged cliffs tied to sheer drop-offs with rocky chasms and deep canyons. The footing was extremely dangerous. We knew one slip could mean serious injury or death.

Josh warned me to be careful. The climb was difficult for seventy feet until we came to a high peak, viewing below us what appeared to be another beautiful valley with an eroded dry creek. All of these challenges posed a huge hurdle to both man and beast. We proceeded slowly and carefully off the peak, heading along a heavily used game trail. In several more clearings along our walk, we eased into them, spotting a variety of game, axis, addax, and other antelope, but still no monster aoudad.

The long afternoon had been glorious. It was still overcast. The sun hiding behind the clouds made it feel colder. After we had walked in stealth mode for another half mile spotting many of the same species of animals, we detoured slightly to our right, gaining immediate altitude heading eastward three hundred more yards along an obscure, constricted route until we came upon a nice, cozy spot located on an elevated ledge about fifty feet off the trail. This open spot was about two hundred feet in diameter. I immediately noticed a handful of old fire pits in this cleared area dating back to the 1800s.

Josh and I were tired. We sat and rested ourselves on the side of this high ridge overlooking a small intimate valley eleven hundred feet below us.

The view was at least thirty miles. I felt like I was in heaven.

"This is the highest peak in this pasture I was telling you about," Josh said.

He was right; the distance views were amazing. I took a deep breath and blew it out slowly. *What a glorious day in the outdoors*, I thought.

"I've found a lot of arrowheads and artifacts up here on this ridge," he added. "It looks to me like this place was an Indian camping ground."

"I think you're right."

"The Comanche named this peak *nanisuyake toya nanisu wukaitu*." Josh said the words slowly. His pronunciation sounded funny.

"And what is that supposed to mean?" I asked.

"Beautiful mountain of the great spirit."

I smiled and nodded. "That's perfect. Sitting here, where we can touch the clouds, and with these heavenly views, I can feel the great spirit of God," I said. "It's easy to see why the Indians called it that."

Josh grinned, and he chuckled a little.

After a few moments, I turned back toward him. "Are you making this Indian stuff up, brother?"

"No way," Josh stared at me. He appeared insulted. "I just thought you might like to hear a little bit of the old folklore and learn some things about the history of this place."

I sat quiet. I knew Josh had a reputation for being a big jokester. I didn't know what to think.

Finally, I spoke.

"Of course, I want to know about all these old stories and history."

Josh smiled large.

I waited a couple of seconds. "I was just making sure you weren't pulling my leg."

He was still grinning from ear to ear. "I'd never do that to you, my brother."

I still wasn't sure. He looked mischievous and guilty.

I quickly put Josh's history lesson out of my mind and focused on the hunt.

The grade down to the valley on our side was probably fifty-five degrees. On the other side of the valley, the wall of the hill went straight up at about eighty-five degrees. Only sheep, goats, and antelope could ascend that sheer face.

6:02 p.m. We glassed with our binoculars for several minutes, finally spotting several species of sheep and goats standing on the rocky ledges across the way. We also saw four small male aoudads and several females. They were flirting and chasing each other through the brush on the valley floor. The long dark shadows in the valley made it difficult for Josh and me to see anything. Our monster trophy aoudad was not in sight.

Sitting next to this awe-inspiring drop-off, Josh and I enjoyed resting and loitering with the animals, bugs, crickets, locusts, hawks, and other birds, sharp rocks, cactus, mesquite thorns, flowers, and native grasses. We shared a strong fellowship with the landscape and wildlife around us.

Only in the outdoors can one sense our connection to earth and truly appreciate our kinship to all of God's creatures.

The wind started picking up now. The cold air felt colder. Five minutes later, the clouds in the west finally broke apart as the sun began drifting toward the horizon. Josh looked at his watch.

"Only one hour until sunset," he whispered.

"If the aoudad shows up in the next thirty minutes, I think we still have enough time to climb down this mountain and get him," I said.

Josh looked at me but didn't respond.

I was sitting beside a large rock that was cantilevered over the drop-off. I looked below, down to my right, and saw several animal protein feeders approximately fifty to seventy yards away. The feeders were located in an expanse where a rough rock caliche section provided a sizable flat area approximately seventy feet in diameter kissing against the mountain wall. There were several different kinds of animals enjoying a meal.

"Are these the protein feeders where the trail cameras showed the big aoudad eating?" I asked quietly.

"Copy that. He likes it here around these feeders."

"If he shows up down there, I definitely know I can get him," I said quietly.

Josh nodded at me and whispered.

"Seventy-yard shot to the furthest feeder."

Our long afternoon hunt of spotting-and-stalking and walking stealth had now turned into an ambush hunt. We waited silently and patiently on the highest ridge in the pasture for the monster aoudad to show up at those feeders.

We could hear the intermittent bugling of another lone bull elk a couple of miles away. There was also a constant roaring and bellowing of several red stags to our southwest. It was remarkable how the sounds carried for miles through these mountains. It sounded like a symphony orchestra. It was an experience I will never forget.

The few clouds in the western sky were now a bright yellowish-orange surrounded by a purple-haze with a few ruby-red streaks. The colors were a brilliant example of God's artwork. And, the wonderful sounds provided by the animals continued to fill the cold evening air. All bound together, the animals, the sounds, our long walk through the steep hills and mountains, our hunt, and this beautiful ending to a glorious day had been an inspiring and extraordinary experience.

6:15 p.m. Josh tapped me on my shoulder and motioned for me to look down to my left. I studied the terrain for several seconds, but there was nothing, then I saw it. The trophy aoudad was lying motionlessly inside a cedar thicket where the dark evening shadows were guarding him.

He was three hundred-fifty plus yards away, too far for a bow shot. The aoudad was extremely difficult to spot, camouflaged well by his surroundings, but once I spotted him, he stood out like a white flag. I took my binoculars and examined every inch of him. I marveled at his impressive, heavy horns and his long thick flowing chaps laid out on the ground. He was surrounded by three frisky females who were vying for his attention.

"What a beautiful, old Barbary Sheep," I whispered. "You're right; both of his horns are at least thirty-five inches."

I kept looking at the monster aoudad with my binoculars.

"You know, Josh, when he stands up, his horns could be longer," I added.

"I told you he was a huge toad," Josh whispered back.

Both of us were stoked. You could feel the excitement in the air.

"He's pretty incredible," Josh added.

For another long minute, we continued to watch the aoudad lying on the ground.

"He's definitely a one-of-a-kind trophy," I said softly.

"Copy that."

With my binoculars, I followed his massive horns as they circled around his front shoulders and touched the ground.

"He's the biggest aoudad I've ever seen in my life, and I've seen hundreds of them out here on the ranch," Josh stated.

"He's unbelievable. What an animal." I stared a long time. "You're right, Josh. He is a monster."

After another minute, the giant aoudad finally stood up. He was massive, heavy-boned, and very muscular. He drifted to our left, heading southward, careful to keep himself in the dark shadows.

His girlfriends never wavered, constantly flirting with him.

"There's still time for us to get him," I said mostly to myself.

Josh nodded at me in agreement while patting his heavy rifle.

My mind was churning. I began immediately planning how I could put myself in a position to be close enough to shoot this animal with my bow. It was obvious the aoudad was keeping close to the brush. He was making sure he had a fast-track exit.

This old-timer was a thicket-busting escape artist who could climb the imposing face of the opposite hill in a matter of a few seconds. But there was one thing that Josh and I had on our side that the big aoudad didn't have with him—the element of surprise.

Neither he nor any of the other animals in the valley knew Josh and I were there. That was the key piece of the puzzle and the vital part of our plan to spot, stalk, and make a perfect long-range bow shot. I was ready to slip quietly into the brush to our left, then slide down off the ledge very slowly on my butt, staying in the brush along the opposite side from the feeders and ultimately getting myself into a good position to shoot him.

"He's standing in the wide-open down there now," Josh whispered. "He's perfectly still and broadside for you."

"You're right," I replied softly. "He's in a perfect position for a bow shot." I was excited. "We just have to find a way to get down there."

"Why don't you shoot him with the gun?" Josh asked. He was poised, ready to hand me the heavy rifle.

"No, brother. All we need to do now is sneak down off this ridge and get within seventy yards of him," I said.

My eyes were still on the giant aoudad.

"I'm definitely going to get him with my bow tonight."

"Trying to go down off this ridge is too dangerous," Josh whispered back. He tried to hand me the rifle again.

I ignored it. I motioned with my left hand for him to follow behind me and walk along the ledge. Josh got up, and we walked for twenty yards along the ledge and stopped.

I pointed. "Let's go down right over there." I was staring at a couple of small openings and narrow trails in the brush below the ledge. They looked promising.

Josh looked at me. "I don't think we can safely make it down to the valley floor."

"Sure, we can. We can do this."

He shook his head no.

I pumped my fist at him. "Come on, brother, let's do it." I was eager to get within seventy yards of that monster aoudad. I was ready to make the perfect shot. I sat on the ledge, hung my legs over, and waited for a few moments. "You know we've done this before in the past," I added.

"Yes, and we were young and stupid."

After a couple of more seconds, I turned looking at Josh. He was still standing on the ledge, holding the rifle tightly with his eyes locked on the steep, hazardous drop-off.

CHAPTER FIVE

6:25 p.m. Climbing down this mountain and traversing the perilous hillside to the valley floor had not been included in our original calculations for this hunt.

We both knew the dangerous consequences of this brutal landscape. There was no safe footing, the slope was too steep, and the jagged rocks too slippery. A cold breeze blew out of the north, cutting across our faces from right to our left. The wind energized me.

Josh, who was five yards to my left, squeezed his heavy 300-Win Mag with both hands as he sat down on the ledge. He turned to me, shook his head, and whispered, "You know this is crazy stupid, brother."

"We can do this," I stated. "Just go slow and be careful."

Josh shook his head at me before he dropped off the cliff. I watched him slide and coil, quickly disappearing into the heavy brush out of my immediate view. I could hear the rocks, tree limbs, and foliage twisting and moving as he began to maneuver downward.

Now it was my turn. I held my bow with my left hand and my quiver of arrows in my right hand. I slid forward and immediately felt the gravity pulling me downward. I began a twisting uncontrollable slither down the unforgiving, steep drop-off. The brush and cactus were thick and prickly. It was brutal trying to get my bow and arrows and body through it. The sharp, cutting rocks and precipitous incline made for an almost impossible descent. As I slid, I clung to limbs and roots and rock outcroppings, attempting to control my speed and direction.

In less than a minute after we started, Josh jumped up two big male aoudads. They sprinted away below us across the hillside, heading southward.

Josh called out to me in a low voice, "They're both good shooters."

I never got a good look at either of the aoudad, but I heard their hooves striking the rocks as they vanished into the brush.

Four minutes later, Josh stopped 450 feet down the hillside. He had struggled through the dense brush and fought his way down the rocky precipice to a small, semi-flat resting spot to catch his breath. When I got to him thirty seconds later, I stopped as well.

Our hands, arms, and faces were bleeding from the miserable thorn pricks and rock scrapes. Our legs and buttocks were bruised. Our clothes were partially ripped and torn. The terrain was cruel and merciless.

Josh looked over at me with an uncharacteristically concerned expression. He pointed to his right and the next drop off below us.

"It's pretty much straight down from here on," he stated.

I could see the next drop-off was about seventy degrees.

"We gave it our best shot just to make it this far," he said.

"We can still do this," I replied.

"No, sir. It's way too hazardous for us to go any further. It's totally unsafe. We're going to turn around and go back to the upper ledge," Josh instructed.

I looked down at the drop-off. It was extremely steep, but there was a lot of brush, large rocks, and tree roots to grab onto. I believed strongly we could make it down the mountain safely the rest of the way if we took our time. "Come on, Josh, we can do this. We're really close now," I said. "All we need to do is descend the mountain another five hundred feet, and we'll have a shot at him."

"It's not worth risking our lives," Josh snapped. "We're turning around right now and going back—end of discussion."

I looked at Josh. "Come on, man, we can't quit now."

He shook his head at me angrily, "I can't believe I let you talk me into doing this."

I looked back at the drop-off one last time, and when I turned around, Josh was already gone, pulling himself back up the slope toward the ledge.

I knew the remaining descent to the valley floor was definitely risky. But it wasn't impossible. I still wanted to keep going. I wanted to get a shot at that monster aoudad with my bow. But Josh was the guide and what he said was final.

I sat for a few moments; I could hear Josh climbing up the incline. *He was probably right*, I thought, but inside of me, I knew it was against all my instincts to quit and turn around.

After thirty more seconds, I began my return ascent.

A long ten minutes later, we both made it back up to the main ledge and sat there with our chests heaving, sucking in the air and resting. Our arms and legs and hands throbbed with pain. Neither of us spoke.

It was 7:06 p.m., and the sun had set. Miraculously, on the valley floor, the monster aoudad and his harem were still grazing at a large round hay bale.

Josh offered me his heavy 300-Win Mag. "I'm telling you, brother, take this gun right now while you've still got the chance to shoot him."

I shook my head. "No, sir, it's our first afternoon to hunt. And, like I said earlier today, I really want to try to get him with my bow."

Josh was clearly unhappy with my response.

I didn't say anything.

He took a deep breath. I could tell he was mad. "Do you know how lucky you are?" He whispered to me. "I mean, it's your first day here at the ranch and in this enormous 52-Pasture, and you have a chance to shoot this record-breaking aoudad."

Josh moved over hunkering down beside me. "You know, you may never get another shot at this monster."

I didn't answer.

"Brother, you just can't waste this once-in-a-lifetime opportunity."

Silence.

"I'm not going to be able to keep this monster aoudad a secret much longer. As soon as one of the other guides finds out about him, they'll be over here in this 52-Pasture with a rifle hunter to get him."

I was listening but not talking.

"That would be horrible." Josh took another deep breath waiting for me to answer.

I finally responded without moving my eyes from the aoudad.

"Like I told you, if I haven't shot him with my bow by tomorrow evening, then I'll consider using the rifle on Wednesday morning."

Josh shook his head in frustration. "Why are you so stubborn?"

I turned toward Josh. For several seconds, we looked each other in the eyes.

Then he leaned toward me and whispered, "Think about what you're doing, brother."

I didn't respond.

"You're never going to get this chance again."

"I don't care if I shoot him or not," I snapped. "I just want to try to get him fair and square. Me against him with my bow."

After that, we both sat quietly for about a minute before I turned and pointed to my left.

"I remember seeing a heavily used game trail about a hundred fifty yards back down this ledge. I noticed it when we were walking up here."

Josh was looking at the aoudad through his binoculars now.

"It appeared to me that's where the animals go up and down this side of the mountain to the valley floor," I added. "Maybe we could use that trail and make it down there."

Josh pulled the binoculars away from his eyes. He was noticeably upset.

"Oh yeah, brother. I know that pesky little rabbit trail very well. It's a trail to the end of the world and back—unless, of course, you're a wild sheep or sure-footed goat or antelope. And the last time I checked, neither one of us fit any of those categories."

I couldn't help myself. I had to laugh. Josh's sarcasm was downright funny at times, especially when he was mad or trying to make his point. I covered my mouth so the animals couldn't hear me laughing.

Josh frowned.

"If I thought for one second I could safely use that trail or any other route to scale down this cliff with you, I'd get you down there with your bow so you could shoot the aoudad," he said. "Look, we tried our best, but honestly, there's just no safe way to get us down below this drop-off to the valley floor from this direction."

"Doesn't that trail have switch-backs?"

"Yes, it does."

"Well then, with those switchbacks, wouldn't that make it a lot easier and safer for us to get down off this ridge to the valley floor?"

Josh shook his head. "Those switchbacks won't help us at all. That trail is more wicked and dangerous than what we just tried to do. It's straight down over there, almost a ninety-degree slope."

I thought for a few more seconds. "I just can't believe there's not a way down to that valley floor."

"Do you ever give up?"

"No, sir. I don't."

"Well, the answer is still no. There's not a way down there from here. Just forget about it."

I stared down at the prize aoudad, squeezing my bow with my left hand, listening and watching as Josh continued.

"If you won't use the rifle, then we'll have to wait until tomorrow morning to hunt him with your bow."

"Okay, fine," I said.

Josh knew that was a major concession for me to make.

"It's for the best, brother."

I nodded. "Whatever you say. You've got the last word. You're the boss."

I knew I sounded disappointed, but I knew Josh was the guide, and hunting on this ranch meant I had to follow his instructions.

"Anyway, it's going to be dark in about twenty-five minutes," he added.

I didn't look and him, and I didn't answer.

"I think we've had a really great hunt today," Josh said.

"It was a good hunt," I answered. "It's definitely been a beautiful Monday afternoon."

I knew Josh meant well and was only looking out for my best interest. I knew he was right about the steep, dangerous slope. It was extremely risky, and he didn't want me to hurt or kill myself.

The day was coming to an end as we kept our eyes focused on the sheep, goats, and antelope moving in the valley below us. In the far distance to the southwest, the bellowing from the herds of red stag filled the air.

Ten minutes later, the muscular aoudad and his girlfriends filtered away from the hay bale and disappeared into the brush.

We watched until we saw him and his harem climbing the extreme face of the mountain on the opposite side of the valley. When the small herd evaporated into the landscape, I knew our hunt was over for the day.

Josh and I sat in silence for about thirty seconds. He finally spoke up.

"You see that fat raccoon sitting down by the protein feeders?" he asked me. He was looking through his binoculars to our right.

I looked down through the dim light and saw the masked animal at the furthest protein feeder.

"Sure, I see him. How could I miss him? He weighs forty pounds or more."

"Well, shoot that worthless dude before it gets dark."

I knew Josh was throwing me a bone and trying to appease me. He knew I was not a happy camper because we failed to scale down the cliff and take the aoudad. Now, what he was asking me to do was definitely not normal here at this ranch. No hunter was ever allowed to shoot any animal without paying for it. Nothing was free here—not a raccoon or rabbit or armadillo or anything. I was shocked. I stood up slowly; the cold had stiffened my whole aching body. I hunkered down and then looked over at Josh.

"You sure it's okay for me to shoot that raccoon?"

"Yes, sir. We hate them here. Now show me what you can do with that bow."

"You know what I can do with this bow."

Josh grinned a little, winked, and finally shot me a big smile.

"Stop wasting time and shoot him."

"Okay, I'm on it." In a crouching position, I maneuvered around the big rock and then ducked into the thick brush to my left. I stood near the ridge drop-off, hidden from the animals below. I located a hole in the foliage where I could see the raccoon down below and make the shot.

Josh watched the raccoon in his binoculars. The raccoon was gorging on protein pellets.

"Be sure you don't hit any of those other animals standing around the feeders down there," Josh said.

"Don't worry. I won't hit any of the other animals."

"Just shoot that thing before it runs off. He's no good for nothing."

A couple of seconds went by. I was trying to figure the distance.

"Just shoot him."

"All right."

I had already nocked an arrow I normally used for hunting hogs. Without hesitating, I drew back my bow.

"They're horrible scavengers," Josh said. "They steal the feed the big game animals need to survive."

I anchored the bowstring in the middle of my nose. "What's the distance to the raccoon in your binoculars?" I asked him.

Josh studied the image in his binoculars. "Approximately sixty-seven yards."

"What's the angle?"

"Fifty-five degrees."

I found my sixty-yard pin in my peep sight. *That should do it*, I told myself.

"Okay, I'm ready."

"Then hurry up and do it."

The raccoon jumped, bounced around, and wiggled under the feeder as he ate the pellets. Then he raced about for several seconds before he finally stopped. For a moment, he was broadside. I stood, aimed through a ten-inch hole in the brush, and rapidly calculated the steep slope of the mountain, the yardage to the target, and the compensation for the gravity pull on my arrow. I figured sixty yards was perfect.

When I touched the release and watched the arrow buffet downward, I knew it was a good, clean shot.

"Youuuuu smoked him," Josh said loudly.

The sound of his voice caused the other animals to scatter in all directions.

"Great shot, brother."

As always, his words put a big smile on my face. This was Josh's patented response to my perfect bow shots. Over our years of hunting together, Josh never missed a chance to use the same reaffirming catch-phrase—"Youuuuu smoked him." It was one of those small traditions born out of a close kinship of brotherhood.

"Thank you, Josh," I said.

I walked out of the brush then knelt down by the big rock. I wanted so much to rib Josh really hard. I wanted to tell him I could have done the same thing to the trophy aoudad had we gotten off our butts and tried harder to scale down the cliff so I could get a shot. I really wanted to say it, but I didn't.

Josh looked over at me with a big smile. "That was some shot, brother."

I smiled back. "Thank you."

He was pleased and sincere. "You're dang good with that bow."

I was still grinning. "We always have fun hunting together."

"Yes, we do," he said.

And just like that, Josh and I were back to being great friends.

CHAPTER SIX

Josh and I sat on the edge of the cliff, talking about our long history of past hunts together. We talked about the old stories and memories that always brought big smiles to our faces and made us laugh. Great hunting and the outdoors. Great memories and fun. Great brotherhood and camaraderie. Both of us loved the animals and wilderness.

I looked out across the stunning landscape fading in the waning daylight.

"I guess we need to get started working our way back to the truck," I finally said.

Josh checked his watch. 7:40 p.m.

"Yes, sir, it's about that time."

We stood and collected our things. The sun had long dropped from the sky, and it was dusk. In a few more minutes, we would need our flashlights.

Josh knew a shorter and easier route back to the truck that took us down a steep path for a quarter-mile, then we traveled the mountains another half-mile toward the southwest, keeping a fast pace the entire time. After a while, we were walking directly south, leveling out on some flatter ground after we had gone two-hundred-fifty yards.

Further down the trail, we heard red stags bellowing and saw several darting through the brush pursuing the hinds.

"We're in the red deer neighborhood," Josh said.

By now, it was zero-dark-thirty, so we had already turned on our flashlights to see the trail.

"We're not too far from the truck now," Josh said. "Maybe a little less than a mile."

I couldn't believe how close the red deer were to us as they ran past.

"This is where the herds of red deer like to hang out. It's what we call the central west area of the 52-Pasture," Josh said. "It's a little more than a three-square-mile area."

They seemed to be everywhere around us now.

"They like being on this flat terrain. It's easier on them than those rocky hills."

A large stag bolted out of the thicket and then stopped fifty yards in front of us. Josh highlighted him with his flashlight. The stag turned and stared at us, his enormous antlers shown in the light beam for several seconds before he bounded away into a grove of cedar, blackbrush, and cactus.

"These red stags are absolutely beautiful. Their racks are tremendous," I said, amazed at what I had just witnessed. "They're mesmerizing. I love the crowns and drop tines."

Several more stags ran out onto the trail before us. We caught them in our flashlight beams. Two of them had monumental antlers.

"We're in their territory, but they don't care right now," Josh stated. "I love it. They're in a total frenzy chasing the girls." He laughed. "They're like a bunch of high school boys."

"You're right," I said. Their roaring was like music to me. "They're just so majestic."

"Yes, sir, the rut always makes every male species do stupid things. It makes them irrational and vulnerable. It causes them to make mistakes."

"I can't believe some of these giants are running past us at forty to fifty yards away."

"Well, brother, you're just lucky you came down here to hunt right now. Honestly, we never see these big boys except during the rut. The rest of the year, you won't catch a glimpse of one of them. In another ten days, they'll suddenly regain their senses and become totally nocturnal and invisible as always."

I nodded my head that I understood.

"It's like a magic spell comes over the males," I said. "They suddenly are crazy fools."

"Exactly. And, if you come back here in a week or so when the rut is over, you won't think there's a single red stag in this 52-Pasture."

We resumed walking. After fifty yards, Josh stopped, squatted down, and focused his flashlight on an older red stag that darted from the brush in front of us. The intense bright light from Josh's flashlight lit up the stag's antlers."

"His antlers are huge," I said. "He's got to be near world record."

Josh turned toward me. "He's a real giant, all right, but he's not the biggest one on this ranch."

The giant stag roared and then trotted away.

"You've got to be kidding me. There's a bigger red stag on this ranch?"

Josh nodded as we resumed our hike out. "Yes, sir. He's here in this 52-Pasture."

We were walking fast.

"One day, I'm going to take a nice adventure to New Zealand and get me a red stag well over 500 Boone and Crocket with my bow," I stated.

We could hear the animals running wildly through the dark.

"It's been a life-long dream of mine."

The night was filled with the clatter of flinty hooves striking the rocky ground everywhere around us.

"I guess hunting a giant red stag has been on my bucket list since I was a kid," I added.

Josh didn't reply as he walked ahead of me.

After another hundred yards, he stopped without warning and pulled out his cell phone. I almost ran over him in the dark.

"I want you to take a look at this photo. Check out this monster red stag."

He held the phone for me to see.

"Wow. What a magnificent stag."

The animal in the photo was beyond belief.

"This animal is running around here on the 52. He's the biggest red stag any of us on this ranch have ever seen. We believe he's going to score... mmm, probably well over 550 Boone and Crocket. Maybe even close to 600."

The red stag looked like something out of a fantasy comic book. I did a double-take. The antlers were so wide and massive he didn't even look real to me.

"Can you believe your eyes?" Josh asked. "That monster is indescribable, isn't he?"

"He's by far the biggest red stag I have ever seen in my life," I replied.

"Take a look at this video I took of him three days ago."

Josh showed me a video of the monster red stag.

"I got within fifty-five yards of him when I took this."

In my opinion, the red stag looked even more impressive in the video than it did in the photo.

"It won't be many more days, and he'll be invisible again," Josh said. "They'll all be invisible once the rut is over."

I took in a deep breath and exhaled slowly, processing everything.

"I'm going to text you the photo and the video so you'll have them. You might want to come back here next year and hunt one of these stags."

I stood in the darkness thinking. A crazy idea danced through my brain. I turned to Josh.

"Do you think we can bow-hunt that magnificent red stag here in the 52?"

"Sure thing," Josh answered back quickly. "The stags are in full rut right now, and you can see how active they are running around like a bunch of idiots. Look how close they're coming to us."

I nodded in agreement.

"We should be able to get you a close shot at that monster stag."

"That's good."

I could tell Josh was excited. He shined his flashlight at me.

"That enormous stag is going to be much easier to bow-hunt than the aoudad."

"So, the 52-Pasture won't be too dense or brushy to shoot that red stag with my bow?"

He was still shining his flashlight toward me.

I was listening.

"No, sir. You can easily use your bow down here in the central west. The terrain to hunt that trophy stag will be much different."

"Okay, I understand."

"With the rut," Josh continued. "I know we'll be able to catch him out in the open. All we have to do is stay patient, and we'll get him."

"I agree."

"There's no question in my mind that red stag is going to make a mistake. He's going to give you a clear shot with your bow."

"I think so too," I said.

Josh stopped talking. He was thinking.

"But hold on, I don't want you to feel pressured into hunting that monster stag. I mean, that's a lot more expensive hunt than the aoudad. I'm not pushing you, brother. If hunting him doesn't feel right to you, then don't do it."

There was another long block of silence.

"It's no big deal to us here at the ranch one way or another. We can sure get back to hunting the aoudad in the morning if you want."

"I understand," I said.

We were still looking at each other with our flashlights.

Josh continued.

"One last thing, brother. I think if you really want to get that stag, you will need to start hunting him in the morning. The rut is probably going to end soon."

"I understand the situation. I'll decide tonight what I'm going to do and tell you."

"Just let me know as soon as you can. I'll start thinking about an ambush as well as a good spot-and-stalk plan so we can have a chance to get him."

"That sounds good."

Josh and I stopped talking. We directed our flashlights out into the darkness. We could hear a loud crashing through the brush coming toward us and watched another red stag run past us at thirty yards, displaying an extraordinary rack like he was a crowned king.

"These animals are very majestic," I said.

"Yes, they are."

"I think you already know I really want to hunt that magnificent stag."

Josh smiled at me. "I know you do. It's a big decision and an expensive hunt, but it's going to be the hunt of a lifetime for you. Something I know you've dreamed about all of your life."

"I just need to think about it and talk to my wife."

"Copy that," he replied.

We resumed our trek to the truck. My mind was filled with conflicting thoughts. It all seemed crazy to me. When I departed Austin this morning, and up until a couple of minutes ago, my mind was solely focused on hunting the aoudad. Now in a matter of a minute, I was completely transfixed on hunting the magnificent red stag I saw in the photo and video.

When we arrived at the truck, I felt totally confused. I didn't know what to do. At the same time, Josh was calling Mr. Randolph, the owner of the ranch, on his cell phone, negotiating the cost for me to hunt this magnificent red stag. When Josh hung up, he told me Mr. Randolph was amenable to selling me this red stag for a dollar amount trophy fee equal to what a comparable size red stag trophy fee in New Zealand would cost.

"That's fantastic," I said.

"I just need to get on the internet and find out what the trophy fee costs in New Zealand would be for a red stag like this one I showed you."

I nodded I understood.

The news made me very happy, but I still needed time to talk to my wife and sort out the pros and cons of a Texas red stag hunt as opposed to traveling to New Zealand.

CHAPTER SEVEN

I knew the cost of a red stag hunt in New Zealand would be far more expensive than hunting a stag here in Texas. In New Zealand, besides the trophy fee, there would be tipping the guide, the daily rate charge, the extra costs for airfare and travel, the charge for lodging, the cost for transporting the meat, and getting the red stag cape and antlers back to Texas from New Zealand for the taxidermy. There were a lot of extra costs, charges, fees, and several variables to consider. With so many moving parts to this expensive red stag hunting transaction, this was not going to be a knee-jerk decision.

All of these things needed to be thoroughly discussed, examined, debated, and agreed upon with my wife before I could commit to hunting the red stag in Texas or anywhere else in the world. In my mind, through all the uncertainty of the hunt, there was one piece of criteria that was clear. New Zealand was halfway around the world, and the Champion Exotic Trophy Ranch was right where I was sitting.

When Josh and I arrived back at the lodge, we entered the building and proceeded directly to the dining room. We looked around. It was very late. Everyone had already eaten and gone home or to their rooms.

I quickly noticed Mr. Randolph sitting across the empty room waving at me. I waved back at him. "I'll be over there in just a few minutes, Mr. Randolph," I called out to him.

He nodded back at me he understood. "Okay, see you soon," he replied.

I informed Josh I was heading to my room to speak with my wife to discuss the potential red stag hunt. It was a big decision.

"Take your time. Discuss it thoroughly with your wife. Just let me know what you decide tonight if you can," Josh said. "I'll text you the cost of the stag hunt as soon as I check the internet and talk to Mr. Randolph."

"Just let me know the costs."

Josh nodded. He was also going to explain my situation to Mr. Randolph.

"I'll let you know in about thirty minutes after you get me the text."

"Copy that," Josh answered.

I was still looking at Josh. "Whatever we do, brother, we're going to have fun." I shot a big smile at him.

He winked. "Yes, sir, we always do."

Then Josh turned, heading toward Mr. Randolph's table.

After a couple of seconds, I yelled back to him, "Hey, brother."

He stopped and turned back toward me.

"How about saving me a plate of food. I'm really hungry."

"I'll take care of it, my friend," Josh said, turning back toward the dining room.

Heading to my room, I didn't know what I really wanted to do. I was drowning in all kinds of thoughts and questions. I was somewhat mixed up. How in the world could I suddenly ditch hunting the aoudad when I had been planning and practicing to hunt that animal for so many months? I entered my room, sat down on a bed, and stared at the wall. After a few moments, I began rolling it all over in my mind. *Come on, man, hunting the aoudad was what you drove down here to do. You can't switch horses in the middle of the road like this. That's just crazy. Just forget the red stag and concentrate on hunting the aoudad.*

But the more I thought about the magnificent red stag, the more I looked at the photo, and the more I watched the video, the more I wanted to hunt him. I couldn't get that spectacular set of antlers out of my head. My brain was swimming with the crazy idea of spending a sizeable sum of money to hunt an animal I had dreamed of hunting since I was a kid. The idea of hunting the stag on this ranch was less than an hour old, but, in my head, it was an idea I had dreamed about all of my life.

When the rut ends, I'll never see this stag again, I thought. *And, because of the rut, there's an extremely short window of opportunity to get this magnificent stag. The expense of traveling to New Zealand for the same animal will probably triple the costs.*

A few seconds went by.

"I have to do this. I have to hunt this magnificent red stag," I said out loud.

After approximately five minutes, I received a text from Josh, giving me the trophy fee cost that Mr. Randolph would charge me to hunt the magnificent red stag on this ranch. The cost looked comparable to those trophy fees I had seen on the internet for hunting similar giant stags in New Zealand.

I dialed my wife's cell phone and waited. When she answered, we talked for a couple of minutes about how the day went for her and then how it went for me. And when I thought the time was right, I brought up the magnificent red stag. As usual, she listened and offered her invaluable comments and perspective. Together we weighed all the options and especially the costs. During our conversation, she brought up my childhood dream of shooting a giant red stag. We talked about the cost of traveling to New Zealand. We talked about the cost of the animal in New Zealand and the cost of getting the animal back to Texas. It was a great talk for twenty minutes. In the end, my wife encouraged me to do the hunt at the Champion Exotic Trophy Ranch. She told me it was the right thing for me to do.

"I'm very happy for you, sweetheart, especially since you will be fulfilling one of your childhood dreams," she told me.

"Don't worry about the money. Everything will be okay. Never look back, sweetheart. Just do it and have fun," she said to me.

I felt so lucky—what a wonderful woman and wife. She is the very best.

"Thank you, baby-doll; I love you," I said to her and then hung up the cell phone.

I exited my room extremely excited. I hurried through the trophy room then turned into the dining room, where I spotted Josh and Mr. Randolph sitting at a table in the back corner. All the other hunters and staff had eaten, cleaned up, and left.

A glass of iced tea and a big plate of chicken-fried steak with mashed potatoes and gravy sat on the table waiting for me.

As I neared the table, I gave Josh a wink and grin. He smiled big.

"It looks like we'll be hunting the magnificent red stag in the morning," I said, with an emphasis on *magnificent red stag*.

"That's great news," Josh said.

Josh and Mr. Randolph stood up at the same time. First, Mr. Randolph and then Josh shook my hand and patted me on the back. They were clearly excited as well.

Mr. Randolph was particularly pleased, and it showed in his voice. "That's wonderful news, Marty. Glad you're finally getting to fulfill your childhood dream."

"Thank you, sir." I was smiling. We all sat down, and I began eating.

"I'm really happy for you, brother," Josh said.

My mouth was full of food, so I nodded my head at both of them.

"That giant red stag is an incredibly special animal. Pretty near a world record from what Josh tells me. I'm really happy you're going to be the man to go up against him," Mr. Randolph said.

Mr. Randolph stood up, walked over to my side, and patted me on the back.

"Good luck on the hunt tomorrow," he said, reaching down for my hand. "From what Josh tells me, I know you'll get him for sure with your hunting skills."

I immediately rose to my feet and looked Mr. Randolph in the eye like my father, the World War II Marine hero, taught me. We shook hands firmly.

"Thank you, sir. If that stag gives me a good shot, I'll get him, sir."

Mr. Randolph nodded at me and smiled. Then he took a few steps away from the table and looked back over his shoulder. "For many years, a lot of accomplished hunters have tried to shoot that record stag and failed. He's old and smart. I look forward to seeing the photos of you holding those antlers of that red stag," he said.

"Yes, sir," I answered. "Hopefully, I'll get him tomorrow."

And with that, the owner of the ranch left the building.

Josh waited while I finished eating.

I'll pick you up at 6:00 in the morning out in front of the lodge."

"All right, I'll be ready."

"I think we need to get an early start."

I agreed. "Sounds good."

"Sunrise is at 7:26," Josh said.

He turned to leave. When Josh was at the door, he looked back and waved.

"You know, brother, I'm thrilled about the hunt tomorrow. This is going to go down in history as a hunt of a lifetime for both you and me."

He shot me a big smile.

"I'm just proud that I'm going to be a part of this great hunt," he said.

"Me too," I replied. "This is a dream come true."

And with that, Josh waved and then exited the building.

As I sat eating the final bites of my dinner, I recollected the hundreds of times I had been in the outdoors hunting. So many great times with so many great people and friends. The lifetime of amazing hunts, the special moments, and the lasting memories flooded my brain. I knew I had been blessed by God many times over. And now I was going to be given the chance to make the greatest memory of them all.

I looked around the big dining room and saw that no one else was there. I was all alone. I finished my dinner and then took my plate into the kitchen and washed it out in the sink.

When I returned to my table, I took one last sip of iced tea before I walked out into the middle of the trophy room and stood there in the empty silence alone. There was no one there to honor this blessed moment I was feeling. I bowed my head and closed my eyes.

"Thank you, dear God. Thank you for my many blessings. And thank you for my wonderful wife and for giving me this great opportunity to enjoy the outdoors."

The words of my prayer echoed off the walls.

"Thank you for giving me the means and the opportunity for this once-in-a-lifetime hunt."

I could hear my words reverberating in the empty room. I was as excited as a kid in a candy store on the way back to my room. I felt blessed and on top of the world. In the hallway, I stopped and turned around to look back at the cavernous and vacant dining and trophy rooms.

"Thank you, dear God, for all you have done for me and for all of your love."

No one else had heard me, I thought to myself. But I knew God did.

CHAPTER EIGHT

Tuesday morning, October 22, 2019. I awoke at 4:00 a.m. I couldn't sleep. The giant red stag hunt weighed heavily on my mind. I took a quick shower with scentless soap to help eliminate any odor in the field, dressed in a clean set of camouflage gear, selected my five best arrows to take along on the hunt, and checked my bow for any potential problems. I felt strong and confident that I could make any shot with my bow. I couldn't wait to get into the outdoors.

I left my room at 4:28 a.m. and walked to the large dining room, where I stood alone just as I had done the night before. But this time, I didn't stop to pray. I was carrying my bow, my release, a quiver of arrows, and a practice target. I placed the target on the floor and the remaining items on an empty table near the coffee pot. I poured myself a hot cup with a splash of cream and then sat there with my coffee, a piece of toast with grape jelly, and my bow and arrows in front of me and waited for Josh.

I could not stop thinking about the 52-Pasture and starting the hunt. I knew my stag was out there rutting with the others, and my goal was to take him today, not tomorrow. I was quite sure if he made a mistake during our hunt and gave me a good shot, I would be taking photos with him and celebrating the success of the hunt of a lifetime tonight in the lodge.

I'm going to get that stag today, I told myself. *I know my bow-hunting skills are very important but, it's my good luck that will bring him to me.*

I finished my second cup of coffee, and then I took my bow, arrows, and my release out onto the porch. On my way out, I glanced at the wall clock hanging in between an impressive collection of elk and deer mounts. It was now 4:50 in the morning. The other hunters would soon be stirring.

The expansive lodge porch was glowing with bright lights. No one was on the porch but me, so I took one of my practice targets and placed it thirty yards away. I took two practice shots and hit the bull's eye both times. Then I moved the target to forty yards and hit the bull's eye. That was all I needed. I was ready. I retrieved the practice target and arrows; then, I took a seat in the nearest rocking chair. I prayed to God for my many blessings and thanked Him for giving me this once-in-a-lifetime hunt. Around 5:20 a.m., I took the target back to my room, brushed my teeth, relaxed on the bed for several minutes, then returned to the porch.

When Josh arrived at 6:00 a.m., we loaded into his truck and then drove out of the complex toward the 52. I stared to my right and then to my left. I rolled down my window. The thick black air swallowed everything up. I knew, somewhere out in this massive darkness, my red stag was waiting. Somewhere on the 5,200 acres, I knew he and I would meet for the opportunity of a lifetime today. I prayed for a good and righteous hunt.

I thought about the strategic and tactical elements of the hunt, the encounter with the magnificent stag, and how we were going to get close enough for me to get a good shot. I also considered I might not get the stag today, and that would only give me one more day to hunt for him.

Time was of the essence. By tomorrow night, I would be on the road back to Austin with or without this elusive prize. I knew hunting on the last day puts undue stress and pressure on the guide and hunter. I did not want to take my hunt for the magnificent red stag into Wednesday. That was something in the back of my mind I had not shared with Josh.

Finding and taking the stag today would eliminate a potentially stressful, pressure-filled tomorrow.

When we were about fifteen minutes out from the 52-Pasture, Josh began explaining to me his plan. It was a good one that I hoped would put me in a position to take the red stag.

We arrived at the large iron gate at 6:31 a.m. As usual, I jumped from the truck and opened it. My energy level was off the charts. We drove down the rough caliche road for over two miles. Josh began slowing the truck, and in three hundred more yards, he stopped the ranch vehicle and hid it in a thicket.

"We're a long way from the hills and mountains," I whispered.

"Yes, sir, this is the area where that monster stag likes to hang out," Josh answered softly. "This is his neighborhood."

I nodded my head. I knew we were in the central west.

It was now 6:39 a.m. The sun had not yet risen. It was still pitch dark.

"We need to be very quiet. No flashlights," Josh said in a voice I could barely hear.

He put his finger to his lips, "Shhhh."

I nodded at him, then eased out of the truck with my bow and arrows and made sure not to slam the truck door.

"I'm ready," I said.

Josh exited the truck, closed the driver's door without a sound, and then whispered to me, "Don't make any noise. Follow close behind me."

I had no idea where we were going. I could barely see Josh in front of me. I just knew we were walking slowly and as quietly as mice in the dark.

After about ten minutes, I could tell Josh wasn't happy. We had walked less than three hundred yards at a snail's pace because we just couldn't see. Josh stopped us abruptly. The terrain was flat and thick, but there was not as much impenetrable vegetation as the mountains to the north.

"We've got to pick up our pace," he whispered.

"You're the leader," I whispered back.

"Then stay right behind me. We're going to go faster."

He turned and took off.

We headed west, but now at a much quicker pace. It was dark, but there was enough starlight to maneuver. I followed closely behind Josh. We were walking fast. I could not believe he knew where we were going in this dense brush. I followed him like a good sheep, hoping we didn't step off a cliff or pitch off into a ravine. Josh knew this game trail like the back of his hand, but we were hampered by the occasional cedar limb or mesquite branch that struck us across the chest or arms, and occasionally our face.

After a quarter of a mile, the cloud cover broke, and the moon cast its light enough for us to pick up our pace even faster. Before long, we reached our destination. Our brushy hideout was near a dry creek bed. We arrived around 7:10 a.m.

This was a great location where we could stay hidden and wait until it was light enough to see the animals—kneeling inside the hideout we were facing south. From here, we planned to ambush the magnificent red stag. But if those plans failed us, we would start our spot-and-stalk of the red stag from here.

Another five minutes of waiting and a chorus of roaring and bellowing began. We hunkered down low in our hideout. Staying hidden from sight was the key. We could feel the animals moving all around us. Ten minutes later, the first rays of light fractured the eastern skyline and began to color the bleak shadows around us.

I couldn't believe my eyes. The landscape looked completely different than where we had hunted the aoudad. This area—the south end of the central west—had large clearings but with clusters of live oaks, mesquites, granjeno, and stands of cedar trees dotting the landscape. With our 360 degrees perspective, we could actually see different distances from where we were kneeling. We could see twenty yards up to one hundred fifty yards depending on which direction we looked. The roaring and bellowing got louder and louder. This was the area where Josh had photographed and videoed my red stag a few days before. The photo I had on my cell phone was proof positive the stag liked this area.

"I know your monster stag likes this location. I'm sure he'll show himself in one of these open areas this morning," Josh said quietly.

"Hope so, that would be fantastic," I whispered.

And then, the brush around us began to crash and move. Several large stags ran hinds out in all directions, blowing out of the undergrowth and into the clearings right in front of our position.

"Yes, sir. The rut is on." I could barely hear Josh.

Next came a handful of hinds pouring out from the brush to our right with a group of larger stags in hot pursuit.

It was now 7:37 a.m.

Josh signaled me to get ready. "I think your monster stag is going to come out at any time now."

He pointed to our left. "The trail cameras show him consistently entering this clearing from the east. He likes to come out right at daybreak and go to that water trough over there." Josh pointed to his right at the water trough about eighty yards away.

I nodded.

"He'll probably be with several hinds."

"Okay."

"You'll just have to wait for a clear shot."

"I'm on it."

Josh looked at me. "You ought to get a fifty to seventy yard shot at him. You can do it."

I nodded. "If he shows up, I'll get him."

The arching top portion of the sun showed itself at the horizon. I had an arrow nocked and ready. Everything was illuminated by the brightening sunlight as my eyes methodically scanned the thickets and the open areas to my left and front. If the red stag came into the clearing from the east, I was prepared to bring him down at any distance.

The minutes felt like hours as more stags and hinds danced around us; then, the herd of red deer began to gather roughly a hundred yards directly in front of us.

We waited.

I had an opening in the brush right in front of me, which allowed me to make any shot I needed. I could feel the cool south breeze hitting me in the face. The wind was absolutely perfect. Josh had done his homework. This was a flawless setup.

Another two minutes ground by.

Then, Josh alerted and pointed to my left.

"I can see his giant antlers. He's coming."

I turned slowly and looked.

"Yes, that's him," Josh whispered. "He's about to come out of the thicket."

I could feel the tension and excitement coming from Josh—"Get ready."

I swung my bow slowly to my left, then brought it up in front of me, drawing the string quickly to my nose. I took a deep breath—let it out slowly. I was ready—my trigger finger on the release.

Josh gave me a thumbs up. "Here he comes."

The loud roaring echoed from all directions.

I watched the big rack of antlers above the brush, moving slowly toward the clearing.

"Where he's coming out, it's going to be right at a seventy-five-yard shot." Josh's voice sounded like it came from miles away.

My heart rate and thinking stayed dead calm. I waited, taking each measured breath like a steady cadenced metronome. This was exactly the kind of shot I had spent long hours practicing for six months. I was confident and ready.

Peripherally, I could see the enormous animal coming through the brush to my left. My right eye was focused on my peep sight and yardage pins.

My right eye locked on my seventy-yard pin. When the magnificent red stag emerged from the dense thicket, he would present himself broadside.

Perfect, I thought as I held steady and waited.

An eternity passed—still no magnificent red stag.

"Something's wrong," Josh said.

The younger stags coming out of the thicket to the east stopped abruptly and looked directly at our hideout.

The roaring of the stags stopped. The stags and hinds in the clearing in front of us stood utterly still. They were all looking toward our hideout now. At that moment, the earth seemed to stand still.

And then, a coyote yipped and howled nearby, and then another and another until a pack of almost a dozen or more joined in howling and barking loudly. I let off my bow and remained absolutely still. The coyotes were so close it seemed like they were in our pockets.

"They're right behind us." Josh sounded worried.

I nodded that I knew.

The howling and yelping made the hair on the back of my neck stand up. The coyotes definitely had everyone's attention. The stags and hinds keep staring in our direction like the coyotes were in our hideout with us.

Josh and I both wished we had brought the 300-Win Mag, but we had left it in the truck. The only weapon we had in our possession was my bow and five arrows. With every second, we could feel the coyotes getting closer and closer. I pulled back my bow at full draw.

Josh was kneeling to my right. "Be ready to shoot," he said.

A foot to my left, there was a large oak tree blocking my presence from the red deer in the clearing. I slowly rose to a standing position and waited.

"I'm ready. I've got a handful of arrows for them."

Josh cut his eyes at me. I could see he was concerned. I could see him mouth the words.

"Stick 'em."

Then I knew—this could get serious.

The pack of coyotes continued to howl and close in on us. They were thirty feet away, and it felt like they were getting closer. It was an intimidating feeling knowing we might be defending ourselves with no more than five arrows and no backup firearms.

Neither Josh nor I were in the mood for getting attacked by a cunning pack of vicious coyotes. I honestly thought the whole pack was standing behind our hideout, watching our every move. The strong south wind was carrying our scent straight toward them. They knew we were there, and their actions were calculated and deliberate.

We waited in anticipation of one bold move by the pack that could escalate into a full attack on us. I remained at full draw with my eyes constantly scanning our perimeter.

This unnerving psychological standoff continued until four big male coyotes bound by our hideout on the west side at a full gallop, running the red deer, strategically looking to get lucky with a kill.

When the first of these savage animals appeared at fifteen feet away, I was fully prepared to use all my arrows and kill as many of them as possible.

The red deer darted in all directions through the brush as another group of five mature coyotes ran past us on our east side. It was like a scene out of a horror movie watching these two groups of predators execute their orchestrated ambush.

As they ran by at close range, I could see the killer instinct and the primeval look of death in their eyes. The spit and slobber dripping from their fangs as they raced past us. Nature's well-thought-out survival of the fittest all playing out before us. And here we were, delicately balanced in the food chain, probably the least well-designed of all the animals in that simple plan.

There was no doubt these coyotes had surprised the stags and hinds in this attack. There was an enormous amount of commotion in the brush around us. The thundering of nervous hooves, branches cracking, the terrified bleating, and loud cries of pain and death sent a signal of the reality of nature in action.

And then, as quickly as it started, it seemed to be over, as the red deer and coyotes had vanished.

I looked at Josh, who was standing now. He shrugged his shoulders. "Brother, that was scary crazy," he said, turning toward the east. "Too close for comfort."

"I thought they were coming after us."

He nodded his head at me. "Me too."

Turning to my left, I looked where the coyotes had run. "I'm glad they were after those red deer and not us."

"Yes, sir," he replied. After a moment, Josh stepped toward me. "I guess we need to go to plan B now," he finally said.

"That sounds good." I waited to hear the new plan.

We stayed in the brushy hideout while Josh explained the general layout and landscape of the 5,200-acre pasture. From the afternoon before, I had already learned a lot about the terrain and impenetrable brush areas of the 52-Pasture. I knew, for the most part, the whole 52-Pasture was a thick, impossible place to hunt. Therefore, nothing was going to be easy about plan B. But at least our fresh strategy didn't include the treacherous mountain areas. The new plan was to locate other open areas as we walked along the highly used game trails in the central west location of the 52. In those clearings, we would then spot-and-stalk each field to try to locate the magnificent stag.

"There's no way any of the coyotes touched your monster red stag," Josh stated. "He would have easily killed them with that rack."

I nodded in agreement. Then I was back to listening.

"I don't think he's traveled very far to escape the coyotes. Maybe a mile or so." Josh looked to his right and then back to his left. "We're still in his neighborhood," he kept telling me. "And I don't think he's ever going to get very far away from this area."

I looked over at Josh, "And his neighborhood is a little more than three square miles, right?"

"Yes, sir," he answered. "I don't think he'll get much up in the hills."

So, this is my magnificent red stag's home base, I thought. *It's at least three square miles where he has at least fifty hinds or more to service.* I looked over at Josh.

"I guess this is what we bow-hunters call real hunting."

"Copy that," he replied with a chuckle. "Anytime you're in this 52-Pasture, it's always real hunting."

We walked about a hundred yards and stopped.

Josh checked the wind. It had switched and was blowing out of the north now. "I think we need to head straight north," he said. A new front was moving into the area.

"My gut feeling is that your stag will be circling around from the east and stay in the central west. Right now, he's rounding up all of his hinds that the coyotes didn't catch, then I suspect he'll be moving his harem north and then back toward the west. And that's where we're heading," he added.

"I'm ready to go."

I turned and saw Josh already walking swiftly down the game trail toward the north.

"We've got a lot of work to do. No time to waste," he yelled back at me.

I kicked myself into high gear. My eyes were looking at this new trail Josh had chosen. I was moving fast, watching my familiar old hunting boots lay down one footfall after the other, silently hurrying to catch him.

As far as I was concerned, my hunt of a lifetime officially started at 8:17 in the morning. We began our journey moving north, trying to locate my red stag and his harem. Josh was sure my stag would stay in the central west, and we would intercept him.

Because of the rut, I was confident Mr. Magnificent would ultimately make a critical mistake giving us a great opportunity. We just needed to outsmart him. And once we spotted him, I knew we would put on a great stalk and get close enough to make the perfect shot.

CHAPTER NINE

In a matter of fifteen minutes, the roaring and bellowing of the red stags echoed from everywhere across the 52-Pasture. After a half-mile, we slowed down. We began a slow and steady walk northward, making sure nothing could hear us. As most seasoned hunters know, walking stealthily takes a lot of patience, practice, and energy.

We followed a handful of game trails along the way, where we located several small clearings, spotting-and-stalking as we made our way through this rough, unforgiving country. The wind was blowing harder now. The front had arrived, and the weather was turning colder.

Everything felt good about the hunt. I knew we were in the heart of the central west, the stag's neighborhood. We saw thirty or more mature red stags and even more hinds, but we never saw Mr. Magnificent. I believed it was just a matter of time, and we would find him.

We continued to walk a mile and a half through the thick brush, inspecting several open areas but seeing no sign of my red stag. We stopped for a brief minute for Josh to check his compass, then we started down a skinny path to our left.

When we were approximately a mile from the steep hills, not far from where we had begun our hunt of the aoudad, we turned slightly eastward, staying below the elevation. Then we walked steadily and quietly on the flatter ground for two hundred more yards before turning back toward the northeast walking slowly for another three-quarters of a mile looking intently in the small clearings to the left and right with each step.

The brush was less dense in this area, and we were spotting numerous stags and hinds. After two hundred yards, we immediately came upon a split where the trail divided into three directions. Josh determined we take the far-right trail because there was a water trough further down that way, and the trail was clearly most heavily traveled.

We pressed on for another grueling half hour and finally found a good clearing in the dense brush where Josh thought the water trough was located.

We stopped, faced north, and let the cold air dry the sweat on our faces.

"This wind's perfect," Josh said, speaking in an uncharacteristically soft voice.

I nodded, enjoying the cooling effect of it.

"If your stag's in that clearing, we're going to get him."

I nodded.

We couldn't be sure exactly how large the clearing was, but we had already spotted at least twenty hinds in the native grass well beyond the opening. It was a good sign, and they had not seen us. Off to our right, we could see one young red stag and three older ones. The males typically graze separately, keeping their distance from the females. This told us there must be a dominant stag somewhere nearby.

The tall grass from the trail to the mouth of the opening provided the cover we needed. Josh felt there was a good chance my stag might be somewhere in this clearing, so he suggested we hunker down for a lower profile and move closer.

My knees were on fire from the stress of squatting and low walking, and the long distance we covered through the tall grass was excruciating.

When we finally reached the mouth of the opening, we spotted my stag in the far-end corner. My heart raced, and my adrenaline went into high gear.

There he stood—that majestic creature—a perfect example of nature's best with his commanding antlers and his head held high, lording over his harem of breeding-age females and bugling a fearsome warning to the other stags. We could see four potential challengers pacing with great uncertainty as we imagined them weighing the consequences of battle with the primeval drive that told them one day that fight would come. But not today.

We scanned the clearing for our stalk and guessed it to be roughly a football field long by three-quarters of a football field wide. The clearing included a scattering of cedar, scrub oak, blackbrush, and mesquite, along with a large mott of live oaks right in the middle. There was adequate cover to conceal ourselves on a stalk to the mott. That location would put us sixty yards from the big red stag and his harem.

I saw Josh staring at the cover, and I checked my watch. 10:52 a.m. He turned to me, "If we can make it to that large group of oak trees without being seen, then I think you can get a really good shot at that monster stag."

"Let's do it," I said.

Josh did another quick assessment of the animals at both ends of the clearing, and then he sized up the oak trees with more intensity.

"I'll follow you," I whispered.

Josh measured the distance to the live oaks with his range-finder. Forty-three yards. If we stayed low in the grass and small shrubs, the stags and hinds might not see us.

To our right, the big stags were roaring and running around the east end of the field in a frenzy. Their testosterone was off the charts. My magnificent stag was on the west side of the field to our left, roaring and circling his girlfriends.

Every few minutes, one or two of the challenging stags would make a charge to the west end of the field to test my stag and attempt to run off the females. Mr. Magnificent firmly held his ground. His show of great force, plus the intimidation factor he held over the other stags, frightened them away. After each victory, he proudly strode back to his hinds, standing amongst them like he was king.

We watched this happen two or three times in ten minutes. The other stags were attempting to put on a show hoping to lure some of the hinds their way. The roaring and bellowing were deafening.

I stood behind Josh. "I'm ready to go when you are."

Josh nodded. Ten seconds later, he gave me the go signal, and we began the slow knee-killing trek through the native grass and shrubs toward the oak trees. As I crawled, both of my knees popped and shot horrible pain through my legs. It was pure torture—all of this while carrying my bow and arrows.

We were within yards of the trees when the hinds suddenly got restless and began bleating and calling loudly. We froze.

"The winds in our face. No way they can smell us," Josh whispered.

I nodded.

"We're almost there," Josh said. "Stay down."

Then we heard a few deep grunts, and the hinds took off running in a circle. We laid low in the grass, listening as the clatter of their prancing hooves echoed through the trees.

"This is part of their romantic mating dance," Josh joked. "Don't move."

I followed Mr. Magnificent with my eyes as he watched his females dance and flirt. They had no clue we were there hidden in the tall native grass. To our east, the four other big stags were in a frenzy, running back and forth.

"We have no choice. Get ready to run," Josh said. "Let's try to make it to the trees."

"Okay."

He glanced behind us, then scanned the ground ahead, where my red stag and his hinds continued with their mating ritual.

"Let's go now," he said.

We sprinted the last few yards across the clearing, dashing into the mott of oak trees, hoping we hadn't spooked anything. Several seconds passed. We were all clear. Somehow, we had made it to the oaks without being seen or heard.

"How lucky was that?"

Josh and I high-fived.

"We've got him now," he said.

We positioned ourselves in the trees and thick brush, well concealed and in a good shooting position. I found a perfect brushy-camouflaged area with three large oaks where I could stand hidden for my shot.

After three or four minutes, the monster stag and his hinds began walking slowly towards us.

"Get ready."

I smiled at Josh. "I'm always ready."

He gave me a thumbs up and grinned.

My favorite arrow was already nocked to my bowstring.

I scanned the west end of the field and watched as the herd of hinds and my red stag were inching closer.

Josh turned to me. "Hopefully, he'll leave his herd of hinds."

I nodded, but my eyes never left Mr. Magnificent.

After a few more seconds, my stag began roaring. The other mature stags waiting at the east end of the clearing reacted like they were on testosterone overload, indecisive about whether or not to follow their natural instincts to answer his challenge or to play it safe.

"He's going to make a mistake at some point and step outside his group of hinds," Josh said quietly as he watched through his binoculars. "At some point, he's got to give you a shot."

My adrenaline rose as I gripped my bow, waiting for the right opportunity.

"When he steps out from the hinds, you'll have a few seconds to take a fifty to sixty-yard open shot," Josh said.

We waited motionless and in silence for approximately forty minutes, then it happened. In less than a minute, my red stag began striding toward the mott of oaks. He made his way through the group of females, pushing forward as they calmly gave him room. He appeared to be taking inventory of the hinds as he moved near the outer circle of the herd and then stopped. His enormous one-of-a-kind antlers were a breathtaking sight reflecting in the sunlight.

Josh continued glassing him. "He's seventy-two yards out."

The stag waited. He checked his females one last time and then raised his head and tested the air—it was a precautionary duty of the dominant male as primitive and old as time itself.

Josh stood next to me. "He's going to give you a shot any time now."

My heart pounded. I breathed in slow and steady, calming myself. *This indeed is the hunt of a lifetime*, I told myself. *Now all I need to do is make the perfect shot.*

My bow and the nocked arrow felt wonderful in my hands. I watched Mr. Magnificent turn his head, staring toward the opposite end of the field where the interloper stags pranced and roared. He watched them for a few seconds, and then he roared back at them.

I couldn't believe we had actually found him in this enormous, impossible 52-Pasture. We had made an incredible spot-and-stalk, and now I was going to get the chance of a lifetime to make a single shot that had to count.

My heart and pulse were calm now. I took another deep breath. I felt good and confident. Everything was perfect. I drew back my bow and waited, staring through my peep sight at my yardage pins. Seconds later, my giant red stag stepped beyond his group of hinds, walked slowly into an opening, and stood broadside.

"What's the distance?" I asked Josh.

Josh was zeroed in with his binoculars. "Sixty-one yards."

I couldn't believe it. It was the same distance and the same shot as the fat raccoon. I quickly calculated any necessary adjustments for distance, slope, and windage. There were none.

"Take him," Josh said, his voice soft and urgent as he held the stag in the viewfinder of his binoculars. "Shoot him now."

I held the tight bowstring resting across the center of my nose. My right eye quickly focused through the peep sight, locking onto the sixty-yard pin. The arrow was set to target the crease behind the front leg where the stag's heart rested. Now, I needed one more second to reach up with my trigger finger to gently touch the release and let the arrow fly. *This is truly an honor*, I told myself.

But then it happened.

The second before I released the arrow, Josh and I heard a loud snort and bellowing and then a chilling bark directly behind us. At the same time, my magnificent red stag jerked his head and body, dashing off into the brush.

It was a real shocker—one of the interlopers, a big stag from the east side, had quietly entered our hideout, spoiled our cover, and signaled the world. The animal sprinted, snorted, and barked his way through the mott of oaks where we were hiding, missing us by three feet, then he crossed the clearing into the thick brush where he disappeared. Of course, the other three big stags and all of the hinds had already departed the area and disappeared as well.

In a matter of seconds, our hunt and good fortune had been turned upside down.

Josh looked over at me. "Can you believe that?" he was shaking his head. He looked alarmed. "That was a total surprise to me," he said.

"Me too," I said.

Josh looked down to his right, spotting the tracks where the large stag had run through our mott of oaks, then he stared up at me. "I could have reached out and touched those giant antlers as he ran by us."

"Yes, sir." I nodded in agreement. "I guess that big red stag did a better job of spotting-and-stalking us than we did of him."

Josh laughed.

We both looked around the clearing, staring at the emptiness of it all.

"Man. We almost had him," he stated.

"Yes, sir." *Indeed, we almost had him*, I thought.

I was disappointed, but the adventure, excitement, and thrills that bow-hunting always gave me were exhilarating.

"I only needed one more millisecond to touch my release and shoot the arrow."

Josh smiled at me. "That's why bow-hunting is called real hunting. There are never any guarantees when hunting with a bow."

"That's for sure. The uncertainty makes it difficult but fun," I said.

"Copy that," Josh replied; he was staring at the area where my stag left the clearing. His mind was working on a new plan.

Then for a few seconds, we knelt down and took it all in. The silence was nice. I looked over at Josh.

"You know, I believe bow-hunting is like an addiction because every hunt is different and because every time we walk through the wilderness, our journey is filled with an unknown mystery."

"You're right," he said. "Just like today."

"Exactly. Not knowing what's around the next corner or what the day is going to bring makes every bow-hunting experience something new," I added.

Josh nodded his head at me. "Yes, sir, I'll agree with that. Just think about our two hunts this morning. The coyotes could have attacked us, and the red stag could have trampled us."

We both laughed.

I smiled in agreement, "You're right about that."

"Both hunts were definitely filled with more than our fair share of excitement, and there is always something magical about being out here," Josh said.

"Agreed. It is awe-inspiring, and there is definitely a kind of romantic connection between man and beast. Honestly, that's why I love to bow-hunt," I said.

Suddenly, a loud roar echoed from our southwest. Josh stood up.

"You hear that stag?"

I nodded.

There were a few seconds of silence. The giant red stag roared from a few hundred yards away.

"That's your monster stag," he said.

I looked at him. "You sure it's Mr. Magnificent?"

"I'm positive that's him. I've heard him roar many, many times before."

We both listened for a moment.

"He's moving back toward the southwest. Deeper into his neighbor-hood," Josh said.

"We'll get him this afternoon," I told him.

Josh looked around the clearing, giving it one final assessment. "Yes, sir. I guess we're finished here," he said. He checked his watch—12:03 p.m. "It's a shame we didn't get him this morning, but hey—we've got a few more days left in the rut to hunt." He hesitated a moment. He was still looking over the field.

I squeezed my bow.

"I guess I should have taken a quicker shot."

Josh snapped his head around toward me. "No, sir," he stated loudly. He was looking me straight in the eyes. "You're dead wrong, my brother. We did everything right this morning."

I didn't speak.

He stepped closer. "Yes, we had that monster stag in the palm of our hand for a short time, but when you're hunting, things just don't always work out like they're supposed to. I'm glad you took whatever time you thought you needed. Sixty yards is a long bowshot. I mean, that's a very difficult, extremely pressure-filled shot."

"You're right about that," I answered.

Josh stepped even closer to me. "And honestly, brother, other than you, I'm not sure I'd ever consider letting another bow-hunter take that kind of shot on this ranch. You know, there's a lot of bad things that can go wrong with a shot at that long distance."

"I understand."

I knew Josh was absolutely right.

Josh pointed at the spot in the field where my stag had stood minutes earlier.

"You know, there's a significant risk of only injuring an animal when you're shooting an arrow at such a long range."

He turned toward me.

"I know you've spent a lot of time practicing those long shots."

I nodded. "Yes, I have."

"I'm very glad you didn't rush that shot. I know you care about the animals. I'm glad you took your time and wanted your shot to be perfect. That's who you are, my friend. That's what I like about you. Don't ever change that."

"Thank you, Josh. I do try very hard to make every shot a perfect shot."

"I know you do. And your shots through the years have proven that."

Josh was wound up now.

I didn't know exactly where he was going with this conversation, but usually, when Josh got deeply passionate like this, he had some important, meaningful point to prove.

He was staring at the area where my stag left the clearing.

I waited.

After a few moments, he turned back toward me. "I mean, sadly, there's a lot of hunters who would have rushed that long, difficult shot, hit him poorly, and injured that monster red stag, so he might never have been found."

Josh was still looking at me.

"I can't imagine this one-of-a-kind, glorious, divine animal being lost—that would be horrible."

"Yes, sir. Because, if he was wounded and lost forever, that, my brother, would be a real travesty," he added like it was the final word on the matter.

"Yes, it would." I looked Josh in the eyes. "You know, I've never shot and lost any animal in my life."

"I know that. But unfortunately, as a guide on this ranch, I've seen that happen here a few times."

"That's totally unacceptable in my book," I replied.

"I agree. But sometimes people come here to the ranch who have never shot a gun or hunted before, and they want to shoot an animal, or they come here to hunt, and they get very nervous before a shot, or they rush the shot," he said. "Then they wound the animal and end up losing it, and we never find it."

"That's terrible."

Josh looked over at me and winked.

"Yes, it is terrible, but I'm not worried about that happening with you, my brother."

I smiled at Josh. "Come on, man, let's go get something to eat."

He let out a hefty laugh. "I'm on it."

We began the long hike back to the truck.

"We'll get your stag this afternoon. I've got a great new plan," Josh said.

CHAPTER TEN

Josh knew a quick shortcut back to the main caliche road. We reached the ranch truck at 12:45 p.m. and then arrived at the ranch lodge for lunch at 1:17 p.m. He was anxious to resume the hunt and said we needed to be back in the 52-Pasture hunting by 2:30 p.m.

"We don't have much time to mess around. We've got to hurry and get back out there," Josh insisted.

He explained the afternoon hunting plan to me while we were eating our lunch. We would begin our quest to hunt my giant red stag somewhere near the wide, cavernous ravine in the 52-Pasture, a daunting proposition by any measure.

"That dangerous ravine cuts across the southwest part of that big pasture in the central west. It runs for about two and a half miles, and then it continues out of the 52 for another three miles, where it drains directly into Reasz Creek," Josh said.

He stopped eating and continued.

"Where the deep ravine runs out of the 52 at the south boundary, we've had a dozer push and dump a lot of rock material there for several years. So, we've slowly filled up the ravine along that boundary fence. About three years ago, we finally made it where we could cross. The ravine is twelve feet deep there at the boundary fence and somewhat passable by foot. But no vehicles. And the constant erosion from the floods still makes it a tricky spot to maneuver."

"I understand."

Josh stopped talking and took a bite of his food before he went on with his explanation.

"We're not going down to the southern fence boundary today, but if you don't get your red stag this evening, then we may try to walk across the ravine at that location tomorrow morning and check out that undisturbed southwest central west area of the 52-Pasture."

"Sounds good."

"That's not really a part of the monster stag's territory. But since he's in the rut, some of the other guides and I feel like he might go anywhere on the 52 to service a hind."

"So, the entire 5,200 acres is in play for us to try to hunt him?"

"Well, probably not, but I'm not counting anything out because of the rut. You know how crazy and stupid all the animals are acting," he stated.

He looked over at me. "Let me tell you the rest of the plan."

"Go ahead."

"For the most part, the ravine in the 52-Pasture has high, steep rocky walls and is approximately thirty-five to forty-five feet deep in most places. And, in a couple of spots, the ravine might even be fifty feet deep or more. No one actually knows the depth of it because it appears bottomless."

I was listening.

"Frankly, it would probably be suicide to ever attempt to climb down those sheer, jagged walls of that treacherous ravine. Our plan this afternoon is to walk to the ravine but not cross it. Remember what I told you?"

"I remember."

"That ravine is no man's land, and it is off-limits."

"I completely understand."

"Most of that place is impassable and so dangerous, no one even thinks about going in there, not even the animals. It's pretty much solid brush with thorny vines, cactus, blackbrush, mesquites, cedars, persimmons, and a few big live oaks."

"I hear you, Josh."

"I'm not sure the Comanche ever went down into that death hole. It's got rattlesnakes and water moccasins, and other poisonous snakes. It's just not a place for humans."

I nodded my head.

"Okay." I was trying to eat my grilled cheese sandwich and tomato basil soup and listen to him and respond to him all at the same time.

"Don't' worry, brother, I'm never going down in that ravine," I said with a mouthful.

Josh was stuffing his mouth at the same time. I looked up at him over my food.

"Go ahead and finish. Tell me the rest of the plan."

"In one particular area of the 52-Pasture, the area I call the central west, where the big ravine begins to enter the pasture territory near the western boundary, it's about ten-foot deep and passable."

"Okay."

"The central west really begins on the east side of that deep ravine and occupies a little over three square miles."

I nodded.

"Well, at that particular spot, I think we have a great chance for you to shoot him. There is a highly used game trail where the animals like to cross the shallow part of the ravine from the southwest side and enter into one of the few open places in this pasture with native grasses. In that large clearing, the foliage isn't very dense. Hackberry, pallida, acacias, juniper, and mesquite beans are plentiful food sources along the perimeter. The clearing is approximately one hundred-twenty yards by seventy-five yards, where the red deer and other species of animals come to the east side of the ravine and feed into this central west area. The grassy field with mostly bluestem and sideoats grama, mixed in with a bit of lovegrass, wildrye, sacaton, and panicum is a favorite spot for lots of the animals."

"Okay, so I assume we're going to find a place on the edge of this clearing to hide out and see if my stag shows up. And when he does, we're going to spot-and- stalk him."

It was more of a question than a statement, and Josh answered accordingly.

"Well, sort of. I'm really thinking more about ambush. My plan is for you to take him while we're sitting in a blind I had built."

"I got it."

We paused the conversation long enough for both of us to shovel in more food. Josh began speaking first.

"So, our plan is to sit in the camouflaged net blind I had the ranch hands build eight weeks ago in anticipation of the red stag rut so my hunters could use it for hunting," Josh said.

"All right, I like it."

"We'll be approximately one-hundred-fifty yards off the ravine. I've hunted that clearing with my hunters many times before in the past years, and it has been a very successful area."

"Sounds good."

"About fifty feet inside the opening of the clearing is where I had the blind built. I think we will sit there for over an hour and hopefully get a shot at your stag. But if he doesn't show by 4:00 p.m. I want us to pick up and move away from the ravine very quickly."

"Okay."

Josh nodded at me and then checked the dining room clock. I glanced up as well. 1:35 p.m. Josh shot to his feet.

"We've got to go right now."

I was on my feet and right behind him as we hurried for the door. We left our half-eaten sandwiches and soup on the table.

We sprinted for the truck and, by the time I had slammed my door shut, Josh had the truck running and in gear. The back tires spun as we fishtailed across the dry caliche road and finally lined out for the 52.

Within ten seconds, Josh was telling me more about our hunting plans. "We need to be sitting inside of our net blind near the ravine no later than 2:30 p.m.," he said as he shifted gears and hit the accelerator, hauling butt to the 52.

He gripped the wheel and flew down the road with his eyes fixed on avoiding every rock and pothole while still trying to explain the after-noon plan to me. He took a deep breath and continued with his hunting proposal.

"After we leave the net blind, we'll need to go a mile north, and then northwest for a half-mile, before turning toward the east with the sun to our backs. That will get us near a watering hole. We must get to that spot no later than 4:45 p.m. I have another make-shift hideout there of cactus, cedar, and brush where I want us to hunt until dark."

"So, would that still be considered my stag's neighborhood?"

"Oh, yes, sir. That's right in the heart of the central west."

"Great."

Josh glanced at me, "We'll be hunting about a mile southwest from where we hunted the second hunt this morning."

"Okay."

"The central west includes all of those areas. Anything to the north and east of that ravine for up to three to four square miles should be in his neighborhood."

"Good. I just wanted to confirm we'll be in an area where you know he likes to hang out."

"Anything below those mountains on the 52 is his territory."

"Good to know his habits."

"Approximately three hundred yards from the watering hole is the remnants of an old broken-down game fence built years ago by one of the former owners. This old, dilapidated fence forms a perfect nine-ty-degree angle we call *the jog*. It's where the animals traveling out of the lesser hills from the west must take a hard right and then jack-knife back to the left in order to get down the trail to the watering hole."

"Sounds like a good spot."

"Yes, sir. It's a good place for us to sit concealed to wait for your stag to come down. You should get a good shot when he gets to the jog."

Josh had the pedal to the metal with a vortex of dust swirling up behind us.

I looked over at Josh. "How far do you think the shot to the jog is there?" I asked.

"Probably around fifty yards."

"That's perfect. I can make a fifty-yard shot in my sleep."

He glanced over. "Copy that. It's nothing for a stepper like you, my brother."

"I'm ready."

"I know you are."

Josh looked over, smiling at me, and I smiled back. He was working hard at trying to keep the truck on the road as I watched the landscape fly by until I began to see familiar landmarks I recognized as being near the approach to the large iron gate we passed through earlier.

"Only a mile to the big iron gates," he hollered.

"I'm on it."

Josh looked over at me and continued.

"At our hideout near the jog, we're going to have to squat or kneel the whole time—no stools at that one."

"That's okay."

"Will your ol' football knees hold up for a couple of hours with us kneeling?"

"I'll be fine. No worries."

We were getting close to the large iron gate now.

"Go ahead and finish the plan."

"Well, we're going to hunker down until dark. I'm hoping your stag picks that particular watering hole. There are approximately a dozen watering holes in the 52-Pasture, but none are as convenient and assessable to him as this one."

We hit a rough spot in the road, and Josh had a white-knuckle grip on the steering wheel.

"I understand. It's the best guess proposition, so we'll deal with it."

"Yes, sir."

Josh swung to the left and slowed the truck.

"I can guarantee you one thing—before the sun goes down tonight, your stag will go to water somewhere."

I chuckled. "Brother, I think that's a safe bet."

"I was just making sure you were listening."

We laughed.

"Okay, well anyway, the watering hole we're staking is, I believe, his top choice because it's very close to being in the middle of the central west. I feel like this is the best place for us to catch him in his own neighborhood."

"Sounds perfect. I believe tonight is the night. I can feel it."

"Amen, brother," Josh said.

We pulled up at the iron gate, and I jumped out, swung it open, and waited for Josh to drive into the 52-Pasture. There was a familiar and exciting but ominous feel to the place.

I swung the gate shut, locked it, and jumped back into the truck. And just like that, we were off, driving into the enormous pasture to have fun. The crunching of the dusty caliche road base was like a musical score to this adventure playing out in real life for the next two miles as it drove the adrenaline through my veins like some kind of excitement-inducing drug.

Josh's voice jarred me back.

"Okay then, to sum this up. So, if your monster stag comes across the shallow part of the ravine into the clearing, you could have anywhere from a twenty to seventy-yard shot. If he doesn't show up, we'll move a couple of miles northeast to the jog."

"Got it."

"If he shows up at the jog going down to the waterhole, I estimate you'll have a downhill shot somewhere around fifty yards."

"Love the plan. It's a winner."

Josh looked over at me, "I believe strongly you'll take him at one of these spots."

"Me, too," I said.

At 2:10 p.m., we parked the truck in a thick stand of blackbrush and juniper, about two and a half miles inside the iron gate. We were well east of the ravine.

We had a little over a mile and a quarter to hike. Exiting the truck, we double-timed to the southwest, heading in the direction of the deep ravine. Fifteen minutes later, we changed course, heading northwest at a grueling pace until we reached the opening of the clearing where we would set up our stake-out.

Josh checked his watch.

"2:35 p.m. and we're at our hideout," Josh said.

"Pretty much, right on time," I said.

We settled in. This was it. The uncertainty and the waiting. Nothing to do but remain silent and motionless, waiting patiently in this well camouflaged blind to ambush the magnificent red stag.

At this point, the hunt became an unlikely mix of boredom and excitement, exhilaration and discipline—every ancient survival skill and prehistoric instinct on display. From Darwin's survival of the fittest theories to Freud's psychoanalytical theory of personality. Every element of mankind coming down to this moment, at this place in time, surrounded by the unquestionable beauty of God's hand in this humbling environment. I can never adequately express how blessed I felt to be there in the outdoors.

Our blind was well-designed, sporting a thick camouflaged netting staked and running approximately four feet high completely surrounding us. Plus, we had some decent stools to sit on. It was perfect for this hunt. I loved it. We were about one hundred fifty yards from the notorious deadly ravine the locals liked to call "no man's land." I had never seen this infamous abyss, but that was okay with me. I hoped to never see it.

Over the next hour and a half, we watched well over a hundred animals pass through the upper side, and then over the shallow section of the ravine behind us just as Josh had predicted, each of these animals followed the worn trail entering the field to our left. They were instinctively cautious, stopping at the edge of the clearing, watchful for danger. Then, after a pre-emptive look, they walked out calmly in front of us and began to graze the lush weeds and native grasses and the variety of bushes along the perimeter.

The animals paid us no attention as they grazed and fed. The roaring of the stags and chasing of the hinds was still apparent as several of the larger stags circled the clearing, hoping to entice a few of the hinds for mating.

I had a choice of at least three giant stags parading in the open field in front of me, each of whom scored right at 500 Boone and Crockett points.

Josh leaned over and asked me if I wanted to shoot one of these giants.

I shook my head no.

I knew each one of these beautiful animals was a grand trophy, and at some point, they all presented me with a perfect broadside shot between thirty to forty yards, but I declined. Not one of them could hold a candle to my dream stag. I knew Mr. Magnificent was a special,

God-given, one-of-a-kind specimen. I knew my stag was born out of a divine creation by God. I believed God had put Mr. Magnificent in my dreams since I was five years old. *I would hunt and shoot Mr. Magnificent or nothing at all,* I told myself.

We witnessed a tremendous amount of exuberant game in a short period of time. Their charm, magic, and imagination—romping and running in the outdoors right in front of us—were indescribable.

Josh rechecked his watch. Exactly 4:00 p.m. With military-like precision, he stood and motioned it was time for us to leave. We moved out swiftly to the north, on our magnificent red stag hunting adventure.

CHAPTER ELEVEN

Our unexpected appearance and exit from our blind near the deep ravine panicked the nearby grazing herds of animals. The animals spooked at the sight of us, and they scattered in all directions. In the blink of an eye, they were gone, and we were on a good, well-used trail.

We double-timed north for a mile and a half from the ravine, and then, at Josh's direction, we angled off at forty-five degrees for another half mile onto a lesser traveled trail that ended at a fork. A few minutes after, Josh and I stopped at the fork to rest, he checked his bearings on his compass, and we proceeded down the left trail heading due east.

Three hundred yards more, with the sun at our backs and still well above the horizon, we arrived at "the jog," our new hideout. It was now 4:43 p.m. The afternoon sun was tempered by a cold breeze rolling in from the north.

Our cedar, cactus, and brushy hideout angled downhill toward the jog that circumvented the pile of rusty wire created by the dilapidated, old game fence. Stepping into the hideout, I began surveying the entire area.

I was happy we were still hunting in the central west portion of the 52-Pasture. I felt we had a much better chance to get my stag in his home territory.

It was reassuring to see the heavily worn game trail to our left, where it twisted back and forth up a short hill with a slight slope. At the top of the trail, a little more than seventy-five yards away, the skyline was a beautiful sight—slightly cloudy with the sun almost touching the top of a picturesque hill that I knew was the ideal setting for the glorious sunset to come. I looked around at our location. This was a great spot. Now, all we needed was for my giant red stag to show.

Josh was kneeling to my left, approximately five yards away. We had a superb view of the approach, where we knew the animals would eventually be coming down the trail straight toward us. The jog provided us the perfect location for a perfect shot.

I focused on the switchback near the broken fence, which caused the animals to change their course and required them to take a few extra steps at a new angle in order to avoid the old wire. At that particular spot, when an animal swung out wide to the right, it forced them to make an immediate hard-left turn to come around the debris. At this point, the animal would be broadside and completely exposed, momentarily presenting the broadest target before turning and following the trail off the hillside and down toward the watering hole.

By 4:50 p.m., we were finally situated and comfortable in our new hunting hideout with a tall grove of cactus to our front and left. We also were provided with excellent ground cover to our right. Agarita, black brush, autumn sage, hackberry, brasil, and other thorny bushes, shrubs, conifers, and succulents all camouflaged us. Behind us were a few cedar trees, a handful of live oaks, as well as junipers, persimmons, and yaupon. All of this natural vegetation and foliage guarded us well and provided us a textbook setup.

Before us stood several tall patches of native grasses—buffalo grass, wild rye, bluestem, and love grass, all covering the downward slope and streaking out toward the jog from where we were hiding.

I knelt down on the right knee, wishing I had that stool to sit on. I meticulously inspected my shooting lane, checking and rechecking every detail, making absolutely sure there was no grass or cactus or anything else that might deflect my arrow between me and the jog. I didn't see anything with my naked eye that bothered me.

We were hidden well. There were a couple of small cactus groves between our location and the target area, but they were nothing to worry about. I used my rangefinder to pinpoint the exact distance to the jog and to each spot around the jog where I might have a shot. It was precisely forty-six yards to the shooting area, from my position to the broadside turn at the jog. The measured elevation drop from the hideout to the shooting area was precisely eight feet. I calculated the downhill shot at an animal in the jog to be right at forty-one yards. I believed my forty-yard pin would be perfect.

Josh and I knelt quiet and motionless for several minutes.

As I waited, I recalled the wisdom of Aristotle, "We are what we repeatedly do. Excellence, then, is not an act, but a habit." I smiled. Aristotle was right. For over six months, it was my daily routine to practice long-range bow shots. Repeatedly hitting the bulls-eye at fifty, sixty, seventy yards had become a habit. I was more than prepared and confident to bring down the enormous stag.

When Josh figured it would be about time for the herds to be coming to water, he whispered for me to get ready. I had my best arrow nocked, my release in hand, and the bow resting against my left leg. I was ready. Within five minutes, several different species of animals began parading by in front of us, a colorful procession of wildlife, all timed to nature's cycle, just as Josh had predicted. We knelt and watched a long time as the caravan made the hard left turn, entered the jog, and then made their way down to the waterhole.

All in all, there are twelve waterholes in the 52-Pasture, so relying on this particular one was not a sure thing. It was a calculated guess at best and a bit of an odds-on long shot that this is where my stag would show up this evening.

The animals continued to pour out of the brush and down the hill. Forty-five minutes later, they were still coming, strolling past us to the watering hole. The large number and varied species passing through the jog was a memorable sight I will never forget.

Each minute we waited, I mentally documented the beauty of the outdoors and cataloged every detail of this hunt of a lifetime, vowing never to forget any of it. I wanted to capture this magical moment forever.

Forty more minutes passed. The sun began to disappear into the greying line between heaven and earth. There was still good light, but I knew it would be dark in about an hour, and darkness was definitely our enemy.

In the next few minutes, roughly twenty-five more animals meandered down, heading to the watering hole.

And then it stopped. 6:54 p.m. That was the end of it. The trail was empty and void of movement of any kind.

After a few seconds, Josh's voice, a raspy and resigned whisper, broke the quiet. "I guess the stag went to another watering hole."

"There's still some good daylight left," I said quietly. "I know he's coming. I can feel it."

Josh glanced at me. He seemed less certain.

"You're always thinking positive, brother—I hope you're right."

"I know he's coming," I whispered.

I wasn't about to budge. We waited another two minutes. Nothing.

"I told you, I know he's coming."

Josh gave me a thumbs up, "Maybe your good luck will bring him."

I looked over at Josh and smiled.

We stayed still and quiet.

7:01 p.m. The sun was setting, and I couldn't wait to see the masterpiece God was painting for us this evening.

The sun began to light up the puffy clouds with a subtle blend of red, yellow, and orange. A couple of minutes later, with the sun barely dropping below the horizon, we witnessed those last rays of sunlight turn the cloud formations into an incredible sight.

God's paintbrush was phenomenal; I let my heart, mind, and soul melt into the sunset.

"I love this time of day," I whispered.

Josh winked and smiled, and it was the smile of a man truly blessed by God's nature.

"Me too, brother. Me too," he whispered to me.

"We'll wait here until dark to see if he shows up. I know a good shortcut back to the truck," Josh said softly.

And then, as an afterthought, he continued. "We have flashlights, so it shouldn't take us long to get back."

I smiled back at him. No matter where we hunted or how many miles we walked, Josh always had a shortcut back to the truck. He was amazing.

Now, we were all alone in that twilight emptiness between night and day—no sign of the red stag. We sat there in silence, waiting for the hammer of darkness to fall.

The light of day was still hanging on, the heavy shadows creeping across the jog. Daylight was fading into darkness, but my hope was not fading with it.

My eyes were focused on the top of the hill to our left.

We were still sitting and waiting when we caught a glimpse of a small band of hinds. The sunset lit them up. They came twisting and flirting and bouncing down the trail, clearly within sight.

And then it happened.

Movement at the skyline. A solitary stag crested the hill, regal and majestic in his sudden appearance. That enormous rack of antlers with the drop tine silhouetted against the reddish-orange sky to the west.

When he moved into full view, the sight of him was breathtaking. He was truly indescribable. God's divine powers had definitely created him. I had no words to adequately express the vision before me. We both just stared and marveled at this big, glorious animal.

"That's your boy," Josh said. His voice sounded almost giddy. "Here comes the legend of the 52."

Josh held his binoculars locked on the enormous stag.

"He's even bigger than I thought."

I could tell in his voice Josh was excited. He kept his binoculars glued on Mr. Magnificent.

"I can't believe you're going to get an opportunity to take this monster."

"It's exciting," I whispered. "I'm ready for him."

My eyes followed every step the stag took. This was my childhood dream. My once-in-a-lifetime hunt was coming true.

Josh barely turned his head, looking at me now.

"You're a lucky man," he mouthed softly. "Through the years, lots of hunters have come and gone from this ranch trying to shoot this giant beast, but all have failed."

He slowly turned his head back toward the stag.

"You came here to hunt at the perfect time. Only in the rut would you ever have a chance at this one," he whispered.

We both focused on the giant stag, then Josh looked at me and smiled.

"I'm so proud and stoked for you, brother."

"Thank you," I said softly, never taking my eyes off of the stag.

We watched him take two steps and then stop. Two more and stop. Then he walked five steps and stopped, tested the air, took two more steps, and then stopped, taking every precaution that made him the illusive, dominant leader he was. It seemed like an eternity watching him descend the hill. All the while, the sky and night air were beginning to turn dark.

"This guy didn't get that massive rack by making a mistake," I said.

"Absolutely. He's going to score 575, maybe 600."

"I think so too."

Within a second, the stag stopped and stared straight at the cactus grove where we were hiding. His eyes were fixed on our hideout for a good fifteen seconds.

It was just plain eerie. It was like he knew we were there. We didn't move. Then the north wind picked up and began to swirl and change direction.

"Oh no. Our scent is blowing straight toward the stag now," Josh warned.

"It's okay. We're going to get him."

My heartbeat, my breathing, and my mind remained rock steady. I was calm and had positive thoughts. After a few moments, the wind stopped swirling and blew straight out of the north. The stag continued his walk down the trail. He moved very slowly toward the jog, keeping a keen eye out for danger. Josh and I knew, with each of his deliberate steps, the clock was ticking toward darkness. About forty yards down the slope, the stag stopped. He looked around and threw up his noise in the air.

"He's just being extremely cautious," I said, my voice barely audible.

"He's the best and biggest stag I've ever seen in my life," Josh said.

When the stag started walking, I could see he quickened his pace to catch up to the hinds that were now out of his sight. He was determined to catch them.

I anticipated he would make the jog faster than normal in order to get to his herd before some interloper stepped in to distract them. I knew his hard left turn at the jog would be a fast one, and I got ready for it.

My right kneecap rested on the ground, straining and throbbing with pain. I ignored it. My left knee was bent at a ninety-degree angle, with my left foot resting on the ground. My left knee had stayed bent for over two hours now, aching, shooting with pain too, but I didn't care. I was focused on Mr. Magnificent.

Josh was being extra cautious. "Get ready," he said.

7:06 p.m. I put everything out of my mind and concentrated on making a perfect shot. This was why I had diligently practiced those long-range bow shots for six months. I was calm and confident. At first, my focus was solely on the red stag. Then I told myself he was walking at a fast pace, so I needed to watch him and the jog at the same time.

I felt relaxed. My grip on the bow was light but deliberate. My favorite arrow was nocked and sitting perfectly in the rest. My left hand and wrist were snuggly fitted into the loop. My release was tied around my right wrist and rested gently in my right hand.

With each step the stag took, I was watching him and, alternately, the jog. My eyes darted from one to the other. He was moving quickly into the target zone.

He was coming fast now, ten yards from the jog. I took my eyes completely off of him and drew back my bow. My eyes were now entirely fixed on the exact spot in the jog where I believed he would turn broadside to me, and I would let the arrow fly. As always, I was focused on making the perfect shot. Light was dimming fast but remained bright enough for me to see the giant stag and my pins.

My right eye held the forty-yard pin on the jog. I held my trigger finger steady, prepared to release the arrow when the stag came into view at the perfect angle.

I waited. Calm. Steady. Unwavering.

Five seconds, ten seconds, fifteen seconds. No stag. No movement. Nothing.

Where is he?

Five more seconds. He did not show in the peep sight.

What the heck? Something's not right, I told myself.

I moved my nose off the bowstring and turned my head to the far left, looking around my bow, stretching my neck upward to see over the top of the cactus.

There, my giant stag stood. Five yards shy of the jog with his wary eyes burning into the cactus grove where Josh and I were hiding. He was facing me, looking straight at me. And when his wild eyes locked onto mine, he panicked and began a fast turn-around through the jog.

"He's moving fast," Josh whispered.

It was obvious the unsettled stag saw me and knew something was wrong.

"He's running. *Shoot him.*"

My head was away from the bow. My nose was off the bowstring. I had absolutely no way to shoot.

A second later, the stag was accelerating at a faster pace, trying to race through the jog in order to avoid the danger.

"*Shoot him now,*" Josh said, his voice sounding impatient.

I pulled my head back to the bow, hurrying to get the middle of my nose on the bowstring and locate my peep sight. My eyes were watching the stag begin to rush out of the jog.

"*Shoot,*" Josh said.

Everything was happening in a blur of speed. I located the forty-yard pin inside the peep sight with my right eye. My left eye was focused on the big stag. He was now moving even faster, mostly out of the jog and quartering away. I had lost my optimum broadside shot.

"*Do it!*"

I was hurrying.

"*Now,*" Josh demanded.

I was rushing to make the perfect shot while the stag was running and on the verge of getting out of position and giving me no shot. The magnificent stag was slightly further away now, a little past the jog heading swiftly toward the waterhole.

There was still good light. In a millisecond, I guessed he was forty-eight yards downhill. I quickly calculated the slope and figured the real distance was probably forty-three yards. I knew I had to lead him because he was running. This was a new shooting lane. One I had not checked out. The distance was slightly longer than the distance to the jog. I expected the arrow to drop two inches from my aiming point at the top of the crease behind his right front shoulder and be perfect. I aimed two feet in front of the stag, parallel to the top of the crease. He was moving away, quartering from me. I hurriedly aimed the forty-yard pin, reached up in one smooth movement, and touched the release.

I watched my arrow with its lighted nock buffet the air at 325 feet per second, flying like it was in slow motion. I watched the stag move precisely into the path of the arrow. My eyes followed the arrow as it hissed along on a flawless flight path watching it drop the two inches I expected to make it a perfect shot. But then, just before the arrow struck the red stag, I noticed it redirected itself slightly upward about two inches. I knew immediately the arrow had clipped an invisible piece of native grass, causing it to deflect and fly slightly off-line. This made the shot slightly high.

Wham. I saw the arrow hit. On impact, the enormous red stag leaped forward, staggering for several moments. I was sure the shot was deadly. Then he stumbled to his left, lost his balance, looking all the while like he was going to crash to the ground. Death was upon him. The arrow and extensive blood were clearly visible on both sides. My heart raced. *He's going down right there,* I thought.

And then suddenly, my eyes could not believe what happened. The stag miraculously regained his strength and balance and galloped away.

It was obvious he was hit extremely hard.

7:08 p.m. I knew I had rushed the shot, and the arrow had deflected upward, hitting the animal a little high. I watched the stag closely, trying to make sure exactly where the two-inch broadhead penetrated the kill zone. This big-boned, thick-skinned, powerful beast was jacked full of adrenaline now, searching frantically for a quick exit from the clearing.

After the stag rebounded, he ran ten yards and then suddenly made a hard U-turn and ran back toward our hideout. As he neared our cover spot, he made a hard-left turn and raced toward the nearby brush. I could hear his hooves pounding the hard ground and loose rocks as I watched him sprint past us, only fifteen yards from our position.

In those important moments, I was clearly able to see the exact spot where the arrow entered the stag and ascertain the sizeable amount of blood flow from the wound. I was now certain the shot was slightly high, but I was also relieved to see it was, unquestionably, a lethal shot. At the very least, the arrow had clearly penetrated the tops of the stag's lungs. My eyes followed the animal as he disappeared into the brush sixty-five yards away.

I was still kneeling. Glancing over at Josh, I waited for his assessment. He was focused intently on the brush where the stag had exited the clearing. He hadn't said a word yet.

Five seconds later, we heard a thunderous crash deep within the brush where the stag had run.

Josh turned and looked at me.

"Did you hear that?" he asked.

I dipped my head to him, "Yes, sir."

He smiled at me.

"You got him, brother. He's already dead."

CHAPTER TWELVE

Josh was exuberant. He gave me a big thumbs up. "Youuuuuuu smoked him. Great shot, brother."

"Thanks, Josh."

After every other hunt we shared together in the past many years, those congratulatory words from Josh routinely brought a big smile to my face, along with an immediate high five and lots of enthusiasm.

But this hunt was a little different. I hadn't made my usual perfect shot. My shot was slightly high, two inches off-target, but I knew after watching the stag run past us it was certainly in the kill zone and definitely lethal.

My mind was quickly filled with lots of thoughts. I knew the stag was moving at a fast pace when I released the arrow. I knew the shot was difficult, but I also knew I had made shots like this before. I was shocked by the stag's miraculous recovery after being shot. The amount of super strength he possessed leaving the field was inexplicable. In my mind, the shot was lethal, but his supernatural powers and determination to live gave me doubt. *Had Mr. Magnificent really crashed in the brush and died, or was that loud, strange noise something else? If the stag was still alive, how long would it take for the stag to bleed out?* I was disappointed for breaking one of my three sacred hunting rules. I had indeed rushed the shot, and that was unacceptable. But mostly, I was disappointed with my shot placement. I believed because the shot deflected slightly high and was not perfectly placed, it would probably take several hours—possibly all night—before my giant stag would expire. And to make things more difficult, I knew if I were wrong and my shot placement was actually better than I thought, and my red stag was dead, the coyotes would surely find him within a short time and totally destroy him. I definitely did not want the stag suffering through a coyote attack and becoming a tasty meal for them. My slightly off-target shot and coyote problem in the 52-Pasture were presenting me with a big dilemma—should I wait until morning or go after my stag tonight?

Having to make myself wait until morning to recover Mr. Magnificent was going to test my mettle. It was clear, the timetable for my stag's recovery was going to be tricky. I knew very soon; I would need to make a decision on what course of action was needed to locate and recover the legendary stag. And lastly, with all this uncertainty and indecision running through my mind, there was a very good chance I might break another one of my hunting rules before the night was over.

I stood up in the hideout and quickly put all of this out of my mind. This was my childhood dream, and my hunt of a lifetime rolled into one. This hunt was a special memory for the ages and a time for Josh and me to celebrate. I was euphoric, bursting at the seams with joy and excitement. I had dispatched Mr. Magnificent, the legendary red stag who had evaded so many experienced hunters through the years. This was indeed the greatest hunt of my life.

I walked over to Josh and held up my right hand. "Give me a high five, brother."

Smiling large, Josh stepped toward me and slapped my hand.

"I'm off the charts excited for you, brother. You just shot a world record stag. What an incredible hunt, and as always, you made another perfect shot."

"Thank you, Josh." I patted him on the back. "But don't you think the shot was a couple of inches high?" I asked.

"What are you talking about? I saw where your arrow hit and all that blood when the stag ran by us. You hit him perfectly in the kill zone."

I turned toward the spot where the stag was shot. In my mind, I could see the arrow deflect and hit high. I knew it wasn't perfectly placed. I quickly turned back to Josh. "You're right, it was definitely a lethal shot, but I know the arrow was slightly high."

Josh shook his head, "No way."

"Yes, sir, and we're going to need to wait until morning to go after him."

"What do you mean we're going to need to wait until morning? We heard the big stag crash and go down."

Yes, we did hear him crash, I thought.

Josh shot me a big smile. "Your giant stag is already dead, brother."

"Hopefully, you're right," I answered.

"You got him good. Okay."

"You're right; it was a deadly shot."

"Copy that."

I knew Josh was ready to go retrieve the giant stag.

I still felt uneasy about how long we needed to wait.

I looked at Josh, "I don't feel comfortable about rushing into the brush after him right now."

He was listening.

"If the broadhead only caught the tops of both lungs, then it's going to take several hours, if not all night, for him to bleed out."

"You're over-thinking this, brother," Josh said.

I shook my head. "No, I'm not. I just want to be careful not to run him."

He didn't speak.

"Look, if the stag is alive when we go after him, he might run, and the coyotes will get him, and then we might never find him," I added.

"I don't think so." Josh shook his head back at me, "Remember, we both heard him crash. He's dead."

That seemed to be the final word.

We both remained quiet for several long moments.

Then I broke the silence. "He was hit a little high. Why not let him bleed out for a while? There's no reason to take a chance and maybe push him."

Josh shook his head at me. "I told you. You smoked him," he said in a loud voice.

His words were very convincing.

Josh placed his hand on my shoulder. "Come on, brother, stop worrying. The broadhead did its job. Your stag's lying dead out there in the brush."

"I hope you're right."

"I know I'm right," Josh shot back. "I've been guiding hunters out here for almost twenty years. Your arrow hit the stag hard in the kill zone. You double lunged him."

"I agree with you on that."

"Your stag is dead."

I was listening. Josh was right; I had double lunged him.

"You put a good shot on him."

I nodded. "Thank you."

I didn't want to argue this point any longer with him.

"Look, I agree with everything you're saying. Okay."

"Okay. Good." Josh smiled, looking at the spot where the stag had exited the field.

"You're right; the stag is probably dead. And hopefully, he's right over there where we heard the crash." I pointed to the northeast.

"That's exactly where he is," Josh stated authoritatively.

"But right now, I think we should play it safe…" I hesitated. "There's no reason to rush the recovery."

He was listening.

"I feel like we need to back out of here and give that big stag some time to expire if he needs it."

I sensed Josh still wanted to race into the brush right now and recover the stag.

He pursed his lips as he thought about what to say.

"I'll tell you what, brother, just for good measure, let's wait thirty minutes, and then we'll go take a real, quick look at the blood trail. If the blood looks promising, then I say let's stop right there, turn around and ease back out for a couple of hours. That way, we can make a plan on recovering the stag, and if he's alive, give him more time to bleed out if necessary."

I nodded. "I think that's a great idea."

I already felt better.

Josh looked at me. "Look, no hunter ever feels completely certain until they are gripping the animal's antlers firmly in their hands."

"You're right about that," I said.

I definitely felt that way tonight. I couldn't wait to find my giant stag and grip those massive antlers, but I had to stay strong and hold off my urge to rush into the brush and try to find him.

Josh put his arm around me.

"Look, brother, I want you to think about something."

I looked him in the eyes.

"You and I both know your shot was downhill."

I nodded.

"So, think about it. It's not where the arrow goes in the animal; it's where the arrow comes out."

I was looking at Josh and listening. He continued.

"The shot may have looked a little high to you on the entry side, but remember, the arrow was traveling at a steep downhill angle, so it came out much lower on the exit side. It's all about angles and geometry, brother."

It sounded logical, I thought.

"So, because of the steep downhill angle of your shot, the broadhead on the exit side was much lower in the kill zone. Therefore, wham and crash, and it's over. Your monster stag is dead."

I nodded. "You're probably right."

"Of course, I'm right. It was a perfect double-lung shot. You got him good, okay?"

"Okay. Agreed."

If Josh was correct, and the broadhead caught the center of the opposite lung, I knew my giant stag probably did crash and was already dead, I told myself. My mind was spinning. *If true, this information would certainly change the timetable for the search and recovery.*

Josh looked at me. "Stop second-guessing yourself. We need to be celebrating. This is a once-in-a-lifetime hunt, and you made a great shot. You did what no other hunter has been able to do. You shot the monster stag—the great legend of the 52."

"It's definitely been a great hunt," I said. "I can't thank you enough for all of your help."

Josh leaned over to me.

"Brother, I need for you to relax and start enjoying this special moment."

"You're right."

"This has been an amazing hunt. You just bagged a near world record red stag. You've accomplished something that no other hunter has been able to do."

We high fived.

He smiled at me. "All right now, that's much better, isn't it?"

I nodded. "I can't believe I got him."

"Like I always say to you, brother. Youuuuu smoked him." Josh laughed loudly.

I laughed loudly too. "Yes, I did," I answered.

I felt on top of the world now.

"We're going to have a celebration at the lodge tonight," Josh stated. "I've got a great bottle of red wine I've been saving for several years for a special occasion like this."

He grinned, "You're one of the best bowhunters I've ever seen. You make those long-range, pressure-filled bow shots look easy."

"Thank you, brother."

I was ready to get to the lodge and celebrate.

"And your red stag is the biggest one I've ever seen in my life and as close to a world record as you can get."

"I can't believe it. I've been dreaming about this since I was a little boy. And now it's come true. It's a real blessing."

"I'm very proud of you and happy for you." Josh always had a good way with words. "It's time to party and enjoy these glorious new memories."

Now, I felt better about the shot placement and the upcoming recovery of my giant red stag.

Josh and I were full of energy.

During this wait time, we walked back the mile and a half to the truck, then drove north on the main caliche road, parking not far from the jog. With flashlights in hand, we exited the vehicle and walked about two hundred yards in the direction where the stag was shot. We located our hideout; then, we stood at the spot from which we took the shot.

Josh checked his watch. "It's been at least thirty-five minutes since you shot him."

7:45 p.m. The sun had long set over the 52. Josh gestured in the direction of the jog. "Let's go check out the blood trail at the beginning," he said.

It was almost dark. We followed our flashlight beams to the spot on which the big stag stood when the arrow hit him and then onto the trail and location where we saw him enter the brush. At first, the bright lights shone on a clear but sporadic blood trail.

Then, within the first fifty yards inside the brush, the blood was consistent along the trail, and we spotted several noticeable large drops of blood. A few steps further, and we came upon a big sample of frothy lung blood about the size of a softball.

Josh knelt down and checked the bubbly blood with his fingers. He looked up at me with a big smile. "This is exactly what we wanted to see. Frothy lung blood. It was definitely a lethal hit."

Even in a whisper, Josh sounded excited.

I nodded. "That's great news."

"He can't be too far now," Josh said quietly, pointing his flashlight down the trail. "He's already lost a lot of blood." He shined his flashlight down the narrow path lined with thick brush. "I bet he crashed within two hundred yards of here."

We followed the blood trail another fifty yards and then stopped. There was a lot more blood and another big deposit of frothy blood.

Josh squatted and inspected several large areas of blood, but mostly he inspected the lung blood. "This blood trail looks very promising," he said softly.

"Yes, it does," I whispered. "Let's not go any further and ease out of here, just in case he's alive."

Josh looked at me.

"We don't want to push him. Let's leave him alone," I added.

Josh pointed. "I think he's dead right up the trail."

"Brother, let's please wait and give the stag some more time to bleed out."

"Okay," Josh said softly.

I could tell he knew I was uneasy about the shot placement and recovery. I was glad we were finally on the same page.

Josh reached down, picking up a rock. "I'll tell you what. I'm going to mark those two big frothy blood spots with some rocks so it will be easy for us to find them when we come back to retrieve the dead stag."

"Good idea," I whispered.

We turned around, walking back in the direction where I had shot the magnificent red stag. Josh was busy marking the trail and diligently placing additional rocks near several other good spots of blood.

We stayed like that, just processing it all in for a few more moments until finally we came out of the brush and found the main road. Josh pointed in the direction of the truck.

"Let's you and I go back to the lodge and eat a good dinner."

"Sounds great." For some reason, we were still whispering.

"I think it would be a good idea for us to talk to some of the other guides. Maybe get their expert opinions on the shot placement and the blood trail."

"Another good idea," I said.

"Let's hear what they have to say. Then we can decide on how we want to handle the search and recovery."

"I like the plan."

8:00 p.m. We had only walked the blood trail for approximately a hundred yards inside the brush. Josh was right, everything looked very promising, and I tried to hold back my excitement.

When we arrived back at the truck, Josh turned to me.

"From my many years of hunting, guiding, and tracking, I think your shot was deadly, and this blood trail is evidence of that. Everything I've seen so far points to a great shot and a positive recovery."

"I think so too," I said.

Josh was fired up now. And I was fired up too.

"I want you to stop worrying. You saw the first hundred yards of the blood trail. And we heard him crash. I can promise you we're going to find your monster red stag one way or another. With that blood trail, it's a sure thing."

I nodded in agreement.

Josh grinned. "But for right now, I want us to go back to the lodge, be happy and relaxed, and mostly, to celebrate this accomplishment."

"You're right, Josh." I smiled at him.

"Let's go party."

"I'm ready." I appreciated his friendship and kind words. I was definitely ready to relax and have fun.

Josh opened the driver's door; then, he paused to mull over a thought.

He finally looked across the truck at me. "If it's okay with you, I'm going to call Sean McElroy and see if I can get him and his dogs to come over here tonight to track and find your dead stag."

I hesitated. "I'm still thinking maybe we should wait until morning before we start the recovery."

Josh shook his head. "Let's at least hear what the other guides have to say before we decide the timeline for your stag's recovery."

"Okay, I agree with that."

Josh stared at me. "And, of course, I know you don't want those coyotes getting him tonight."

"No, I don't." I took my seat in the truck and shut the door.

"Those coyotes are a threat. You know they have to be a major factor in our timeline."

"I understand."

Josh jumped up into the driver's seat. "I really need to reach out to Sean right now and see if I can get him and his dogs on the hook."

I thought about the tracking dogs and how that might hurt or help the search and recovery. I didn't respond.

Josh was impatient. "I need to call him right now, brother, if it's okay with you."

"I understand," I said. I thought for a couple of seconds. "If you think it's necessary, then go ahead and call him."

Josh nodded his approval.

"I think you know," I looked over at Josh. "I trust your experience and expertise."

He smiled. "And I'm going to listen and do whatever you and the other guides think is best in the search and recovery of my stag."

"Then I'm going to have Sean ready to come tonight if that's possible. Hopefully, he's available. I think for sure he and his dogs will find your dead stag," Josh said.

"Whatever you think is best."

Josh smiled at me. "Right on, my brother."

He fired up the ranch pickup truck, and we quickly headed toward the big iron gate. When I jumped out to open the gate, Josh was making his calls.

I felt good as we left the formidable 5,200-acre pasture behind us and headed for the lodge.

Josh had already called ahead and made arrangements for the chef and ranch staff to hold our dinner until 9:00 p.m.

When we left the 52-Pasture, we were very happy. As usual, Josh drove like a race car driver. It was time for us to celebrate.

CHAPTER THIRTEEN

I felt a sense of excitement brewing in the lodge when we arrived at the building at 8:45 p.m. We were greeted by several other hunters plus a handful of ranch staff who stood at the door waiting when Josh and I entered.

The place was buzzing, and several people greeted us.

"Can't wait to see the photos of your prize stag," one of the staff members said as we walked into the room.

"Wow. Congrats on shooting that legendary stag," another staff member stated.

"Yes, sir, looking forward to seeing those giant antlers," one of the hunters added.

We were shaking hands and high-fiving these people as we walked through the lodge.

"Congratulations. Can't wait to hear about the hunt," another hunter shouted out.

Apparently, the news had spread fast after Josh made his call to see if any of the other guides were still available. Someone in the lodge had communicated the news to these people that the legendary giant stag—talked about and hunted for many years—had finally been taken with a bow. And, just like Josh and me, these people were pumped up and wanted to celebrate and party.

"Thank you for your kind words," I said to everyone. "Hopefully, we will find him tomorrow morning."

The congregation of well-wishers didn't appear surprised that we had not yet recovered the stag.

"Congrats, big guy," an unidentified voice yelled from one of the back dining tables.

"Best of luck on recovering him," another hunter said.

"Can't wait to see that monster stag," one of the staff added.

I waved to each of them.

Apparently, the reputation of my legendary stag was more widespread than I imagined. The enthusiastic gathering of hunters, guides, and staff buzzed and celebrated the grand news. Even the ranch chef and his crew came out of the kitchen and congratulated me.

We mingled with the crowd and had a lot of fun. Then we stood in front of the warm fireplace and chatted with different people. After twenty minutes, several came to shake our hands and congratulated us one last time before heading to their rooms or leaving the lodge. Around 9:05 p.m., the trophy room was still buzzing, but the dining room was fairly empty.

Josh and I sat down at a table near the back wall. We toasted and celebrated our stag hunt with Josh's special bottle of red wine. Now that the celebratory crowd had filtered away, we both wanted a few minutes to calm down. The glass of wine was excellent. We both were relaxed and laughing, and best of all, we felt on top of the world.

Sheldon Hamilton and Jon Carlos Morales, two highly regarded guides and veteran hunters approached our table at 9:15 p.m.

Josh invited them to pull up a chair and join us for dinner. I had met these two fine gentlemen many years before and was mindful of their outstanding and distinguished hunting careers that included some of the most exotic and challenging game in Africa, Europe, Canada, and North and South America. More importantly, I was aware of their extraordinary skills in hunting, guiding, and tracking. Each of them had served as guides and professional hunters for several years on this ranch as well as several hunting concessions throughout the world. Their reputations preceded them. Their abilities and talents were unmatched.

In a matter of a minute, we had all shaken hands and were sitting comfortably around the table usually reserved for Mr. Randolph. The staff served up heaping plates of rib-eye steak, baked potato, and green beans. The food, as always, was over the top delicious. We all dug in, very hungry and happy.

The conversation about the stag began immediately. Josh had apparently brought Sheldon and Jon Carlos up to speed on all the details of our hunt and the fact we had not yet recovered our animal.

"Josh said you made a great shot," Jon Carlos said. "Congratulations on a great hunt and taking a tremendous trophy."

"Thank you, it's been the hunt of a lifetime for me," I said.

Jon Carlos was six feet tall and a muscular, wiry, middle-aged man, with the rugged good looks of an outdoorsman.

I nodded at both Jon Carlos and Sheldon; then, I leaned forward in my chair toward them. "Josh and I really appreciate your help and advice on the recovery of my stag."

"We're happy to listen and offer our opinions in any way we can," Sheldon said.

"Thank you. First of all, I believe it's important for us to consider that my arrow hit the stag a little too high."

"How high?" Jon Carlos asked.

"I'd say approximately two inches high," I answered.

Jon Carlos and Sheldon didn't speak. That information didn't seem to faze them.

I continued. "Immediately after the shot, I watched the big stag stumble; he looked like he was going down right there."

"The arrow hit him hard," Josh stated.

I looked at Josh and then continued. "I really thought he was dead right there but, miraculously, the animal regained his strength, then he ran toward us and made a hard-left turn toward the brush. He was about fifteen yards away from Josh and me when he ran by us, and we were able to clearly see that my arrow caught the tops of both lungs."

Sheldon leaned forward, "You got both lungs?"

"Yes, sir."

"Then the animal is dead," Jon Carlos stated.

"How much blood was coming from the wound?" Sheldon asked.

"It was a significant amount of blood," Josh interjected.

Sheldon looked over at Josh and smiled, "That's good information."

"Did the arrow pass completely through the stag? Jon Carlos asked me.

"No, sir. The arrow was visible on both sides."

"But the wound was producing lots of blood?"

"Oh, yes," Josh stated.

"Well, I wouldn't worry about the shot being high," Sheldon stated. He leaned toward me. "All I can say to you is, in all my many years of hunting, I really don't think you can ever hit one of those red stags too high. It's pretty much impossible because the top of their lungs come close to touching the backbone."

Sheldon, a big man about six feet five inches tall, in his late fifties, had a barrel chest and a booming voice. He looked me directly in the eyes.

"Keep in mind; your red stag is a much larger animal than what we normally shoot here in Texas. He probably weighs in at over 500 pounds," he said.

I nodded.

"On an animal of this proportion, his vitals and organs expand and occupy pretty much the entire area inside of the body cavity."

"I understand that," I said.

Sheldon glanced over at Josh.

"It's my understanding y'all found a good blood trail."

"Yes, sir, it was a substantial blood trail. A real, good one."

"Well, animals that aren't mortally wounded don't leave good blood trails," Jon Carlos said, with an air of finality.

Sheldon looked over at Josh and me. "Jon Carlos is exactly right. This animal was obviously hit hard in the kill zone."

"He was definitely hit hard in the kill zone," Josh replied, shifting his gaze from Sheldon to Jon Carlos and back.

Jon Carlos and Sheldon were eating and still listening intently.

"And add to that, the large frothy blood deposits we found on the blood trail in the first hundred yards," Josh added.

Sheldon nodded in the affirmative. "Well, there you have it," he said with certainty.

"If the stag was shot through both lungs and there was good frothy lung blood found early on the blood trail," Jon Carlos stated, "Then the animal is already dead."

"That's right. The animal was double-lunged." Josh reconfirmed what they were all saying. "I know a good blood trail when I see one. And this one was really good. I also believe the stag is dead."

I had stopped eating now. It was more important for me to listen to the conversation between these experts in order to learn from them what decision I needed to make about the recovery.

"That's it, then." Sheldon looked at me. "You made a great shot, Mr. Akins, and the animal is dead," he said.

Jon Carlos took a sip of his iced tea and weighed in. "I agree 100 percent. The indicators are all there. It's a done deal. Go get him."

Josh nodded at them, then he forked in another bite of steak and spoke as he ate. "Plus, we heard him crash in the woods not long after he was shot."

"You heard him crash. Well, that pretty much sums it up," Sheldon said.

"Yep, game's over," Jon Carlos said as he resumed eating like that was the final word on the matter.

Josh was caught up in the excitement of it all and couldn't just let it go at that. He grinned at Sheldon and Jon Carlos.

"Like I told y'all, my brother here smoked that monster stag."

They all smiled at me.

"Well, once again, Mr. Akins—congratulations on a perfect shot and the great honor of being the one to bag that legendary stag," Jon Carlos said.

"Definitely, he's a one-of-a-kind trophy animal," Sheldon added. "You know, the past several years, we've all tried to hunt that monster stag."

"He was just too sneaky and clever," Jon Carlos said.

Sheldon tipped his head. "That stag was a smart cookie. Amazing you got him."

"He never gave any of us a shot."

"You're a lucky man, Mr. Akins."

"Thank you, guys," I said.

Everyone was finished eating now. I waited a few more seconds before I asked the big question still on my mind. "So, because the shot was not perfectly placed, do y'all think we should wait until tomorrow morning to recover the stag?"

Sheldon had a shocked expression. He shook his head at me, "Why in the world would you want to wait until tomorrow morning, Mr. Akins?"

"Just in case we're all wrong. I mean, he was clearly hit high in the lungs. What if the stag isn't dead? I don't want to take a chance and run him so we might never find him."

Sheldon was still shaking his head, "By tomorrow morning, Mr. Akins, the coyotes will have devoured your stag. He'll be more than half gone. And the rest of him will be dragged off where you won't ever find him. And besides, don't you want that delicious meat for your freezer?"

"Of course, I want the meat." I looked at all three of them. "And I sure don't want those coyotes touching him either," I stated.

"Then you better go get him tonight."

"Coyotes are all over that 52-Pasture," Jon Carlos warned.

"Tell us something we don't already know. We almost got eaten by a pack of them this morning," Josh answered.

Sheldon cleared his throat. "I think you boys need to get out of here and go get that trophy stag rounded up while he's still in one piece," he said, his voice sounding more authoritative than ever.

Jon Carlos turned to me.

"Your stag's coyote bait right now. There won't be much left of him to collect if you don't get going right away."

Josh jumped into the conversation.

"I called Sean McElroy. He's meeting us at the gate tonight."

"You've got Sean coming?" Jon Carlos looked surprised.

"Yes, sir. He'll be at the 52 in approximately one hour."

"That's very impressive, Josh." Jon Carlos reached over and patted Josh on the back. "Great job."

After a moment, he turned to me.

"How lucky can you get Mr. Akins? You know the odds of getting Sean to come over here and find your trophy stag on such short notice?'

"Zero," Sheldon stated. "You're a very lucky man."

"Sean's one of the best trackers in the state. Normally his schedule is so full and committed he can't respond for a week," Jon Carlos added.

Sheldon was nodding. "The man has some great dogs. He will definitely find your red stag tonight in no time."

Josh looked over at me.

"I promised Sean some extra money to get him over here tonight. I didn't think you would mind as long as it means finding that magnificent red stag of yours."

"That's fine," I said.

It was clear to everyone at the table that the discussion was over. We all pushed back from the table, shook hands, and were beginning to walk away. The handwriting was on the wall. Everyone, Sheldon, Jon Carlos, and Josh, all voted to go out immediately and recover my stag.

Strangely enough, I was still uneasy. Something was telling me not to go after my stag. I saw the strength of the stag as he left the clearing. My Grandpa Schultz's third hunting rule was pounding in my head. *Never seek to recover a wounded animal if you believe your shot was not perfectly placed in the kill zone. Wait at least ten hours or until the following morning.* I knew my shot was not perfectly placed in the kill zone. It was two inches high. I had already violated one of the hunting rules by rushing my shot. Surely, I wasn't going to violate another one.

With all that had been discussed and said, I still wanted more reassurance from these experts.

We were all walking toward the lodge door now.

"So, what if the stag's not dead and the dogs run him tonight?" I asked.

"Then you'll take a rifle and shoot the stag," Sheldon said without hesitation. "Sean's dogs will bay him, and you'll get the job done in short order."

Then Sheldon stepped closer and leaned in toward me.

"Coyotes, coyotes, coyotes."

"Amen," Jon Carlos added.

Sheldon stared at me. "Look, Mr. Akins, here's the bottom line— dead or alive, the dogs will lead you right to the stag. And when you locate the stag, you can do what you need to do, but, either way, it needs to be done tonight."

"I understand that," I said.

"Then there you go. End of story," Sheldon stated.

Jon Carlos chimed in. "That's right, Mr. Akins, you have no other choice. Either way, alive or dead, finding your stag tonight is a win-win for you. If you find him and he's alive, then shoot him. The piece of mind alone that you will get from recovering him tonight will be worth it."

Josh put his arm around me, "Not only that, brother, think about how great it's going to feel for you to put your hands around those enormous, massive antlers. We need to recover him tonight. He's one of the biggest red stags in the world."

"That's for sure. He's the biggest red stag I've ever seen, and I've been all over the world hunting them," Sheldon said.

"He's nothing short of a world record," Jon Carlos said. "I've never seen a bigger stag in my life."

I was listening. It all sounded so good. They made me want to rush out to the 52-Pasture and find my giant stag. But I dreaded the thought of possibly running the stag and losing him. I hated the thought of never being able to find him. I just didn't want my magnificent red stag lost to the world forever.

All of us had stopped walking and were standing in the lodge doorway.

I leaned against the lodge door. I didn't know what to do. We all shook hands. I thanked them for their time, advice, and help. I truly appreciated their expert opinions and support. As they walked away, they congratulated me again for shooting the record stag. They wanted to see photos of our recovery tonight.

These men had more guiding, hunting, tracking, and animal recovery experience than the great majority of outdoorsmen in the world. Who was I to disagree with their decades of experience and expertise? They all had listened carefully, offering their valuable opinions and sound advice.

There was only one thing left to do—find my giant red stag tonight.

When I stepped out onto the porch, Josh informed me that Sean McElroy had agreed to meet us with his dogs at the 52-Pasture at 10:15 tonight.

"The dogs will find your dead stag fairly quickly," Josh said. "I'll bring my rifle, just in case he's alive and we need to put him down."

My inner soul was telling me to wait until morning, but I knew we needed to find him tonight and do it fast because of the coyotes.

Josh's truck was parked thirty feet from the wooden fence.

"Are you ready to go, my brother?" Josh asked.

I shook my head no.

My brain was locked. I couldn't make a decision. I walked toward Josh's truck, stopping suddenly. I didn't know what to do. Then I walked a few more steps, resting my arm on the wooden fence, gazing upward at the bright moon.

Only you, God, and Jesus Christ, and that lonesome moon up there know exactly where my red stag is lying tonight, I mumbled softly to myself, thinking no one else could hear me.

Josh stood right behind me.

"Well, brother, someone else knows too. Those mangy coyotes know," he whispered.

At that moment, I couldn't help myself. I broke out into loud laughter. Josh's way with words, his unexpected comment, his being a jokester at this stressful time was just the tension breaker we both need. We laughed a long time. The laughing took away my anxiety. And, when we stopped laughing, we both stood silent. Josh took a deep breath. This was hard on both of us. There were the unspoken reservations we both had if the outcome of the recovery wasn't good. Five seconds went by; then Josh stepped toward me, our faces were six inches apart. Our eyes locked together. "It's do or die now, brother. We're out of time. What's it going to be?" Josh was putting everything out there on the line for me to make a decision.

"Jon Carlos and Sheldon are the best there is," he said.

"I know that."

"It's your decision."

I didn't answer.

"We can call off the search."

I was torn. I stared out into the darkness, caught up in this terrible dilemma.

"Come on, brother. What do you want me to do?"

I was struggling. I looked Josh in the eyes.

"If the dogs run him, we'll never find him."

"I understand."

I shook my head. "I can't let that happen."

"You heard what Sheldon and Jon Carlos said."

Josh was still looking me in the eyes. I could see the hope and confidence there.

"I promise you we're going to get him tonight."

Josh's cell phone buzzed. It was Sean. It was a ten-second conversation.

"Sean and his dogs will be at the gate in twenty-five minutes. What's it going to be?"

I glanced at my watch. It was 9:49 p.m. on the dot.

"Trust me, brother."

I stared into Josh's eyes.

"We're going to find your red stag tonight."

The stress and anxiety of making this decision were almost unbearable. I wanted to make the right choice, but honestly, I didn't know what to do. I glanced into the darkness. The tough choices paralyzed me—try to find my red stag tonight, or wait until morning after the coyotes have destroyed him.

One thing was for sure; I wanted to do the humane thing for the animal. I wanted to keep the stag from suffering. I looked into Josh's eyes.

"Do you really think he's dead?"

"Yes, sir, I do," he answered quickly. "We heard him crash. He's dead."

I still wasn't convinced the stag had crashed and died, but it was game time, and I knew I had to do something. It's called decision-making under stress and uncertainty—making the correct decision under extreme pressure. Something I had dealt with all my life as a quarterback, a trial lawyer, a husband/father, and a hunter. At that moment, I knew exactly what we had to do.

I looked Josh in the eyes. "All right then, let's do it," I said. "Let's go get him."

Josh jumped high into the air.

"All right," he shouted. "Yes, yes, we're going to get him."

"Let's do it, brother," I said, now caught up in Josh's enthusiasm.

"I can't wait to see you grab ahold of those big old antlers," Josh said.

"I can't wait either."

I jumped in Josh's truck and held on. I knew the decision was, ultimately, all mine. And, right or wrong, I also knew only time would tell. I felt like the weight of the world was lifted from my shoulders, and I wasn't going to worry about it anymore. No looking back. No second-guessing. Just plunge ahead and find that monster stag. That was all that mattered to me now.

CHAPTER FOURTEEN

Jon Carlos and Sheldon had concurred with Josh that the placement of my bow shot was perfectly placed through the lungs, clean and lethal. Their certainty the stag was dead, and my desire to do the humane thing for the stag and the horrible coyote problem in the 52-Pasture were the deciding factors in my decision to begin the recovery without delay. The way it sounded to me, this was going to be a routine search and retrieval of my stag.

Josh and I headed out of the complex in a hurry. Time was wasting, and we needed to meet Sean and his dogs in less than twenty-five minutes. Once again, we were on the caliche road with Josh driving like he was trying to win the Le Mans. We were rushing to the 52-Pasture faster than ever before.

10:20 p.m. We pulled up to the big iron gate. There stood Sean McElroy in our headlight beams, waiting outside his small truck smoking a cigarette, petting the heads of his tracking dogs secured in the pickup bed. He shined his flashlight on us as we parked and stepped out of the truck.

Sean was whistling a catchy tune and getting his dogs ready.

"You're late," Sean hollered in his Irish brogue. "I was only going to wait another couple of minutes; then I was leaving."

"We're really sorry, Sean," Josh said as he leaped from the truck. He was headed for Sean and a handshake. "We got hung up a little bit at the lodge."

"It'll cost you, but it's only money," Sean said through his loud laugh.

He pointed his thumbs at the dogs.

"Can't keep my dogs waiting, you know."

"This should be an easy recovery. I think your dogs will find the stag in just a few minutes," Josh said as they shook hands.

"Same price, short or long. Doesn't matter."

"I understand," Josh replied.

Now that we had some real action going, I felt excited about recovering my red stag tonight. The stress was gone. All the unknown issues felt resolved. I felt good.

I walked toward Sean with my flashlight beam held low and extended by hand as I approached the good-natured Irishman.

"Good to see you, Sean," I said.

He shook my hand.

"How ya gettin' on?" Sean asked.

"I'm fine, Sean. Hope you and your dogs can find my giant stag tonight."

"We'll give it our best. Josh tells me you've shot yourself a dandy."

"I think so."

"A grand one, huh?"

"Yes, sir. I call him Mr. Magnificent."

"Oh, I see. A big one indeed."

I nodded. "Yeah, and hopefully, he should be lying out there somewhere close."

Josh pointed his flashlight at the dogs.

"We just need you and your dogs to find him."

"I was pretty sure it wasn't a picnic you had in mind," Sean said in the way he had of keeping you wondering when he was serious and when he was joking.

"We'll find the boy if those coyotes don't get him first."

I had met Sean several years earlier when he had come to this exotic game hunting ranch to recover a wounded animal for another hunter.

The recovery had been successful, and Josh introduced us in the lodge that day. I remembered Sean was fun to talk with, and he was a very friendly guy. And also, how Josh joked between my strong Texas accent and Sean's Irish brogue, we were a great pair to listen to.

Sean was in his late fifties and still in great physical shape. He had built a good reputation for being one of the best trackers in the state. One thing was for sure; he loved his Jack Russell dogs more than he loved people.

"We're wasting time. Let's get going," Josh said.

"Ready when you are. Me and my dogs been waitin' on you," Sean said.

I got the gate open and held it until Josh and Sean pulled into the 52-Pasture behind me. I shut the gate but didn't lock it this time; then, I hopped back into Josh's truck. We headed east for a quarter of a mile, then turned due north on the rough, winding caliche road. Sean followed close behind us in his small truck while his dogs stared out into the black darkness.

Josh and I talked the entire ride, both eager and motivated to turn Sean's dogs loose on the trail. This was it. The time was now, and we both believed it. Nothing left to do now but turn the dogs out on the scent trail, and, fifteen minutes later, we would have my stag.

As excited as we both were, there was still something in the back of my mind that kept nagging at me. I had this premonition that breaking my own rule about waiting until tomorrow morning was going to come back to haunt me. I tried to force the thought out of my mind and focus on the task at hand.

The three-mile drive inside the 52 took about ten minutes, and then we stopped and parked along the roadside about two hundred fifty yards east of the jog.

The blood trail lay more than a hundred yards north of us. Josh and I watched while Sean put his three dogs on the ground. The oldest dog, a female named Rainey, was about ten years old and a veteran tracker. Sean also had two younger dogs, a female named Bree, who was five years old, and a male named Finn, about four years old.

The two younger dogs were also well-tested trackers. Together, this was a formidable, seasoned group of tracking dogs. When Sean spoke to them, their response to his commands was like watching a squad of Marines in action. These dogs listened with intensity and executed every command with crisp precision—it was an awesome sight to witness.

Almost four hours had elapsed since I shot the stag. It seemed like an eternity.

Sean held his flashlight in his right hand and led his three dogs following closely behind as we walked toward the start of the blood trail at the brush line. It took us a couple of minutes to get there. Sean didn't want to take his dogs to the last marked blood spot a hundred yards into the brush. He wanted them to start at the very beginning of the blood trail.

Sean amped up his dogs, loading them up with adrenaline for the hunt they knew was coming.

"Blood, get him up, blood, get him up," he said, pumping the dogs with energy.

They looked up at him like the ultimate pack leader he was. He amped them up, and then he turned them loose.

10:45 p.m. The dogs immediately found the blood scent and took off, flying down the narrow trail, disappearing into the absolute darkness.

Sean took off right behind them, moving remarkably fast for as little as we could see of the trail.

"Come on, boys. Keep up," Sean said, huffing between breaths and swinging his flashlight across the trail.

Josh and I hurried to keep up, now as adrenaline-charged as the dogs. After about sixty yards, Sean slowed the pace, and we slowed down with him, happy to have time to see where we were going. He continued at a steady but controlled pace, with Josh and me close behind him.

"Go slow. Dark as it is, you can lose an eye in this thick brush," Sean shouted back to us.

"We understand," Josh yelled.

We all went slowly and carefully. As bad as the brush-infested terrain was in the daylight, in the pitch black of night, it was horrific. Every fifteen seconds, Sean shouted out to his dogs and waited to hear their barking in order to gauge their general direction.

The stag's escape route to the east was random and unpredictable, which made it a miserable, winding, bushwhacking challenge that was as painfully difficult as it was dangerous. We went slow. There was no choice. Every step was a struggle, but there was no quit in us or the dogs. About every twenty-five yards, Sean stopped and examined the blood trail.

After about two hundred yards, the blood trail turned due south. Then fifty yards, and it turned west. And finally, after an hour, Sean called out the command for his dogs to stop and come back. When we caught up to them, Rainey, Bree, and Finn stood dutifully over a large pool of fresh blood.

Sean said, "Sit," and the three dogs dropped their butts to the ground at the same time.

Josh estimated we had probably gone three hundred seventy-five yards along the blood trail.

11:45 p.m. The brutal trek through the cedar, cactus, brush, and mesquite left our clothes looking like we had all taken a thrashing. Our shirts and pants were slightly torn, and we had scratches everywhere. We looked and felt like we had come out on the bottom of a barroom brawl.

Sean pulled a bottle of water from his coat pocket and filled his hand for each dog to drink one at a time. The patient way each waited his turn was a testament to their good training and their trust in Sean. It was an inspiring thing to see—that definitive connection between man and beast.

When he finished watering them, he told them to go lie down, and they did so without being told a second time.

Sean knelt by the pool of blood, examining it closely as if he was some sort of frontier hematologist. First, he inspected the edge. He picked a sample of blood with his finger. He smelled it. Then, he rubbed it between his fingers. Finally, visually inspecting the way it appeared on his fingers. Then he thoroughly inspected the center. The ground was completely soaked and bubbly wet with blood.

"I believe the stag laid down here not long after he was shot," Sean stated.

I was stressed and upset. It was obvious we had jumped up my stag and run him. This was exactly what I did not want to happen. This was why I had questioned Sheldon, Jon Carlos, and Josh's expert opinions. This was why I wanted to wait until morning to find him. I turned my flashlight toward Josh, then pointed my light at the large pool of blood and then back at Josh.

"So, is this where you heard the stag crash and die?" I asked him angrily.

Josh didn't answer. But I could see he was shocked my stag was still alive.

Sean looked over at Josh and me. He didn't know what I was talking about.

"The dogs jumped him up, maybe five minutes ago," Sean stated.

"Does any of the blood look frothy?" Josh asked.

"There's lots of froth in the blood," Sean said. "He's hit very hard."

"Yes, he's hit in both lungs," Josh replied.

Josh scanned the immediate area with his flashlight.

"He's lost a lot of blood."

"That's a fact," Sean said as he continued to kneel and examine the samples.

After several more seconds, he looked up at us. "I don't know how this animal is able to get up and run with this much blood loss."

I shined my flashlight, so I could see Josh's face. I could tell he couldn't believe the stag wasn't lying there dead. But he didn't flinch. His reaction was very positive.

"The further he runs, the weaker he gets. He's about finished. He's probably dead by now. Let's get back on his blood trail."

"I agree." Sean whistled his dogs up, and they sprinted to his side. He talked to them, and they were immediately amped and ready to go. He pointed them down the trail, and they were off.

11:55 p.m. We watched the dogs take off due west, vanishing into the dark abyss. And then, we followed Sean, who was right behind them.

After a hundred yards, the blood trail turned southwest. We crossed over the main caliche road continuing our search.

The determination of the stag and the uncertainty of where he was, pushed us harder. I knew my giant stag was running. At every turn, I hoped we would find him, and the search would be over.

We tried desperately to keep up with the dogs. It was impossible. We had to go slow. They stayed fifty yards ahead of us and never let up until Sean gave them the *halt* command. Each time we closed the distance to within fifteen yards, he would give them the *search* command, and they would be off again. We walked at a snail's pace, searching another two hundred yards of blood trail. Sean stopped every twenty-five yards and examined the blood. The thick brush continued to be ruthless and unforgiving.

12:30 a.m. The three Jack Russell's began to bark wildly. Somewhere in the darkness, approximately seventy yards directly ahead of us, we heard a loud commotion.

"They have him bayed," Sean shouted.

His flashlight beam swept the trees erratically with each hurried step he took.

"They've got him cornered."

Josh shouted back at me, "We've got him, brother."

We all tried to hurry through the dense brush toward the barking dogs, but there was no going faster. We struggled as best we could to reach the dogs, but the going was frustratingly slow.

Sean commanded the dogs to continue baying the stag. We heard the barking getting louder. We couldn't see anything yet, but we could hear the big commotion now about forty yards ahead of us.

"Your stag's not far off," Josh said. We could hear his hooves striking the rocks, keeping the dogs away.

I was trying to rush forward.

"We're very close now," Sean said, fighting his way through the brush.

"Almost there," Josh yelled back as his labored steps begin to slow.

We all fought and hacked our way through the brush.

Josh carried his heavy 300-Win Mag rifle. "When we get there and see the stag, I'll give you the rifle," he hollered to me. "Shoot him quick."

"Okay," I answered.

When we were within ten yards of the dogs and stag, we heard them begin to move away from us.

The barking began to fade. We were losing them.

The stag was running.

Sean yelled out the *halt* command. The now muffled barking ceased immediately.

We stopped in the small clearing where Sean was standing and where the dogs bayed the red stag. Our flashlights lit up the space. The area was covered in blood—lots of blood.

Sean shook his head. "Look at all of this blood," he said in disbelief.

"Have you ever seen so much in your life?" Josh stated.

"The stag is on his last leg," Sean added confidently.

We gathered around Sean to find out what was next. Sean seemed perplexed but confident. He looked at me over his flashlight.

"The stag has gone about seven hundred yards from where he was shot. My guess is, he's staying in this area because he's familiar with it," Sean said.

"He's in the central west," Josh said. "This is his neighborhood."

"I'm going ahead to find my dogs," Sean said.

He turned without another word and then set off alone into the brush. His flashlight bounced left and right, disappearing into the darkness as he walked toward a nearby game trail.

I looked at Josh with a questioning expression.

"I can promise you, brother, we're going to find your stag tonight," Josh said.

I nodded. "I hope so."

I stood there alone for a few seconds trying to process it all. I couldn't believe the stag was still alive and on the move. I turned the light on my shirt. It was torn to pieces. My legs and arms, face and chest, and the top of my head were bleeding. My whole body was pricked and bleeding from the mesquite thorns and cactus and shrubs and from being slapped by the cedar branches. My cap was torn. My legs, knees, ankles, and feet were scuffed, hurt, and aching. This southwest Texas brush country had beaten me to a pulp.

12:50 a.m. I knew I needed to catch up with Josh and Sean. It was pitch dark, and I didn't want to get too far behind. I pointed my flashlight southwest, ducked down, and pushed myself slowly through the thicket. I quickly made it to the game trail; it was two feet wide and a lot easier to maneuver.

I hurried, but after about sixty yards, the trail shrunk to nothing. I located a small tight game trail to my right and took it until I heard Josh and Sean standing and talking twenty-five yards ahead of me.

CHAPTER FIFTEEN

Sean and Josh both looked frustrated. I expected the worst as I gave them a moment, and neither spoke.

"So, what do y'all think now?" I asked.

They both turned to look at me.

"In my thirty years of tracking, I've never seen anything like this," Sean stated firmly.

"It's really unbelievable," Josh said. "This stag is a super beast."

"How far do you think he traveled from the jog where I shot him?"

Josh waited. "I don't know. If I had to guess, probably eight hundred yards." He lit the trail with his flashlight as he spoke.

"I've never seen this much blood come out of one animal that wasn't dead," Sean replied.

"Copy that," Josh said, pointing his flashlight toward the southwest. "There can't be much life left in him."

12:58 a.m. I stared into the darkness. The bow-hunt at the jog and my shot at the red stag seemed like it was several days ago. We were all whipped, physically and mentally.

After a few seconds, Sean spoke up.

"We need to stay on him," he said. "The stag can't go much further."

"This is it. He's down somewhere close," Josh said.

Sean called his dogs. They looked fatigued as they came slowly to him.

As much as I hated running my stag, I felt we needed to stay on him. Sean and Josh seemed sure this was it. I, too, could feel how close we were, and I was determined to find him tonight.

Sean held his dogs and looked them in the eyes.

"Dead deer, dead deer... go get him, go get him."

Sean turned to us, "Let's go. He can't be more than a hundred yards."

Sean tried to amp his dogs up one more time, but they were obviously spent. He turned them loose; they charged out a few feet and then slowed as they entered the thicket. We watched the dogs disappear into the brush.

"Come on, we've got to stay up with them," Sean said as he took off.

Sean and Josh, running with their flashlights waving, vanished into the darkness ahead of me. I could hear Sean calling out to his dogs. I hoped the dogs would find the animal dead.

I pushed ahead, knowing there was no quit in any of us. We would stay in the chase until we found the stag. Sean and Josh seemed sure we were going to find him any second now.

The brush was like a jungle, and the going was slow. I hacked my way through, following the sound of the dogs and trying not to lose them.

I had gone about fifty yards and heard the dogs barking and running toward the southwest. I could hear Josh and Sean yelling and the dogs barking for another fifteen seconds. I listened as the sounds began to fade away.

I was still plowing through the brush when I heard the voices of Sean and Josh talking in the distance. A few minutes later, the beams of their flashlights emerged from the brush coming toward me. And there they came, tromping out of the brush with the dogs. I watched them, waiting for the good news.

It was now 1:10 a.m., and I watched them as they approached. No one said a word.

I shined my light on Josh and then on Sean. Their silence confused me.

"Well, did y'all find my stag?"

I was worn out and impatient and hoping to hear something good, but their faces told the story.

"My dogs couldn't find a blood trail. The stag just disappeared," Sean said, shrugging his shoulders.

I listened in disbelief.

"I know it sounds crazy, brother, but the dogs couldn't find anything," Josh said.

Sean nodded. "The trail just vanished."

"I think the dogs got tired," Josh stated.

"My dogs are fine. They can't track without a blood scent," Sean snapped.

I stared at Josh. I couldn't believe what I was hearing. I turned to Sean. He could see by my expression I was disappointed.

"I'm telling you, there was no blood trail," Sean said to me.

"It doesn't matter," I stated loudly. "We're all tired and totally exhausted, including your dogs. Okay?"

"Okay," Sean said. He shrugged his shoulders.

"We'll find the trail in the morning when we get some daylight, and then we'll find the stag," I said firmly.

"I agree," Sean replied.

Josh looked at us both and nodded. "We'll find him in the morning."

Far in the distant night, a pack of coyotes howled repeatedly. We turned without another word and began walking back toward the two trucks parked almost a half-mile away.

Walking in the darkness, all I could think about was where is my stag? Why couldn't the dogs find him?

The entire day had been surreal.

It was 1:35 a.m., and the first thing Sean did when we reached the vehicles was water his dogs and then put them away inside his truck.

I looked in Josh's direction. He stood at the door of his pickup, put the rifle inside, and then slammed the door. He reached into the cooler in the bed of his truck, grabbed a bottle of water, and then took a long drink and stared off into the darkness.

I watched Sean climb into his truck and close the door. He rolled down his window and looked over at Josh and me.

"Josh, it's getting late," he said. "I really need to get going. I'd like to get paid before I go."

Sean held his hand out the truck window. Josh nodded at me.

I approached the truck, disappointed but knowing a deal was a deal. Sean's expression was neither apologetic nor emotional—it was all in a night's work for him and his dogs.

"Is it okay if I just mail you a check?" I asked.

"That's no problem."

Sean wrote down his mailing address and the amount of money I owed him for his services and then stuck the paper out the window. He looked drained and ready to get home.

"Thanks for your help, Sean. I really appreciate it," I said.

"I wish we could have found him tonight," he answered.

"We did our very best. That's all anyone can do."

Sean tipped his head at me, then fired up his truck.

I slipped the folded paper into my pants pocket.

"I'll mail you the check when I get back to Austin," I yelled as he pulled away.

"No worries," Sean replied, waving goodbye.

I watched as he turned his truck south on the caliche road and disappeared, heading toward the iron gate.

The only thing I knew for sure was that my stag was lost, and it was going to be more difficult than ever to find him, particularly since his trail went cold and the dogs had run him too far. I was upset at myself for letting this happen. I made the wrong decision. I should have put my foot down and made us wait until morning to recover him. But deep down, I knew my decision to find him was based on good intentions. I was trying to be humane, and I did not want the stag to fall victim to the coyotes.

Josh walked up and touched my shoulder. "We'll get back here first thing in the morning and find him, brother."

I nodded.

"And, if we don't find him tomorrow, the buzzards will surely locate him for us in the next few days," he added.

I felt sick. My head was about to explode. What had begun as the hunt of a lifetime was now a nightmare spun out of control.

1:50 a.m. Josh and I were loaded up and heading out of the 52-Pasture, staring out the windshield in silence. This was new territory for me. I hated the thought of not being able to recover the stag. For the first time in my life, I had shot an animal and not been able to find him. It was something I never thought I would experience. It was not in my playbook. I was frustrated, angry, and worried all rolled into one. The one thing I knew for sure was that I would never give up the search. I would never accept the idea of my red stag being lost forever. Even if it took me the rest of my life, I was going to find this one-of-a-kind, beautiful, divine creation by God.

Josh and I didn't say much on the way back to the lodge, but it was clear that Josh was trying to stay positive and upbeat. He wanted me to believe we would find the stag in the morning. I sure hoped he was right.

When we arrived at the complex, Josh dropped me off at the lodge. I opened the passenger door and stepped out of the truck. Then, I turned to Josh, leaned inside, reached across the console, and shook his hand.

"I know this has been difficult for both of us," I said.

"Copy that, brother."

"I got mad at you tonight, and I'm sorry about that."

Josh nodded at me.

"Thanks so much for all of your help," I told him.

"No problem. Just don't you worry about tonight. We'll find him tomorrow. Guaranteed," he said.

"I agree."

Josh shot me a partial smile. "I'll pick you up at 8:00 a.m."

"That sounds good," I replied.

I shut the truck door, waved goodbye, and then turned toward the building. I could barely walk. I was beat up and hurting. But I was more determined than ever to find my stag.

I hobbled into the lodge and went straight to my room. I took the note with Sean's contact information from my pocket and placed it on the nightstand, tossed my shredded shirt and camo pants into the trash, and took three Advil.

Staring at my naked body in the bathroom mirror, I saw the many cuts, scrapes, and bruises. The punishment we endured in the merciless brush had taken its toll.

I fought back the exhaustion and pain and the urge to give up.

A few minutes later, I stood under a hot shower replaying the details of the day in my mind. Deep inside my brain, I believed tomorrow, we would find him.

3:00 a.m. My head hit the pillow, my body ached, and a few minutes later, I felt like I simply lost consciousness.

CHAPTER SIXTEEN

I felt like I had barely closed my eyes when the alarm went off. It was Wednesday morning. A little more than four hours sleep, and I felt like I could hardly move when I rolled out of bed. I took more Advil. Already my mind was racing. It was October 23, 2019, and I was scheduled to leave tonight to return home to Austin. It was impossible to imagine getting everything done we needed to do today.

I struggled to get dressed as I pulled on a new set of camo gear.

7:55 a.m. I was waiting on the front porch of the lodge, eager to get started. I wasn't hungry. I skipped my usual coffee with cream and a waffle or piece of jelly toast. Recovering my lost stag was the only thing on my mind.

8:05 a.m. Josh arrived. He looked tired and worn out. A few minutes later and we were headed out to the 52-Pasture—it felt like a bad dream being replayed in the bright light of day. The only saving grace to it all was that we would soon end it when we found my red stag.

As soon as we hit the exit to the complex, I told Josh I had to return to Austin that night. He was a little stunned by this new information, but he understood. He knew I had clients and meetings I had to attend, and that was that.

We bumped along the unpaved road, rehashing the events that led up to this moment—the rushed shot, the high placement, the crashing of the stag in the brush—all of it. Then we walked through every itera-tion of the chase the night before—from the affirmation by Sheldon and Jon Carlos that it was a lethal shot to the buckets of frothy lung blood on the trail. Finally, we talked about Sean and his dogs and the fact they bayed the stag before they completely lost the blood trail. The conversa-tion ended with us debating what else could go wrong.

Of course, what we didn't discuss was the nagging feeling I had that it was going to take a miracle to find my prize stag.

A lot of things were different this morning. There was no laughter. No joking around. No funny stories or reliving memories of glorious past hunts. We both felt dejected and empty and even a little depressed. We both regretted what had happened. Neither of us could take much more stress or anxiety in this foreboding 52-Pasture. I sensed we both wanted to put yesterday's failures behind us. But, one thing was certain. Neither one of us had lost our faith or fight to recover my stag.

When we entered the 52-Pasture and had the iron gate closed behind us, we went back over the details of the night before and con-cluded the stag died somewhere between the jog and the deep ravine—an area covering approximately three square miles.

Josh continued down the caliche road until we reached the central west. He parked the truck when we were eight hundred yards south of the jog. We got out of the truck slowly. We were sore and stove-up. I walked around the truck and looked at Josh. "We need some good news today," I said.

Josh nodded and smiled, "Let's find him."

We left the truck and hiked southwest four hundred yards into the brush. Josh found the large rock he had placed on the blood trail less than ten hours earlier. We studied the stag's tracks and some dried blood in the soft dirt.

"The stag ran to this point last night. He's got to be dead somewhere in this area."

"So, is this the spot where Sean's dogs lost the blood trail last night?"

"Copy that, brother." Josh pointed to the southwest. "It looks like his tracks go up this way."

I began to feel the heat of the hunt pumping through me.

"Let's go see if he's lying dead up there."

"Sounds good," Josh replied.

We walked down the trail, unable to move fast. It took us a while to get the blood flowing. We walked like two old men, thrashing our way through the dense underbrush.

We found another large drop of blood on a mesquite limb lying in the middle of the trail. We spread out, walking two circles simultaneously at twenty and thirty yards, trying to locate more blood. No success.

We came back to the last spot of blood on the mesquite limb. Josh knelt down and touched the dried blood. "I think this was the spot where the dogs lost the trail."

I didn't answer.

"I think he completely bled out after this. So, all we've got to do is find him."

"I agree. He can't be far."

Josh and I fanned out, using an old tracking technique for finding a lost animal by walking in ever-expanding circles around this last known blood spot until the animal is located.

We first tried as best we could, one of us walking a circle at fifty yards and the other at one hundred yards. Then we tried at 150 yards and 200 yards. And then, so on and so forth, until we were attempting to walk circles at 700 and 750 yards around the last drop of blood.

As usual, getting through the unforgiving brush was brutal. It was a constant battle, but at least it was daylight, and we could see. We searched diligently, looking in every direction and under every bush or tree or shrug or plant as we walked the circles. Our effort to find the lost stag was nothing short of super. We gave it our all, but we never located the giant stag or any other sign he was ever there.

1:45 p.m. We called off our search and drove back to the lodge for lunch. We didn't talk much on our drive back.

We finished lunch and went out to sit on the porch. We needed a new plan. We were both tired, mentally and physically. Neither one of us wanted to continue fighting the brush.

It didn't take long for us to come up with a different plan that did not include hacking our way through 5,200 acres of undergrowth.

4:00 p.m. We returned to the 52 and drove around the entire pasture, looking for buzzards. After an hour of driving around in the central west, approximately two hundred yards to the east of the main caliche road, we spotted a big oak tree full of buzzards.

Our excitement rose quickly. As we got closer, we noticed several buzzards were on the ground. Josh and I drove up in the truck and jumped out.

Under the tree laid a giant dead red stag. His head was turned away, and his enormous antlers were lying mostly hidden in a brush pile.

"There he is, my brother," Josh yelled. He was totally energized. "We've finally found him."

I was beyond excited. I felt like the weight of the world was lifted from my shoulders.

"Oh my gosh, this is wonderful," I shouted out.

Josh smiled, "I told you we were going to find him."

Josh and I high-fived.

"I can't believe it," I said happily.

Josh pointed, "There lies the legend of the 52."

"It's a real blessing."

"Yes, it is."

The stag looked freshly killed, and it was obvious his backside was mostly eaten by coyotes.

"Hallelujah." I was over the top happy. "Praise God." This moment would be seared into my brain forever—the day I recovered this God-given one-of-a-kind specimen born out of a divine creation by God.

Together, we hurried toward the dead monster stag as quickly as our sore bodies would allow. Josh turned to me as we got closer.

"Finding your stag in this enormous 5,200 acres is a real miracle."

"I know. It's unbelievable." I was absolutely overjoyed.

This was my stag of a lifetime, and I couldn't wait to put my hands around those massive antlers.

"We'll get the camera and take pictures," Josh added.

I agreed.

As we got closer, the buzzards gave way to our intrusion, jumping back and flying to a safe haven.

Josh stepped into the brush, reached down, and drug the heavy, giant stag out into the open. His antlers were massive, extremely large, and beautiful, but this was not my red stag.

The let-down was hard. We both went from an all-time high to the lowest of lows in a matter of seconds. Suddenly the anxiety and worry, and frustration leaped back into my mind. I couldn't stop it. We were both clearly disappointed but not finished searching.

We returned to the truck and continued driving around the 52-pasture. Somewhere, we knew, my stag lay dead.

Two hours later, we spotted another group of buzzards sitting in a tree near a waterhole at the south end of this endless pasture. This time, I didn't allow myself to get overly excited.

When we walked up, Josh and I spotted three hinds lying dead from coyote attacks. These were fresh kills, too, less than eight hours old. These animals were almost completely eaten.

We got back in the truck and continued our search.

7:00 p.m. Sunset. No more buzzards and no sign of my stag.

Reality was setting in. I was beginning to think there was a good possibility I had permanently lost my red stag. It was a hard pill to swallow, but I knew my stag of a lifetime might be gone for the ages. I rubbed my eyes with my dirty shirt sleeve and tried to fight back the lump in my throat.

7:20 p.m. Josh and I sat on the tailgate of the pickup drinking a bottle of water.

We talked for a few minutes watching the sky turning dark. Finally, we agreed Josh and the others would keep a keen eye out for the next few days. They would watch for buzzards and just generally be watchful for any sign of my stag.

Josh promised he would keep searching for the stag every day, even if it meant employing the help of some of the other ranch workers to help him.

"Don't ever lose the faith. If you believe you'll find him, then I know you will," I told Josh.

"I'll find him for you—and soon," Josh promised.

The coyotes started howling, some nearby and many off in the distance.

"You know they've probably already eaten your stag."

"I know that," I replied.

We sat staring into the night. I felt completely empty. I angled my flashlight in his direction.

"Josh, you know this is not how this fairy-tale hunt was supposed to end."

"I know that, my brother. All I can do is promise you; I'll never quit looking for him."

"And I thank you for that."

"I'm going to do everything in my power to search for him every day."

"That's all anyone could do. Hopefully, one day soon, I'll get the call from you, and we can celebrate."

Josh reached over and put his hand on my shoulder. "I can guarantee you this; we're going to have a major celebration when I do find him."

"I'll come back to the ranch, and we'll have a good one."

Josh smiled, "You betcha my friend."

"We've had some good times and great hunts together," I said, feeling like we were both trying to patch up a broken one.

I directed my flashlight toward Josh.

"One day, we're going to look back on this one with some great memories, too," I said.

I could barely see Josh's face, but I could tell he was smiling.

"With all that's happened, this one could turn out to be our greatest hunt of all time."

"Definitely, it been the toughest and most eventful," Josh said.

We sat in silence. I was running late. I smacked the tailgate with my hand.

"I gotta get back to Austin."

We hopped down from the tailgate, got in the truck, slammed the doors behind us, and were off down the road.

We tried our best, did everything possible to do, used up every ounce of strength we possessed, and we lost. It was the most disappointing twenty-four hours imaginable, but I knew Josh would never quit searching. I knew if that stag was anywhere on earth to be found, Josh was the man for the job.

As we drove back, one thing Josh had said during our tailgate rewind put the fear of failure in my heart.

"Finding your stag in a place as inaccessible as the 52 is worse than looking for a needle in a haystack—it's going take a miracle."

As much as I didn't want to admit it, I knew he was right. I knew what we were trying to do just might be an impossible task.

Everything took on a new perspective now—the iron gate, the caliche road surface, the dark, the ominous brush-covered drop-offs. It was part of me. I felt a sense of loss, almost sadness, knowing, as we approached the big gate, I may never open and shut it again for a long, long time. I looked back at the 52-Pasture, and it felt like part of me was staying behind. The intensity of it all made normal life seem somehow incomplete. Maybe the thing drawing me to hunts like this was the primal need to test myself and live on the edge. Whatever it was, I knew I would never look at myself or my surroundings in the same way again. This was something much bigger than the hunt or the elusive red stag.

I already knew the loss of Mr. Magnificent had changed me.

On our drive back to the complex, I was unsure when I might return to this ranch or if the search for my lost red stag would ever be over. All I had was Josh's promise and assurance he would keep looking.

When we pulled into the complex, we saw Mr. Randolph waiting for us on the porch. We stopped the truck, and he began walking toward us. We stepped out of the truck to greet him.

When we told him we had not found the stag, he immediately promised the services of some of his other ranch workers to help Josh in his search. It was a kind and generous offer.

I shook hands with Mr. Randolph and thanked him. Then I hurried to my room, packed my things, loaded everything into the back of my truck, and waited on the porch of the lodge for Josh so I could settle up my bill.

About fifteen minutes later, Josh and I proceeded to the ranch head-quarters, where I wrote a hefty check for the price of the red stag. It was a big pill for me to swallow.

"It won't take me long to find him. The buzzards never fail. Just be patient, brother," Josh said. I knew Josh was being sincere, and I knew he would do his best. I also knew from the time spent in the 52 searching, that it would take a lot more than determination and confidence to get this one done. I truly appreciated Josh's resolve and good intentions, but I had serious doubts.

"It's all on you."

I could see the weight of it all was on him. Josh just nodded at me.

"Just let me know when you find him."

I shook hands with Josh.

"I will, brother. I will."

9:10 p.m. I walked back across the large complex, physically and emotionally drained. I slid behind the wheel of my pickup and sat there a moment. I had this strange feeling that I might never come back to this ranch after this. I started my truck and yelled out the window at Josh.

"Just find him for me, brother."

"You got it," Josh hollered back at me. I saw him waving in my rearview mirror.

"I'll call you or text you every day and let you know how things are going."

I stuck my arm out the window and gave Josh a thumbs-up. I could still hear his words drifting into the darkness as I drove away.

I departed the complex full of hope. After fifteen minutes, I finally exited the ranch through the main gate. I tried to be strong and positive. I tried to remain confident Josh would locate the lost stag within a few days. But, on my four-hour drive back to Austin, I had a lot of isolated time to think.

1:19 a.m. I pulled my truck into the garage at my home in Austin, feeling low. Everything was out of sorts. I had no one to blame but myself. The problems that lay in front of me—I considered them all to be my fault.

As badly as I felt, I knew my problem with losing the stag paled in comparison to the obstacles so many faced with illness, poverty, and homelessness. Those people were always in my thoughts and prayers.

When I was a kid, I remembered my dad telling me "one's character is always tested during a crisis." Well, to me, this was a crisis. My life had changed in the past two and a half days. I left Austin a happy, strong-minded, confident man—full of life and loving God. I knew I was blessed by God and my family and all the good that was around me. But, here I was returning home unhappy and unsure about the problem I had created. I still loved God, still felt blessed, but, in my mind, this problem didn't have anything to do with God. This problem was about me and my inability to direct and control a situation that should have been straightforward. All I wanted to do was to get back to my old self. I knew that was going to be difficult because I now had no control over the outcome. It was late in the night when I got home. The streets were dark and deserted, traffic on the freeway was sparse. I looked up at myself in the rearview mirror.

Quit feeling sorry for yourself. Be strong. Have faith; I said to the tired green eyes looking back at me. *Josh is going to find the stag. Everything will be okay.*

I had always thought of myself as a tough guy, both mentally and physically—always able to will myself to victory under every circumstance. Tonight, it was different. Something was off. Tonight, for the first time in my life, I came to realize that saying and believing were not the same thing. My thought process had changed completely in the past two and a half days.

I exited the pickup. Inside myself, I could barely think. I looked up at the door from the garage into the house, and there stood my beautiful, sweet wife with that smile that always made me feel like I was the luckiest man in the world. She was special, and she made me feel special.

We went inside, sat on the bed together, and talked for a long time. When she told me this was just a setback and that my life would soon be back to normal, I believed her.

CHAPTER SEVENTEEN

6:45 a.m. I awoke to a beautiful Austin morning in my own bed, a million miles and a thousand years from the hunt that now felt like a bad dream. As my feet hit the floor, the cuts and bruises and the soreness and pain were a quick reminder of the past two and a half days.

It was Thursday, October 24, 2019, and the first thing I thought about was Josh and the lost red stag. That was my reality now, and I knew I could not escape it.

I need some good news, I said to myself. *Josh, you're going to find him today.* It was like my message may somehow reach him telepathically. I figured Josh would call or text me in the next few hours, and I couldn't wait to hear how the search was going.

No camouflage this morning. Instead, I dressed in a pair of slacks with a sport coat. I had an appointment to meet with two clients this morning, beginning at 11:00 a.m.

I wanted to put the stag hunt out of my mind, but I knew shooting and losing the red stag had left its mark on me. Its real impact was still unknown. As usual, I was trying my best to be tough-minded.

I was fighting off negative thoughts, trying to convince myself things would turn out for the best, and the stag would be found soon. But deep inside, I couldn't shake the feeling I had failed and lost control. All my life, I felt I was able to fix any problem that came my way. Now I faced a personal challenge two hundred miles away, and I felt completely helpless to go fix it.

9:45 a.m. I sat in my office drinking hot coffee with cream, reviewing a stack of files on my desk. Yesterday I was thrust, bleeding and torn, into a primal struggle for survival—today, I was dressed business casual sitting comfortably in the quintessential lap of gentrified culture and luxury.

Which one is the real me? I wondered.

I didn't know the answer, but I did know that, even though I knew the facts and laws pertaining to the cases before me, I needed to review each case before visiting with clients. *An arrow missing the target by a fraction of an inch has the same consequences as missing the tiniest critical detail in a legal case,* I thought as I stared down at the files on my desk.

My passion for litigating State and Federal District Court cases was well known. In legal circles, I had a reputation for litigating about every kind of case. As a trial lawyer for over forty years, I was obsessed with the courtroom, the juries, and making things right in the world for all people.

Seeking the truth always appealed to me, and performing under extreme pressure was second-hand nature. Therefore, dealing with what I presumed was a failed red stag hunt shouldn't have been a problem. I just needed time to find a way to fix it.

I went over the files on my desk, reading and sipping my coffee like I had done so many times in the past years. I knew the facts of these cases backward and forward. I didn't need to take much time rehashing these petitions and predicting their legal outcome.

My mind rushed back to the stag hunt. The biggest problem I faced was simple. I had created this terrible mess. I had brought about this unacceptable situation. It was all my fault, and worst of all, I couldn't do anything about it. I wasn't in a position to fix it. This was new territory for me, a problem completely out of my hands.

Growing up, being a student, playing sports, litigating lawsuits, being an artist, or hunting in the outdoors, I had always been in complete control. Now, I was faced with a situation that was out of my control. I felt helpless, and I hated it. The stress and anxiety from not being able to fix this problem were causing my head and brain to hurt.

In my mind, I could never let anything go unresolved. That was part of my DNA. Solving all problems, big or small, was important to me. I knew there were many obstacles and serious situations others faced daily that were more critical than my lost red stag. And if given the chance, I would have tried to help everyone fix their problems too. But for now, the lost stag issue was staring me in the face, and I was not about to turn my back on it.

Looking out my office window, I began to think. *As a lawyer, I represented a client with a broken arm as diligently and passionately as I represented a client in a wrongful death case. And in a football game, I played my very best against a lesser opponent just as strongly and passionately as I played my very best against a championship team. Therefore, my conviction to resolve the problem with the lost stag was not diminished by comparing it to other important issues,* I told myself. *Because, who is to judge the value given to each issue that affects our lives? Only God and each one of us individually can do that.*

I looked away from my office window and checked my watch. I had an hour before my first client meeting.

The more I tried to figure out how to rectify the lost stag problem, the more frustrated I became. Plain and simple, all I could do was hope. I hoped Josh would get lucky this morning and call me to say he had found my red stag. I hoped the buzzards would do their job and show Josh where the stag was located. I hoped the coyotes had not already destroyed the beauty and glory of this divine creature. I hoped the world would become a better place. I hoped for a lot of things this Thursday morning.

That's it. I couldn't hold off any longer. My need to know what was going on in the stag search overpowered me. I dialed Josh's cell number and waited.

Josh answered on the first ring.

"Hey, my brother."

"Hey Josh, any luck?"

I could hear Josh take a deep breath.

"No, sir. Nothing yet, my friend. I drove around the 52-Pasture for two hours early this morning. I saw no sign of the red stag. No buzzards."

I was disappointed, but at least I knew he was trying.

"But don't worry, brother. I think I should find him pretty quick."

I knew Josh wouldn't let me down. His encouraging words were helpful.

"That would be great," I said.

"Like I told you, I'm never going to stop trying to find him," Josh's voice sounded upbeat.

"I appreciate that."

"Keep the faith, my brother. I will deliver those antlers to you."

"I'm looking forward to it," I said.

"I've got everyone who goes into that 52-Pasture looking for him."

"Thanks, Josh."

"It might take a couple of weeks, but we'll track him down."

A couple of weeks? I can't wait that long, I thought.

"Well, you do whatever you have to do to find him. I don't want to bother you."

"You can never bother me," Josh said. "I'm trying to get my schedule arranged so I will have the time to look for your stag."

"Well, hopefully, you'll be able to find some time to look."

"Yes, sir. That's my plan."

"Just call me or text me every once in a while. Let me know how things are going."

"You got it."

"You take good care of yourself."

"Right on, my man. I'll talk to you very soon. Goodbye."

I dug back into my work, trying to put the call with Josh out of my thoughts.

11:05 a.m. It was business as usual. I threw myself into my work, meeting with clients and working on cases and legal issues.

By the end of the day, the stag hunt was completely out of mind, and the few hours spent not thinking about it were good for me.

It was obvious to my wife and me that, as long as I didn't think about the lost stag, our lives were back to normal—no frustration, no anxiety, and no anger. But, when I let my thoughts go back to the red stag, I was consumed with the loss and failure of the hunt and my inability to fix the one problem I couldn't shake.

I was still saying my prayers and talking to God. I was praising Him and thanking Him for my many blessings. As usual, I affirmed my devotion to Him and Jesus Christ. I spoke to Him about forgiving me of my sins and making me a better person. I prayed to keep everyone in the world safe and healthy.

The one thing I could not and did not do was to ask God to intervene in helping find the lost red stag. In my mind, that was crossing the line. I thought that was a selfish request and below the level of things of true importance. That was not something in which God got involved.

Friday morning, October 25th, 8:00 a.m. First thing I did was call my youngest daughter, Angela, to wish her happy birthday and to tell her I love her.

A few minutes later, Josh called me. When I saw his name come up on the phone's caller Id, my heart raced. I smiled. *Yes, he's found him,* I thought. I couldn't wait to hear the good news. The weight of the world lifted from my shoulders.

"Good morning Josh. Tell me you found him, brother." I was clearly excited. "Tell me you're holding those massive antlers in your hands as we speak. Talk to me."

Josh's voice was absent the excitement I expected.

"No, sir. I was just checking in to let you know we haven't found him yet and to give you an update on our progress," he said.

"Okay. Let me hear it."

I felt like I was on a roller coaster. Within three seconds, my mind had gone from kite high to scraping the bottom of the barrel.

Josh cleared his throat. "I drove around the 52 for an hour this morning. I'm probably going to go back out this evening. No stag. No buzzards."

"Just keep looking! You'll find him."

"Brother, I'm never going to stop looking."

"You know I appreciate that."

The phone went quiet.

"Remember that Mr. Randolph said he would let you have some extra guys to help you search."

"I'm going to talk to him about that at lunch today. I'm hopeful he'll give me some men to help me walk a grid of the 52-Pasture. If we can make that kind of search, I think we'll find your stag."

"I agree. That would be a huge help."

"Yes, sir."

"Sounds perfect."

I heard the ranch office calling Josh on his truck CB radio.

"Sorry, my friend. I gotta go," he said and hung up.

9:30 a.m. I left my house in Austin and drove west to my ranch in central Texas. I loved working in the outdoors and taking care of my Brangus cattle and all the wildlife.

Ranching and raising cattle in Texas has been in my family since the early 1830s. I consistently tried to do a good job of blending my legal practice with physical ranch work. Working hard physically is a genetic trait that seems burned into my DNA. The ranch has always been my go-to place to accomplish that. I believe ranching is definitely one of the things in my life that has a relaxing and calming effect on me.

I was feeding range cubes and driving one of my large tractors with a spear-and-fork attachment to put out several round hay bales for my cattle when I felt my cell phone vibrate in my pants pocket.

It was a text message from Josh: *I checked the 52-Pasture at noon. No buzzards and no stag. Going back to the 52 after lunch with Mr. Randolph.*

I texted him back: *Great to hear from you. Did you ask Mr. Randolph about how many extra people he's going to let you have?*

Josh responded: *Haven't found out anything yet. Going to talk with him in about thirty minutes about getting me the extra help. I'll let you know.*

For the next five hours, I was so busy catching up with ranch chores I had little time to think about the stag. I spent the early afternoon welding and installing two H-braces with kickers to support a new cattle guard.

4:15 p.m. I took a short break from the ranch work and texted Josh: *What did Mr. Randolph say about the extra men to help you?*

Josh responded: *I'm here in the 52-Pasture with Mr. Randolph. We're driving around at the moment. No sign of buzzards or your dead stag.*

I responded: *Tell Mr. Randolph I said thank you for his help. And tell him the more people we have searching, the better chance we have of finding the stag.*

Josh texted back: *Copy that, brother. I'm not going to give up.*

My response: *Let me know how many men he's going to let you have.*

I received no answer, and for the rest of the evening, there was no communication between Josh and me.

It was a long day after that, so I ate a late supper. I cooked one of my favorite meals of scrambled eggs mixed with elk sausage and cheese. I was famished, and it was delicious.

After dinner, I sat in my recliner watching the ten o'clock news. The peace and quiet of being alone in the ranch house was a relaxing relief, but try as I did, I could not keep my thoughts from drifting back to the missing stag.

I tried to calculate where the stag may have run to in that huge pasture, given his severe blood loss and dire condition. I quizzed myself. How much more ground was he capable of covering after the dogs lost his trail? What was his most likely choice?—It had to be flight or concealment. The one incalculable variable came down to a single thing—the craftiness of the stag. It was the one factor that defied logic and, along with his unpredictable behavior, it stacked the odds against anyone ever being able to figure out the answer.

Josh and I had never set foot together in the southeastern part of the 52-Pasture, an area considered to be only a tiny portion of the central west and the stag's neighborhood. I knew the southeastern part represented several square miles of uncharted terrain. *Maybe he's there,* I thought.

My mind was running a hundred miles an hour. I debated all the different scenarios. And as much as I agonized over the calculations, the one conclusion I always came back to was the fact that I needed to walk and search every inch of the 52-Pasture to find him. Period.

I was so anxious that night; I couldn't sleep. I needed to text Josh to find out how his meeting with Mr. Randolph had gone today.

11:35 p.m. I reached for my cell phone and texted Josh, hoping he was still up. *How many men and how much help is Mr. Randolph going to give you to search for the stag?*

I was happy to see Josh was awake.

He responded immediately: *No sightings of your red stag today. Still no buzzards. I am not going to give up, my friend.*

My quick response: *How many helpers is Mr. Randolph going to give you? Tell me how many men to help search!*

No response. I waited, watching the phone hopefully, but that was it—no further communications from Josh that night.

I was mad and frustrated.

I rolled back onto my pillow and stared at the ceiling.

I had a premonition that nothing was really happening with the search.

I wanted things to speed up. I wanted the Champion Exotic Trophy Ranch to devote more time and put more men and energy in the 52-Pasture, looking for my lost red stag.

CHAPTER EIGHTEEN

Saturday, October 26, 2019. I rolled out of bed early. I was very irritated. I really needed something to calm me down. I got on my knees and prayed.

> My heavenly Father, full of grace,
> divine mercy, and love. Thank you for being so
> good to me. Thank you for my many blessings.
>
> I humbly pray you will forgive me of all my sins
> and will keep me mentally strong and my mind
> at peace during this difficult time. I pray in your
> name and in your glory. Amen.

Not long after saying the prayer, I began to feel much better. My mind was at ease. Midmorning, I packed up and departed the ranch. Driving back to Austin, I was hoping this weekend would materialize with some good news concerning the search.

Saturday came and went with no word from Josh. Sunday was agonizingly slow as I waited all day long, and still no word. My frustration and anxiety were getting the best of me. Whether they found the stag or not, I expected a daily update on their progress—some information on what they were doing and how many people were on the search, but there was nothing. At that point, the lack of communication was consuming me. The longer it went on, the worse it got.

By Sunday night, I was racked with doubt and concern. The frustration and anger from losing control were killing me.

9:05 a.m. Monday, October 28, 2019. I punched in Josh's number on my cell phone. My pulse was pounding. I wanted to know what was going on.

The phone rang. It picked up. An unidentified voice answered: *Hello, you've reached the voicemail of Josh*—I punched the disconnect button and sat there agitated.

11:28 a.m. My cell phone rang. It was Josh.

"Tell me something good, Josh!"

"Hey, my brother. Cold and windy here. I drove around for two hours this morning in the 52. Still no sign of your stag."

I waited a moment. "What about the extra men to help you search for the stag? What's going on with that?"

"Well, Mr. Randolph rode around the 52-Pasture with me this morning," Josh said.

By now, I was pacing back and forth in my office, trying to remain calm and not telegraph my anxiety and anger.

"So, how many men is he going to give you to help in the search?"

Josh hesitated.

I knew he was dodging the question, but I resisted the urge to let him get away with it.

"Well, he told me this morning he was working on it."

"Working on it?"

"Yes, sir. Right now, there are no ranch employees available who can help me out. Mr. Randolph said he was going to see if he could work something out with Tommy Hemphill, the ranch manager."

My blood pressure was rising. "Work something out?"

"Yes, sir. I'm fairly certain I'm going to get one helper twice a week until the hunting season is over."

At this point, it was all I could do to contain my anger. I stopped pacing, sat, and tried to compose myself. I took a deep breath before I responded.

"Okay. If that's all the help the ranch can spare, then so be it."

"Yes, sir. That's all the ranch can give me right now. I'll get them to help me look early in the morning, and then we'll hit one more time late in the afternoon."

Josh took a deep breath and waited. I could tell he was waiting for me to come unglued. I did everything I could to stay positive.

"All right then, if that's all the ranch can do, then just do it."

"Look, my friend, I'm really sorry, but this is just the busiest time of the year for us."

"I understand."

"It's the peak of our hunting season, and everybody here at the ranch is running ragged."

"I know that."

"It's just a bad time."

I didn't say anything. Josh filled the void with more small talk.

"I guess we were just unlucky," Josh paused. "That we lost your stag at the wrong time."

I cringed when I heard him say *unlucky*.

Luck had nothing to do with this, I told myself.

Now Josh was rambling. "I mean, I'm booked solid with hunts and clients almost every day through the end of January. I know I promised you I would find your stag for you, and I'm going to find him."

I leaned back in my chair. I wanted to let Josh off the hook, but I didn't want to minimize the importance of staying with the search.

"Look, Josh, I know it's a busy time for all of you at the ranch right now. And, I know you're doing your very best to allocate your time and to get help in trying to find my stag."

"Yes, sir, I am."

"I know all you can do is try."

Josh's normally upbeat tone was now beginning to show signs of resignation, which I found troubling.

"Yes, sir. Everyone is so busy here at the ranch; it's just a madhouse." Josh hesitated. "I guess what I'm trying to say, brother, without some good luck, I would estimate it's going to be a long while before I have time to search for him."

I looked down at my desk. I wasn't ready to accept even the slightest hint of defeat, but I knew I had to keep Josh motivated.

"That's okay. You take your time. You look for him when you get the chance. I know you're busy, but one day soon you'll find him. I believe that."

I knew Josh was no quitter, but I also knew the deck was stacked against him in this case.

"Yes, sir, at some point in time, I hope to find him."

"I know you will."

"I'm never going to give up looking for him."

"I understand," I said. "I'll talk to you soon."

I hung up and stared out my office window. At that moment, the Champion Exotic Trophy Ranch seemed like a million miles away. And finding that red stag in that huge 52-Pasture was now so far out of my hands, I had no choice but to accept that fact and live with it.

Tuesday, October 29, 2019. 12:58 p.m. A new text from Josh: *It's a rainy, crappy day here. I checked the 52 this morning. I saw no sign of the stag, but I'm going back out again this afternoon.*

I responded: *Maybe you'll find him this evening.*

Josh answered: *Copy that.*

After these early in the week communications between us, everything went quiet. Josh was dealing with other hunters and didn't have time to text or call for the next two days. During that time, all I could think about was no one was searching for my stag. And if no one was looking for him, then how was he ever going to be found? I was at the mercy of the Champion Exotic Trophy Ranch time schedule with no control at all. The only thing I could do was wait and hope.

Friday, November 1, 2019. My plan was to call Josh for an update around 9:00 a.m., but he beat me to it. He began texting me first thing.

7:05 a.m. *I haven't had time to look for your stag in three days. Sorry, my brother. I've got a hunter with me all day today. No time to look. I'll get back to you as soon as I can.*

I responded: *You'll find the stag one day soon.*

I'll start looking for him sometime next week.

I texted him back: *Have a great weekend.*

Copy that, my brother.

After our Friday morning texting had ended, I sat in my office and stared out the window for about an hour. My stress level had shot up a few notches. In a lot of ways, my obsession and strong desire to never leave anything unresolved was a curse I inherited from my father and his father. It took every ounce in me not to succumb to the reality that my giant red stag might be lost forever.

Over the weekend, I felt mentally exhausted. By all indications and my own self-diagnosis, I suspected I was suffering from anxiety and depression. Both fueled by the immense frustration I felt for rushing the shot and for not waiting until the following morning to track the stag. It was all made worse by the fact I let the dogs chase my stag to the moon and back. I kept blaming myself, all because I had created the problem and lost control of the problem.

I knew, unless the stag was found, those thoughts would never go away. I needed to hear something good, but there was nothing good for me to hear. I needed someone to resolve the issue with the lost stag—one way or the other. Not knowing was the worst of all possible outcomes. And, the way it looked so far, that was the one I was stuck with forever. I needed this problem to go away, and I needed it to go away soon so I could get back to my happy, normal life.

I was still saying my prayers. I was still praising and glorifying God and thanking Him for my many blessings. I spoke to God about my devotion to Him and Jesus Christ. But, consistent with the way I had learned to approach God, I never mentioned the lost stag. In my heart, I felt certain that He was not to be bothered with trivial or selfish issues like I felt this one was. And, true to that belief, the subject of the stag was kept absolutely out of my prayers.

I found my devotional time with God helped ease some of my mental sufferings. The problem was, I knew with each passing day my emotions were getting the best of me. The frustration mounted, as did portions of other dysfunctional symptoms associated with stress, depression, and anxiety.

My wife and children and friends were concerned about me. There was no question this situation was having a horrible impact on me. It was turning me into a grumpy, ill-tempered, unpleasant person. It was driving people away from me, and I knew I had to nip it in the bud fast.

Helen Keller wrote many years ago that "character cannot be developed in ease and quiet. Only through experience of trial and suffering can the soul be strengthened, ambition inspired, and success achieved."

I tried to relate her words to my situation. I knew my character and my soul were being tested. And, I knew being so intensely focused on a single problem like the one I was facing and couldn't fix could lead to serious mental issues, both long and short term.

There was no question my obsession with the loss of my red stag was taking a serious toll on my mental and emotional well-being. At the same time, I was dealing with those personal issues and the effect they were having on me; I began to also recognize the impact the state of my mental health was having on my family.

Letting myself become the victim of this kind of thinking was inexcusable—letting my family be victimized by it was intolerable.

Sunday night, November 3, 2019. After a lot of thought, I decided that any action was better than no action. In order for me to win this battle, I needed to do something different fast. I needed to find a way to deal with my emotions and not be overwhelmed by them. I needed to get back in control at some level and not become a bystander in my own demise.

The way I saw it, I had two options, either get in my truck and go back to the Champion Exotic Trophy Ranch to find my stag or stop thinking about the animal. With my busy schedule, it was physically impossible for me to stop my life and go search for the stag, so that left the latter—I had to purge my mind of my obsession with the lost stag as much as it would be possible for me to do that.

I knew this wasn't an ideal plan for me, but I believed it was going to give me the strength and inspiration to put my mistakes and the stag's loss behind me and move forward. I made the commitment to move ahead with it. It wasn't much, but it was enough. With my new plan, I already felt better.

Monday, November 4, 2019. The sun was barely up when Josh called me and said he was in Iowa on a personal hunting trip and would not be back to the Champion Exotic Trophy Ranch until the morning of November 12. I wished him good luck on his hunting adventure in Iowa, we exchanged a few pleasantries, and then we hung up without a word about the lost stag.

Josh's absence from the Champion Ranch meant no one would be searching the 52-Pasture for the lost stag for eight days. That was not good news.

As disappointed and upset as I was, it did not immediately hit me that I had committed to let the problems with the search go. But, here I was, right on the verge of full engagement once again.

For the next eight days, I did a good job of putting it all out of my mind, Josh, the stag, the 52-Pasture, all of it. I buried myself in my legal work, my painting and artwork, my ranch work, and mostly being with my family. It almost felt normal. It helped that I had absolutely zero communications with Josh and from the Champion Ranch, even though it did irk me some knowing there was no effort being put into finding the red stag. But, for the most part, I was able to put that out of my mind as well.

I knew it was important for me to let go of the lost stag a little bit at a time each day until this problem was eventually not part of my life anymore.

By Tuesday, November 12, I had pretty much let all thoughts of the stag go.

And then Josh texted me.

10:00 a.m. *Back from my hunting trip. I'm at the Champion ranch, heading out to drive the 52-Pasture. Hoping I have some good news for you in a few hours.*

I read the text but didn't respond. I flushed it from my mind.

In the afternoon, I heard back from Josh.

3:20 p.m. *I saw buzzards at 2:15. It was a dead raccoon. I also saw buzzards at 2:45. Just a dead hind. It's been twenty-one days since you shot your stag. As you know, we have had no luck in finding him.*

I responded: *Keep searching.*

Copy that, Josh texted back.

Let's try and think like the stag. Where did he run and hide that night we lost him?

I'm sure he's somewhere in the central west.

Then where?

Ha ha. That's a good question, my man, Josh answered.

Have you had time to walk some of the southeastern part of the central west? I asked.

No, sir. By now, the coyotes have eaten your stag and made our job much tougher.

Then all you can do is keep searching.

They could have dragged his carcass anywhere in the 52. Even into the mountains.

Then the whole 52 needs to be searched.

Josh replied, *Copy that! I guess you know the buzzards can't help us anymore. We're just looking for horns now. Huge Horns. Massive Horns.*

I understand.

Josh didn't text me back for five minutes. *It's beginning to look like trying to find him now in that 5,200 acres; it's worse than looking for a needle in a haystack.*

I quickly replied: *I think the only way we're going to have a chance to find him now is for the ranch to put a whole lot of boots on the ground, searching and combing every inch of that 52-Pasture.*

Copy that, brother!

Please ask Mr. Randolph for some help.

I'll do my best to get it done. Got to go.

I turned off my cell phone and stared at the screen for a long time.

You have to let this go, I told myself.

For the remainder of the week and through the weekend, there were no further communications between Josh and me. Things were quiet and uneventful.

CHAPTER NINETEEN

I was doing well, sticking with my plan of putting the stag hunt completely out of my mind. Five days had passed since I had any communication with Josh. Not thinking about the stag hunt was helping me considerably.

Sunday morning, November 17. Sitting in church, I reminded myself that I was blessed and that the red stag problem was insignificant.

When I got home, I read an article in the newspaper that said, "The unknowns and uncertainties in our life always have a way of throwing our lives off course." It seemed right on point with me. The unknowns and uncertainty I felt from the failed stag hunt had definitely thrown my life off course. It was evident to me and to everyone else around me, keeping the lost stag hunt out of my mind as much as possible was helping me function normally.

But there were days I failed. Days when the urge to check in with Josh was almost impossible to deal with. There were times when touching base with Josh seemed necessary, and submerging myself back into the stag hunt felt mandatory.

Monday morning, November 18, was one of those times. It had been six long days since Josh and I had communicated. I needed to hear something from him.

6:30 p.m. I called Josh.

He answered on the first ring.

"How's it going, Josh? Any news?"

"Absolutely, yesterday morning was exciting."

"Really."

"Oh, yes, sir."

I could feel the excitement in his voice.

"Let me hear it."

"I was driving around in the south part of the central west. I saw some crazy shape in a grove of hackberry bushes a hundred yards away. I immediately stopped the truck. I was skeptical, but the more I stared at it, the more it had the shape of your stag's antlers. I jumped from my truck and ran as fast as I could. I have to tell you, as I approached, my heart started racing."

"Brother, did you find him?"

"When I got there and pulled it out of the brush, it was nothing but a huge ball of roots," Josh said.

I shook my head in anguish.

"I guess it was just another rabbit trail," he added.

"I understand."

"I'm just trying to do everything I can now to find those huge horns."

"Have you been able to get any help from Mr. Randolph?"

"Only one guy. He still comes out to help me search twice a week."

"Well, I guess that's better than nothing," I said.

"Yes, sir. We're still real busy here, but you know we're not going to give up trying to find your stag."

"I appreciate that."

Josh cleared his throat. "I'm not going to sugarcoat this for you, brother. I want you to know; it's going to be pretty much impossible to find him now that we're just looking for his horns."

I didn't like the sound of that, but I suspected Josh was having to let go of the lost stag a little bit at a time, just like I was.

"I understand. You take good care, Josh. Just keep looking. Call me or text me every once in a while and let me know how you're doing and how things are going."

"I'll definitely do that."

"All right then, have a good one."

"Copy that."

Josh and I had no further communications over the next eight days. At the same time, our talking dropped off, my depression and anxiety ramped up. I was miserable. Bad thoughts, guilt, and blame for losing the stag overpowered me.

Tuesday, November 26. I called Josh on his cell phone and left a message wishing him and his family a happy Thanksgiving. I'm sure Josh knew it was a thinly veiled excuse to talk to him about my lost stag. But, I called on all the power and strength in my body and mind to refrain from mentioning anything about the stag in my message.

Josh responded the next day. He sent me a text on Wednesday morning, November 27.

"Hey Brother, I couldn't get to your phone call yesterday. I've been very busy with hunters. I had four guys back there in the 52-Pasture with guides last weekend, and man, nobody, and I mean nobody found your stag's massive antlers. As always, I'll keep looking. You have a good Thanksgiving too. Adiós, amigo."

Thursday, November 28, 2019—Thanksgiving Day. Normally we celebrated Thanksgiving at the ranch, but today we assembled at our house in Austin. My family and I gathered around the table to give thanks for our good health and for Texas and for our country, and for our many blessings. I tried my best to smile and be cheerful. I hugged and kissed my kids and grandkids and wife. I told each one of them how much I loved them. We played board games and cards, then charades, basket-ball, whiffle ball, and bocce ball. I showed as much love and enthusiasm on this special holiday gathering as I could muster, but deep inside, I was hurting.

Intellectually, I recognized my situation with the lost stag was minor when compared to the major problems that others in the world faced, but it was still consuming me.

Every day was now déjà vu. My brain was clogged with invariable thoughts. I had never shot an animal and lost it. The way I had lost the stag made me angry with myself. My total lack of control over finding him was frustrating and unacceptable. My mental state was in the toilet.

I was miserable, but I knew I didn't need a doctor or some kind of brain-altering pills to make me feel better. I knew I needed a lot more help from God.

I had nowhere else to turn. I wanted so badly to talk to God about the stag hunt. I wanted to tell Him how the hunt and the loss of the stag were affecting me. I wanted to speak to Him about things I never thought He would get involved in. But most of all, as hard as it was to admit to myself, I wanted to ask Him about helping me find my red stag.

After everyone left the Thanksgiving celebration late in the evening, I went into my office and shut the door. I began to pray out loud. I spoke to God much longer than I had ever done before. My mental suffering had reached its peak. I needed God's help. I needed Him to take control and fix my problem. I was ready to turn this whole lost stag matter over to God.

In the beginning, it felt uncomfortable for me to pray and ask for God's help on something I had never before believed He would get involved in. But in my mind, for the first time in my life, I was totally defeated. I felt I had no options and no other choice but to ask for God's total and complete help.

I prayed out loud for half an hour or more. The substance of my talk with God was all new territory for me, but I felt at peace in His presence. I felt good about finally coming to Him and asking for His help in finding the lost red stag and everything else that went with the hunt.

I laid out my heart to God. I held nothing back. When I was finished speaking with Him, I felt a new sense of relief and calm. More comfortable than at any time since I had shot and lost the stag. I no longer felt the need to beat myself up. I felt no need to blame myself or to carry the burden of anger and frustration, both of which seemed to disappear. My worrying about finding the red stag or forever losing it was not a problem to me anymore. I had turned everything over to God. God was in control. Now all I needed to do was wait for God to answer me and help me.

After this prayer, I sat in my office for fifteen more minutes. I closed my eyes and rested my head against the back of my chair. My mind was clear and at ease. While I rested, I could feel my blood pressure, pulse, and heart rate slow down and get in rhythm. The burden was lifted. Mentally and physically, God lifted the weight from me. And, I don't mean metaphorically. In reality, I felt Him take the heavy stones from my shoulders.

I stood up and walked toward my office door. I was different. Different than I had ever been in my life. An amazing transformation had come over me. My body and mind were actually in sync. When I reached the door, I stopped. I thought I heard something behind me.

I turned and listened. I heard a deep voice inside my office say, "Go back to the place and seek your stag."

I was sure I heard the voice. It was loud and clear. But I told myself, *there's just no way*. I looked around, trying to make sense of it all. *That was my imagination*, I thought. I was skeptical and more than just a little doubtful. Then I heard the voice again, deep and resonating. The message was firm and clear—"Go back and seek your stag." Okay, I heard the voice. That was not my imagination.

It was Thanksgiving weekend, and I knew no one would be at the hunting ranch until Monday morning. In my mind, I was keenly aware of what I needed to do. I was pumped up. I felt empowered by my new marching orders.

I checked my calendar. I needed to find the first opening in my schedule that would allow me to block out a few days to go to South Texas. The first opening was December 12th through the 15th.

I couldn't wait to call the ranch manager on Monday morning and tell him I was coming back to look for my lost stag.

When I left my office, I was sky-high. I couldn't wait until December 12th. When I entered the living room, my wife turned and looked at me. She could immediately see the change in my walk and attitude.

"What's happened to you?" she asked as she stood and began walking toward me.

I smiled at her, "I finally asked God to help me with the red stag hunt."

Her smile was radiant.

"That's wonderful. Hopefully, you'll get back to being your old self now."

"You know, doll baby, I've never asked God to help me with problems like this."

She put her arms around me and gave me a kiss and a big hug.

"I know that sweetheart, but you should have been asking Him for His help a long time ago."

I squeezed her tight.

"You're right. You're always right. I should have asked for God's help a long time ago."

She smiled and hugged me.

I smiled back at her. "You know, doll baby, I feel better right now than I have in my entire life."

When I was twenty, I read a quote from Edgar Allan Poe that I will never forget. I had no idea, at the time, what he meant. Now, I think I know exactly what he meant when he said, "Never to suffer would never to have been blessed."

Today God had begun to heal my pain. He took control of my problems, and I could feel it. God was in full command now. He would give me the strength and show me the way.

Monday morning, December 2, 2019. I was set to call the general manager of the Champion Exotic Trophy Ranch, Tommy Hemphill, at 8:00 a.m.

I had met Tommy several times over the years since I began hunting the Champion Ranch with Josh. I knew he was all business when it came to ranch operations. He had a reputation with the employees of running the place with an iron fist. My observations had always been that it was his way or the highway unless Mr. Randolph over-ruled him.

On a handful of occasions, Tommy, Mr. Randolph, Josh, and I had eaten lunch or dinner together in the lodge dining room. There was a special table in the back corner where we always hung out. I felt relatively sure I was fairly good friends with all of them. I didn't foresee any problems when I placed the call.

When Tommy Hemphill answered the phone, I was ready. "Hey Tommy, this is Marty Akins."

"Hey Marty, hope you had a good Thanksgiving," Tommy said.

"Everything was wonderful here in Austin. My wife and I had our whole family around to celebrate, and we really enjoyed the holiday. How about you and your family? Did y'all have fun?"

"Everything was good. We had a great time. I ate too much turkey and dressing, but hey, life is good."

I heard Tommy take a breath. I knew he didn't like to waste time chatting. "So, what's up? What can I do for you?"

"Well, I'm just calling to let you know that I'll be coming to the ranch on December 12th early in the morning to begin looking for my lost red stag."

"No, no. There's no way, Marty. That's not possible. We're right in the middle of our hunting season," Tommy stated firmly.

"Well, Tommy, I'm coming anyway," I said.

"No, you're not coming."

"Oh, yes, I am."

"You can't just show up here at the ranch without first clearing it with me and scheduling a time to hunt. We have to prepare meals and lodging."

"That's exactly why I'm calling you Tommy. I want you to write it down and schedule it. From December 12th to the 15th, I'm coming to the ranch to search and find my red stag."

"No, sir. I don't have any openings. That time is not available on our ranch schedule. This is our busiest time of the year, and I don't have any hunts or any rooms in the lodge available. And none of the guides can spare any time with you on those dates."

"Tommy, you're not listening to me. I'm not coming to hunt. I'm coming to walk that 52-Pasture so I can find my red stag. I don't need a room. I'll sleep in my truck if I have to, but I'm coming."

Tommy didn't answer, but I could hear him breathing heavily into the phone.

"And I've got one other thing. I'd very much appreciate it if you and the ranch saw fit to provide me with a few extra people to help me search that 52-Pasture when I get there."

"We don't have anyone available in December or January to help you."

"Yes, you do. You run the ranch. You can find some people to help me find my stag. Josh told me you okayed five or six ranch employees to help another hunter find his wounded stag a week after I left the ranch back in October."

Tommy did not reply.

"Is that right, Tommy?"

Tommy hesitated for a long moment.

"Well, I guess we did provide a few ranch employees to help another hunter find his stag back in late October."

"So, don't you think I deserve to be treated like every other good paying customer who hunts at your ranch?"

There was no reply.

"Look, my plan is to leave Austin on Thursday, December 12th, around 2:00 in the morning. There shouldn't be much traffic. I'm thinking I will probably get to your ranch lodge a little before 6:00 a.m. I'm fully expecting you to have Josh and a handful of other ranch employees prepared to help me search and find my stag."

"I'll discuss it with Mr. Randolph," Tommy said.

"That's a good idea, Tommy. I think you really do need to talk to Mr. Randolph. And I look forward to seeing you, and Josh and some helpers in ten days. You take care now."

"Goodbye," Tommy said.

I hung up the call and then called Josh. He answered immediately. I asked him if he had any good news about my red stag, and he said *no*. Then I told him I had arranged my schedule to be at the Champion Ranch in the next few days to search for my lost stag.

Josh sounded genuinely excited.

"I'm happy you're coming, my friend. This will give us our best chance to find him."

Then I told Josh about my conversation with Tommy Hemphill. Josh laughed.

"I'm glad you finally got his attention," he said.

"I just wanted Tommy to know I was coming to find my stag. And, I wanted him to know that I fully expected him to get the ranch to do something to help me."

"I understand," Josh said. "You deserve the ranch's help. And Tommy needs to understand that too."

"Well, I think I said it loud and clear, brother. There's no doubt he knows exactly what I intend to do."

"That's good. Just let him come around. Give him a chance to think about it for a day or so."

"He can think about it all he wants. But, no matter what, I'm coming to the ranch on the morning of December 12th to begin searching that entire 52-Pasture."

"And I'll be right there with you, my man."

"Good. I knew I could count on you."

"Absolutely. I'll cancel a few hunts and be there."

"Thanks, brother. So, I'll see you in ten days at the ranch."

"Yes, sir."

"Maybe you could give Tommy a call today to get him motivated to help me before I get there on the 12th."

"I told you. Just give him a day to think it over. I know how Tommy works. He's got to believe this is his idea. And that this thing has the potential to make him look good."

"Whatever it takes to get us some help. I just want to find my stag."

"Copy that," Josh chuckled. "I'll call Tommy tomorrow morning. I'll tell him I've heard through the grapevine that he's come up with a great idea to call you and ask you to come to the ranch so we can help you find your stag. I'll let him know I think his idea is going to be a great public relations asset for our ranch website. That will get him all jacked up about this thing."

"That sounds good."

"Then, he'll call Mr. Randolph tomorrow with the idea and seek praise and approval."

"I understand."

"And I'll call Mr. Randolph toward the end of this week to let him know I'm all in with Tommy's idea. And I'll let him know that Tommy's got you coming to the ranch the second week of December so we can help you find your stag."

"That will be really great."

"I know Mr. Randolph really likes you. And I think he'll be very happy to know that the ranch is going to help you find your stag."

"I think you know how much I appreciate your help, brother," I said.

"I know that. I'll see you in ten days, my friend."

And with that, we both hung up.

In my mind, the next ten days couldn't come fast enough.

CHAPTER TWENTY

The next eight days went by swiftly. I had not heard a single word from Josh or Tommy. I didn't know whether Josh and I were going to be the only members of our search party. I was a little worried this trip might begin and end with no help from the ranch. But it didn't matter. I was keeping the faith; after all, this matter was in God's hands now. I was doing what He instructed me to do.

Wednesday, December 11th. I went to my mailbox and found a handwritten note attached. The note read: Believe in Miracles. Neither my wife nor I knew where the note had come from. At the time I had no idea of the significance of that note.

Thursday, December 12th, 1:00 a.m. My alarm went off, and I was on my feet and moving fast—a quick shower, dressed in thick old clothes, grabbed a cup of hot coffee and my old corduroy coat that had maybe one trip left in it. I knew that where I was going for the next few days was rough and brutal, and whatever I wore would be ruined by the end of the trip.

2:15 a.m. I was on the road heading south out of Austin on my way to the Champion Exotic Trophy Ranch. It had been seven long weeks since I arrowed and lost the stag, and I was in a hurry to get on with the search.

My red pickup truck hummed down the pavement. I took the 410-Loop going into San Antonio, where I made a right turn onto US 90, heading west. I had dreamed about this return visit to the ranch to search for my lost stag. It seemed like an eternity since Josh and I knelt quietly in the cactus-brushy hideout by the jog, waiting for the stag. I could hardly wait to get to the 52-Pasture to begin looking for my red stag.

6:20 a.m. I arrived at the ranch's main gate in the pitch dark, right on schedule. In another hour, the sun would be cracking the eastern skyline coming up over the mountainous horizon.

I stopped at the keypad and rolled down my window. The code had not been changed in years and, when I hit the last number, the gate swung open at a snail's pace.

I entered the ranch, driving slowly down the caliche road toward the lodge. I felt a little nervous. I had no communications with Josh or Tommy since December 2nd, and I did not know what to expect when I got to the lodge. Surely, Josh would be there waiting for me. But what if Josh wasn't there? It was an unsettling thought.

I was very familiar with this long stretch of road. I could have closed my eyes and driven this dusty route with one hand tied behind my back. I had traveled back and forth on this road many times through the years. But, today's ride felt a lot different for me.

For the first time, I was not coming to the ranch to hunt. This was strictly a search and find mission. The road twisted and turned its way through the tall trees and thick brush for several miles. This entry into the ranch was nothing short of spectacular. It was absolute darkness, but I knew to my left and right were rolling hills and steep mountains surrounding me.

Along the way, my headlights illuminated some of the most exotic game animals in the world—sable, gemsbok, gazelles, blue wildebeest, eland, nyala, kudu, and oryx, to name a few. Some of these animals stood motionless while others scattered into the dark, waving goodbye to me with their flashy tails. I always felt like I was driving through Africa when I entered this ranch. Nothing had changed.

6:30 a.m. The sky was scattered with bright stars and lit by a beautiful moon guiding my way. When I cleared the last gate and cattle guard, I could see the bright lights of the big lodge rise up before me. The closer I got to the impressive building, the more surprised I became.

For a few seconds, I thought the darkness and my eyes were deceiving me. My heart raced. When I stopped my truck in front of the lodge, I looked at the lighted porch. I knew God was with me.

I exited my truck, smiling with my eyes all lit up and taking in the glorious sight before me. There, on the lighted porch, stood Josh, Tommy, and six ranch hands. All eight of them, seven men and one woman, Brenda, dressed in good walking boots and sporting thick, heavy clothes and caps. They looked ready, willing, and able to cover the long hard walking miles I knew lay ahead of us that day.

Josh hurried toward me with a flashlight in hand as I headed toward the lodge. We met at the wooden fence, and then we shook hands firmly.

Tommy came at me next. He actually gave me a strong handshake; then, he patted me on the back, smiled, and appeared happy to see me. All of this was sending me a good message.

Then the rest of the crew filtered over to me, shaking my hand and welcoming me grandly with open arms. I could tell, as a group, each one of them knew the reason they were there.

They began boasting to me about finding my red stag in short order. They assured me they would scour the countryside, and they would look over every single inch of the 5,200 acres, and they would eventually recover my lost stag.

In my mind, all these extra eyes definitely offered us a great opportunity to finally put an end to what had become my own personal obsession and nightmare. For the first time since I had shot the stag, I honestly felt confident that today I would hold those massive antlers in my hands. I looked around. Everyone was eager to proceed with the search.

"It's time for us to get going," Josh hollered out. "Let's find that needle in the haystack."

The whole group was staring at Josh.

"All right, everybody in the trucks now," he added.

"Yes, sir. We're ready to go," Thomas, one of the ranch hands, shouted.

"It's time to load up," Jesse, another ranch hand, yelled.

"Yee-hah, let's do this," Brenda called out. "Let's find that giant stag."

"Okay," Pacho and Roberto shouted out.

"It's time to get'er done," Johnathan hollered.

Everyone began walking quickly toward the trucks. Tommy raced over and asked if I wanted anything to eat or drink before we headed to the 52-Pasture. I hadn't eaten all morning, so I said *yes*, and he and I headed into the lodge.

Tommy followed me around the familiar dining room while I grabbed a cup of coffee and two cinnamon rolls. He pointed down the hallway to my left.

"You're in room three. You're welcome to stay as long as you need."

"Thanks, Tommy. I appreciate what the ranch is doing to help me."

"It's our pleasure. You've always been a great client here."

"You be sure to tell Mr. Randolph I said thank you very much."

"I'll do it. He told me to take good care of you."

"Please tell him I really appreciate his help."

"He knows that. He considers you a good friend."

Tommy and I headed for the door in a big hurry, eager to get to the trucks and to get this search underway. When I swung the door open, the outside air was like a cold slap in the face. It was invigorating and added to the excitement.

The others had already piled into their trucks. They were waiting for us. I hopped into Josh's truck. He fired it up and turned on the heater—Jesse and Brenda road with us.

Tommy, in the meantime, loaded himself and his tracking dog inside his truck where Pacho and Roberto were waiting in the back seat. Thomas and Johnathan followed in a third pick-up. Josh led the way as we caravanned into the cold dark air on our way to the 52.

Here we were, finally—a search party of nine. I was pumped up with adrenaline and excitement. I was positive we were going to find my stag.

With this much help, I knew we could make a serious effort covering a tremendous amount of geography on the 52 in a more systematic manner. Now we had the help. All we needed was God's guidance, which I felt we had since I was convinced He sent me back here for a reason. Time would tell if that reason was to be a hard lesson in humility or an answer to what I had always felt through the years was possibly a frivolous request.

CHAPTER TWENTY-ONE

7:19 a.m. Our three-truck caravan pulled into the 52-Pasture with the sun already burning off much of the chill of the pre-dawn darkness that preceded it.

One of the ranch hands jumped out from the truck behind ours and ran to the heavy iron gate. He held it open while we all passed through.

We proceeded deeper into the unyielding 52, bumping along the rough caliche road, twisting and turning its way deeper into the rugged interior. It felt normal, like the 52-Pasture was welcoming me back for a rematch.

We traveled through the major part of the central west, continued for another mile, and then stopped two hundred yards from the jog.

At that point, we loaded everybody into Josh's truck and left the other two trucks behind. With all nine of us in Josh's pick-up, we headed north for one mile and then angled off to the right, heading due east. We maneuvered our way along with a series of narrow old vehicle tracks not far from the bottom of the mountains.

From there, we drove two miles straight toward the centerline of the eastern boundary of the 52-Pasture. Josh parked his truck a short distance from the H-braces where the property line shot up into the mountains to the north.

We unloaded and then headed back up the steep incline for two hundred yards, where we assembled by the braces. Everyone was focused on Josh and Tommy as they began to lay out the details of how the search would be conducted.

Josh stepped forward. I stood behind the group and listened.

"From this starting location, we're all going to spread apart along this eastern property line."

He pointed due south down the property line running into the pasture's flatter country.

"Is that understood?"

A collective *yes, sir,* from the group.

"I want everyone to spread out approximately fifty to sixty yards between each other. And when we all get lined up and ready to move out, I want us to start walking in a tight grid due west. It's going to be about two and a half miles back to where we parked the trucks. Take your time and find that monster. Any questions?"

Heads shook, a few *no, sirs,* and it was clear this search party was ready to get going.

"The purpose of this search is to look thoroughly in, around, and under all this thick brush and foliage so we can find Mr. Akins's monster stag. All right?"

More collective nodding and *yes, sirs.* Everyone understood.

Josh held up a photo of my once stag.

"Okay, take a real good look at this and remember those antlers. Some of you saw him a few times in the early fall."

Everyone studied the photo. After a few nods, Josh continued.

"As y'all can see, the stag's antlers are massive—and extremely wide and tall. They're unique and should be easy to spot, especially with the long drop tine off his right beam and those distinctive crowns."

Everyone knew exactly what we were looking for.

Tommy stepped forward and stood next to Josh.

"I want y'all to remember one thing. You're looking strictly for the skull and those enormous antlers. The carcass may or may not be attached."

"That's right. This animal was shot and died over seven weeks ago. Not much chance there's anything left but the skull and antlers," Josh said.

"Y'all know how many coyotes are in this pasture," Tommy said, putting the finishing touch on things.

Josh turned and gestured toward the south.

"All right, guys, let's get going. Spread out down this property line. Leave fifty or sixty yards between you."

The group turned and headed south down the east property line. It didn't take long for us to spread out. And, when the grid line was finally formed, we were ready to find the stag.

Eight of us fanned out to search a strip approximately five to six hundred yards wide. One of the ranch hands drove the truck back to the jog to wait.

7:40 a.m. Our search line of eight, with Josh and Tommy in the center, stood waiting, a human grid line ready to move forward.

When Josh yelled, "Start walking," the line moved forward, toward the west at a quick pace. I occupied the farthest right-hand position in the grid line on the north side. After a few steps into the brush, I rarely saw anyone else in the line. But I could hear people yelling every once in a while to identify their location.

We wore protective eyewear, and we used scarves to protect our faces. Our coats and thick pants also protected us from the overwhelming wicked landscape that lay in front of us. The brush was brutal and daunting, but we walked through it as best we could, slicing, ducking, and struggling our way, constantly searching back and forth.

We attempted to maintain our fifty to sixty-yard intervals, but most of the time, the terrain required us to extend or contract those distances. Within fifteen minutes, I knew none of us had a clue how far or close we were to the others in the grid line.

The frequent initial yelling to mark our positions had faded away, and it was pretty much every man for himself. My eyes strained and combed every inch of the ground within my view. With each glance, I hoped to spot those monster antlers. I wanted to find my red stag so badly that my eyes oftentimes played tricks on me. I'd see a large, thick horn-shaped shrub or several big tree limbs shooting up from the ground resembling a pair of antlers. I would frantically fight through the brush to reach them, only to discover they weren't antlers at all.

Along the way, I did find a couple of small red stag carcasses. The coyotes had decimated them, leaving only the skulls and antlers.

After a mile and a half, we got into the area of the vicinity of where the dogs had first run my red stag.

Eventually, we reached the main caliche road where the trucks were parked, which meant our search toward the west was completed. When the last person emerged from the brush, we rested at this location for several minutes while everyone reported in. No one in the group had seen any sign of my red stag. We each drank a bottle of water and waited for our next set of instructions.

9:00 a.m. Josh gave us a few minutes before he laid out his plan for the next phase of the search.

"Now we're going to turn our grid line to the left and go straight south," he said, pointing his finger down the caliche road.

All heads turned to look.

"I want us to stretch our grid line back toward the east, and when we're all in place, we are going to head south for four miles."

Everyone in the group listened intently.

"This will allow us to search the entire eastern area of the central west. This is a huge area. It's an important part of the stag's neighborhood, and it's the remainder of the 52-Pasture southern boundary. That's our new plan."

Heads nodded.

"I want y'all to take your time. I want y'all to look really well in this area because I really believe someone's going to find that lost stag on this walk."

Tommy stepped up.

"Why don't we increase our interval to a hundred yards?"

"That's no problem, as long as we don't get too far apart and miss something," Josh said.

Tommy seemed to be exercising his authority at the same time he was making a constructive suggestion.

"We can cover more ground, and that should give us a better chance to find the stag," Tommy said.

Everyone nodded in agreement.

"All right. We'll try it. Let's do a hundred yards apart, everybody," Josh said.

At one hundred yards, I knew from walking the first grid line; there would definitely be a substantial gap between each of us that would make it easy to miss something. And, without one of us stepping right on top of the dead stag's antlers, I didn't see how getting wider apart was going to help our cause.

But I wasn't going to complain. At least we had a lot of boots on the ground with people walking and looking. This was what I had hoped for. I was happy and appreciative of the help. And, I still felt certain one of us would definitely find my lost stag before the day was over.

It took five minutes for us to set up the grid line and to get spread out through the brush. The new interval had us covering close to a one-thousand-yard wide strip of land in which it would be impossible to communicate once we began bushwhacking through the dense undergrowth.

By the time everyone was in place, I could no longer see Josh. But, I did hear him yell out for us to start walking. The search for my lost stag was underway.

Tommy had volunteered to drive his truck to the south end of the property to wait for us there. That, of course, took him out of the brutal walk and search. Not surprisingly, it was extremely tough going.

We walked and looked everywhere. As harsh as I remembered the first search to be, this one seemed even worse. The terrain seemed steeper, the brush thicker, the dead ends and backtracking more frequent, and the brush never let up.

As I had on the first pass, I took the far-right hand position where I was given the task of searching fifty yards to my right and one hundred yards to my left. It was a lot to cover, and my eyes never stopped darting from one misleading shadow to the next. I thought, for sure, I would spot those enormous antlers at any moment.

The four-mile trek through the unrelenting brush was exhausting and brutal. Our clothes were already partially ripped and torn, and the two-and-a-half-hour slog through the stag's territory was just the beginning. By the time we reached our destination, we were all bruised, beat-up, and fatigued.

The group reported seeing five red stag carcasses with decent racks of antlers, but my stag was not among them.

11:20 a.m. We all gathered around the ice chest at the back of the pickup. No one complained. No one was ready to quit. I could sense the positive vibes coming from this group. The great attitudes and can-do mentality of everyone inspired me. It gave me confidence that we would find my lost stag.

We had Coke, Dr. Pepper, Gatorade, and bottled water to quench our thirst. Josh even had the foresight to bring several packages of peanut butter crackers, all of which we devoured. We needed all the energy we could muster at this point.

Josh and Tommy huddled up in the shade of a few oak trees about thirty yards away from the truck. I listened in as they discussed a number of areas they wanted to search next. They considered where the stag normally hung out in the central west and the most likely areas we had still not looked in the 52-Pasture.

"I guess we can completely rule out the mountain region," Tommy said.

"I think so."

"So, where should we look next, Josh?"

"I still think that dead stag has to be somewhere in the central west area," Josh said.

"We've already combed the eastern and southern part of the central west," Tommy said.

"And if we don't find him in the middle and upper part of the central west, then we'll search that small area to the southwest behind the ravine before we go to lunch," Josh said.

"You know this 52-Pasture better than I do," Tommy said. "It's your decision."

"Well then, if we have time, let's do the middle and upper central west first, and then the small area to the southwest of the deep ravine second."

Josh turned and walked back to the group.

"We're going to drive up to the middle of the central west."

Everyone nodded their heads.

"First, we're going to search the middle and upper part, and if we have no luck, then we'll turn our attention to that small area southwest of the deep ravine before we go eat lunch. Everybody load up," Josh hollered.

We all felt rejuvenated as we crammed into Tommy's truck and headed north.

When we arrived, Tommy parked the truck about a quarter of a mile north from where the other two trucks were parked near the jog.

11:35 a.m. We formed the third grid line, repeating the one-hundred-yard interval pattern, and began searching the middle and upper central west area. This time, I went to the far-left hand position of the grid line, which stretched across a search area nearly a thousand yards wide.

This new search area in the central west was also large. It incorporated a large portion of the upper territory to the northwest just below the mountains down through the jog down to the middle section where the pack of coyotes busted our hunt. As we walked the area due west, our grid line stretched and contracted. This area was tough going, but it was not quite as thick and unwieldy as the two previous searches we had already endured this morning.

We combed the countryside for another two and a half miles, mostly along the flatter terrain but also through a multitude of hills with valleys. I have never strained my eyes to look for something as much as I did this day looking for my lost red stag.

12:55 p.m. We reached the far west property line and then turned our grid line to the left and headed southwest.

At this point, we were directly on course for the deep ravine. We searched for another mile and a half before we stopped, two hundred yards above the treacherous ravine—still no sighting or word on my stag.

Tommy was parked near the western property line, not far from where the deep ravine intersected the 52-Pasture.

1:15 p.m. We rested just long enough to take on more fluids and give our legs a rest. Everyone looked a little down now, but no one complained.

During this time, I did notice a possible chink in some of our group's attitude armor.

"Josh was right. Trying to find that stag in this 52-Pasture is worse than looking for a needle in a haystack," Johnathan said.

"Yeah, it's just so thick in here, you can't see a thing," Thomas stated.

Jesse stepped forward, nodding his head. "Exactly. This is crazy. If you can't see him, you can't find him."

"I hate this stupid pasture," Thomas said. I could see the weariness in his eyes.

"There's just no way to maneuver through this brush. It's brutal," Johnathan added, sounding like he may be considering giving up.

"Why don't y'all just be quiet?" Brenda said. "All your negative vibes aren't helping us here."

"They're asking us to do the impossible," Thomas shot back.

I turned and walked away from the group. I knew we had all been searching diligently for a little over six hours. I knew these guys were working their butts off, and they were getting tired and hungry. But, I didn't want to hear their discouraging complaints or to feel like this may be the prelude to them calling it a day and quitting. I distanced myself from the group, sat down on the tailgate, and looked over at Josh.

He was studying the high grass and scrub brush area in front of us.

Tommy walked up, and they spoke for a few seconds. Then, Josh turned his head toward the ranch hands and shouted.

"All right, everybody, let's do this last grid search, and then we can head to the lodge for lunch."

The group cheered loudly, finally some good news.

It was time to start searching, but it wasn't that easy.

Everyone stood up slowly, responding in kind to their tight muscles. No one spoke, but there was definitely some moaning and groaning.

When I stood up, my knees were screaming in pain. I did my best to put this distraction out of my mind. Finding the red stag was consuming my brain now.

"We've got a little more than a two-mile hike to cover the entire western side of the deep ravine," Josh said, pointing toward the area right in front of us.

"Watch out for rattlesnakes," Tommy shouted.

I could see the group frowning.

This small area was mostly filled with a dense scrub brush, and provided great cover for the animals, and was approximately two miles long and a third of a mile wide. And, although only a small part of it was included in the central west, Josh was determined to search every inch of it.

Fortunately for us, this spot was nowhere near as thick as most of the 52. But, it was rocky and overrun with nasty, prickly pencil cactus, agarita, high grasses, scrub brush, and of course, small thorny mesquites—none of which would make this search easy. To add to the difficulties of the rocky terrain and restrictive vegetation, this place was infested with venomous snakes. Besides rattlesnakes, there were also copperheads, water moccasins, and coral snakes which were impossible to see in the tall grass that averaged about four to five feet high in most places. It was not going to be fun.

"The northern part of this area has long been one of the prime hangouts for several of the bigger red stags," Josh stated. "I'm very hopeful we will find him here."

Tommy yelled out, "Roberto and Pacho, I need you two guys to go with me so we can bring back all the trucks."

The two ranch hands hurried toward Tommy and waited for more instructions.

"We'll pick y'all up on the main caliche road just southeast of where the deep ravine exits the 52-Pasture," Tommy said to the rest of us.

Josh looked toward Tommy, "Sounds good. We should be there around 2:10 unless, of course, we find the stag in this high grass."

"That would be great news. Radio me if you find him."

"Copy that," Josh said.

Tommy turned and started walking to the truck with Roberto and Pacho right on his heels. When they reached the truck, they jumped in and were off. It wouldn't take them long to retrieve the trucks. We would see them at the rendezvous area in a little over an hour.

"Come on, let's get this thing going," Josh said.

The remainder of the search group stepped toward Josh, ready to form another grid line. I took the far-left position. I would be walking next to the deep ravine. With only six active searchers remaining, we would have our work cut out for us, and the search band would be narrowed accordingly.

1:25 p.m. The grid line stretched all the way across the area from the deep ravine to the boundary. The high grass and thorny scrub brush loomed menacingly ahead.

"If the dead stag is anywhere in this area, we're sure to see his antlers. Keep a keen eye out. This is the payoff. One of us is going to find him right now," Josh said. His words were spoken with such confidence I think we all believed him. Our hopes were up. We could feel the excitement building.

There was a renewed energy in the group this time as we set out.

I wanted to believe this was it. This time we were destined to find him. It wouldn't be long before I was holding those glorious antlers in my hands.

CHAPTER TWENTY-TWO

I walked on the farthest left-hand position of the grid line. I was walking approximately one hundred feet from the deep ravine. After I had walked approximately two hundred yards along the new grid line heading south, the deep distinctive voice told me to stop. I stopped. Then the voice said, "Turn back. Go to the shallow spot at the ravine, walk across, and walk on the other side of the ravine."

I turned around and started heading back. I did what the voice told me to do.

I saw Josh in the middle of the grid line about three hundred yards from me. I yelled out at him, and he stopped.

"What is it? Have you found him?" Josh asked excitedly. He took off jogging in the high grass toward me.

"No, no. I haven't found him," I yelled out.

I put up my hands for him to stop.

Josh stopped abruptly, "What is it?"

"I'm going to cut across at the shallow entrance of the deep ravine so I can walk and search on the other side of it."

"What for? Your stag's gonna be dead somewhere in this high grass."

"Then y'all will find him. I just want to search on the east side of the ravine."

"We've already walked that area."

"I know, but I'm going to walk it again."

"Okay, fine. Just be sure to meet us at 2:10 p.m. on the main caliche road near the southern property line."

"I'll be there."

Josh stared at me for a moment, "You be careful, brother."

I waved at him, then started heading back toward the north.

He turned and began walking south. "Lengthen out the grid line," Josh yelled to the others.

I saw a group of five extending the space between them.

They quickly disappeared into the high grass as I hurried to the shallow swale of the ravine.

1:35 p.m. I began crossing the swale and looked into the ravine where it dropped straight down a five-foot precipice. I stopped and stared down at the jagged, rocky ravine. It sloped sharply downward at a forty-five-degree angle, its bottom disappearing within twenty-five yards.

Here at this ancient location, as old as time itself, the erosion had ripped the soil and rocks away, leaving this inhospitable gorge where no man nor animal was ever intended to travel. God and the elements had sculpted it. This deep ravine was wild, forbidding, and dangerous. Not a place for humans.

Where I was walking, I could see a crisscross of many well-used game trails that cut back and forth from the southwest where Josh and the other four helpers were now scouting. Then I saw three other trails traveling to the upper part of the central west, and there were two heavily used paths turning sharply toward the southeast heading into the lower central west.

It was in that middle central west section where Josh and I had sat in the hideout on the stools overlooking the big clearings two hundred yards away from where I was standing now.

This was the beginning of no man's land, where this wicked chasm stopped men and beasts in their tracks and where its inner boundaries held secrets that no man knew. Josh guessed there might be a few small pools of water on the unexplored floor of this massive formation.

I walked south by the hideout and then another four hundred yards along the east side of the ravine. I noticed the foliage was so thick the visibility was limited to no more than a few feet in any direction. I continued to walk south, searching for any sign of my stag. I was doing what the voice instructed me to do.

A half a mile later, I stopped to take a breather and to assess the sheer rock sides of the ravine that appeared so steep and dangerous that no human being or animal could possibly scale them to get in or out.

After a few more seconds, I was on my way. I searched intently, my eyes like radar on the dense brush. If the red stag was here, I would find him.

I walked another three hundred yards and then stopped. I looked directly to the east. I knew I was only a few hundred yards away from where the dogs had lost track of the blood trail.

On that night, the stag had mysteriously simply vanished into thin air. My eyes drifted over an unusually large brush pile about seventy-five yards away.

This is where a wounded animal might take refuge, I thought. It was a good choice in a pinch—hard to get to and well-concealed.

I made my way down to the pile and began to search. Everything felt right. This is the kind of place we have been looking for. Even though there was no evidence yet of the stag, I was sure this is why God told me to come to this overlooked side of the ravine.

I walked carefully on top of the brush pile and then around it looking at the different possible places for an animal to hide—nothing.

I continued looking, with this strange premonition not to give up. After about two minutes, I saw something buried deep inside the pile.

My heart raced. I was more than excited. *Oh my gosh, this could be it.* I began pulling the brush away as fast as I could. I was in a big hurry. I needed to dig deeper inside the pile to get a better look. I was frantically pulling away from the brush. *Was this really it?* Brush was flying everywhere.

And then I knew for sure. Part of one side of that great rack, and then another until I was able to grip those thick, heavy antlers. I yanked and pulled, and, finally, the skull and antlers broke loose from the carcass.

Once free, it was apparent that the red stag skull and antlers were too heavy for me to drag completely out. I left them lying at the top of the pile.

I was amazed, grateful, and blessed beyond words. The antlers were beautiful. I marveled at them. *But where was the big drop tine?*

Something was wrong. No big drop tine off the right beam, and they were not nearly the size of those on my stag. They were nowhere near as grand. I knew immediately—this was not my stag.

I was disappointed and tired of the endless setbacks. This was another failed attempt in my quest to locate my stag. Despite another letdown, I was still charged with adrenaline from the close call and, when I walked away from the brush pile, I did so filled with faith. I believed in my heart one of us would soon find my lost stag.

I took off walking back to the ravine and then turned south. My eyes never stopped looking.

With each step, I was getting more tired and hungry. I had already walked over twelve miles today. I didn't want to let disillusionment win me over, but I just couldn't understand why no one had spotted my lost stag by now.

Stay positive, I told myself for the millionth time since this ordeal began. But, after several more steps, I was thinking nothing good had happened so far. I was frustrated. I was also feeling a touch of anxiety and stress like I had experienced from late October through late November.

On my drive here this morning, I was sure we would find the stag. But maybe Josh was right. Maybe looking for the stag was indeed worse than looking for a needle in a haystack. Maybe finding the lost stag was an impossible task. Maybe this one particular animal was indeed lost to the world forever. Maybe what I was asking everyone to do was a waste of time.

1:55 p.m. I was dragging. It had been a long day since I departed Austin this morning. I still had another mile to walk to get to the rendezvous spot. I needed to stop these negative thoughts and kick myself into high gear.

I was walking at a fast tempo, my eyes focused on the ground in front of me, and my mind was racing with impossible-to-understand thoughts.

Was the deep voice I was hearing really the voice of God? Was the voice just in my imagination? Something I was making up? Had God actually told me to come back to this ranch and look for my lost stag? Or was it me who really wanted to come back here to satisfy my needs? Had God actually instructed me to walk around on this side of the deep ravine? Or was my brain playing tricks on me? If God was really talking to me and guiding me, then why hadn't I found the stag? And why hadn't anyone else in the group found the lost stag? And what was the reason for all of this walking and searching for the stag, if he could never be found?

I didn't know what to do. This was the reason I had asked God to help me. I needed God's help and answers.

Ahead of me, I noticed a large, smooth rock—a perfect place to take a rest and just ten feet from the edge of the deep ravine. But, I had no time to sit and think. Time was of the essence now. *You've got to keep pushing forward and searching*, I told myself.

2:05 p.m. I needed to keep moving at a fast pace to make sure I was on time at the pickup point at 2:10 p.m. I needed to clear all these bizarre thoughts from my head. I walked hastily past the big rock but, for some reason, stopped after I had gone a few yards. I had no idea why I stopped. I turned around and stared at that large rock for several more seconds. I decided to go back to sit down on it. The rock felt very comfortable. After I sat there for a few seconds, I began talking to God out loud, half talking, half praying.

My heavenly Father and God, you know how much I love you and your Son Jesus Christ. You know my faith in you and your Son Jesus Christ has always been strong.

I came here today because I believe you told me to come here to this ranch and search for my red stag. And I believe I'm sitting on this rock right now because you told me to come walk on this side of this deep ravine.

I've done everything you've told me to do. I've done everything I can to find my lost stag.

And the people who have helped me today have done everything they can to help me find the stag. I believe this incredible animal that you created is too beautiful and too spectacular to be lost to the world forever. I believe the people of the world need to be given the chance to see and celebrate your glorious creation.

My heavenly Father, I know you can hear me. I know you're here with me. I know you've been talking to me. And I know you want to help me.

I slid off the rock and got down on my left knee. Then I looked up toward the sky.

Almighty God, I know there is absolutely no way I will ever find my red stag on my own. And there is absolutely no way anyone else is going to find my lost stag in this pasture.

You know I need your help. And you know I'm asking for your help. You know I'm praying to you, God, to please help me find my stag.

I'm asking you to please take over my body and my mind. I'm asking you to please guide me and lead me to the stag.

I'm praying for you to please tell me where the stag is located. I am asking you to please take over my eyes and show me the path to where this animal is resting. I'm praying that you will let the people of the world see this splendid animal that you have conceived.

And I am praying that when you reveal him to me that this miracle will be all to your glory, my heavenly Father.

Lord, God Almighty, full of wisdom, forgiveness, and love, creator of the universe, and Father of our Savior Jesus Christ, I am praying with all my heart for you to let the people of the world know you're still alive.

I am praying to you to let the people of the world see your great powers.

All of this I leave in your godly hands. All of this I leave in your almighty control.

My heavenly Father, please speak to me again. Please show me, and lead me, and tell me what I need to do.

All of this, I pray to your divine glory. Amen.

When I stopped talking, I looked toward the heavens. I felt energized. Then, just before I stood up, I heard the three trucks honking in the distance and everyone in the group yelling and hollering.

"Brother, where are you? Where are you?" Josh screamed.

"Mr. Akins, can you hear us, can you hear us?" One of the group members yelled.

I could hear others hollering as well. They were scrambling around trying to find me.

I stared at my wristwatch. It read 2:11 p.m. "I'm late," I mumbled. "Yes, yes. I'm okay. I'm okay," I yelled back at them. "I'm coming. I'm coming."

"Everyone be quiet," Josh yelled. "I think I heard him."

"I'm coming. I'm okay. I'm coming," I hollered.

Faintly, I could hear Josh and the group. They had heard me, but the yelling and honking continued. I yelled out one more time, then started south. The moment I took my first step in the direction of the yelling and honking, a power took over my body. My immediate reaction was to resist the power, but it was too strong for me. The power gently pulled me toward the ravine. And when I was finally one foot from the edge of the ravine, I could feel the power let up. I was startled, maybe a little frightened by what was happening. I thought I was imagining all of this. But then I heard the deep voice again.

"Go down here," the deep voice told me. "Go down here in the ravine."

Looking down over the edge of the ravine, I could see it was a straight, sheer ninety-degree drop-off. To me, it was worse than looking into the Grand Canyon. I had no idea how far down it was to the bottom because I couldn't see the bottom. *To try to go down in that ravine was suicide*, I thought.

"Brother, where are you?" I heard Josh yelling in the distance. "Where are you?"

I could tell he was walking toward me and getting closer.

"Mr. Akins, Mr. Akins," I heard some of the group yelling.

They were walking fast and getting closer too.

I turned and hollered. "I'm coming. I'm coming. I'm on my way."

Then I turned back toward the ravine.

"I can't go down in that ravine. It's too steep. And it's too dangerous," I told the deep voice.

"Go down here. You will find him," the voice commanded.

At that moment, I wasn't sure if the voice was God trying to help me or the devil trying to kill me.

"I told you, I can't do it. My knees and my whole body cannot do it," I shouted.

The deep voice did not answer.

"I can't go down in that ravine. I think it would kill me if I tried."

The voice did not respond.

"I've got to go now. They're looking for me," I said to the voice.

I heard nothing. I had no idea what would happen if I tried to leave. I turned my body to the left and took a big step away from the ravine. At that moment, I felt the power release control of my body. I immediately took off, jogging slowly through the brush toward the south. The yelling and the hollering were getting louder with every stride. When I had gone two hundred yards, I finally reached the group. They looked happy and relieved that I was okay.

Tommy stepped up and greeted me with a handshake and a pat on the back. I could tell he was genuinely worried about me and glad I was okay.

"What happened to you?" Josh asked me. He looked exasperated.

"I really thought I had found my stag. It was in the lower central west area. I thought maybe he had buried himself inside of a brush pile that I saw. It was a pile near where the dogs lost his blood trail. I thought it might have been a good place for him to have hidden."

"Did you find him?"

"No, but I found another carcass and a big rack of horns."

"So, you found a good one?"

"Yes, sir, but not my stag. It just took me a lot longer to look in that brush pile than I anticipated."

Josh stared at me, "Was it another coyote kill?"

"I think it was."

Josh turned to Tommy. "We're going to have to do something about these coyotes in this pasture, or we're not going to have any animals left in here."

"I'll call a trapper in the next few days," Tommy replied.

Josh shook his head, "We're going to need more like a hit squad." All the helpers laughed.

Josh patted me on the shoulder. "Well, brother, we didn't spot your stag either."

"I didn't figure you did."

Then Josh wheeled around. "Okay, guys, let's get out of here."

Everyone turned and took off south.

"Let's get everybody fed."

We were back at the trucks in five minutes. We loaded up and drove to the big iron gate.

2:28 p.m. We exited through the iron gate of the 52-Pasture. I didn't say a word. I was lost in some profound thought. I was thinking about the deep voice speaking to me. I was thinking about the power that had pulled me to the edge of the ravine. This was unimaginable. I couldn't explain this phenomenon to anyone without sounding like a crazy man. I mean, who in the world could I tell without appearing irrational and psychotic? I knew the deep voice was real. I wanted to believe I was talking to God. I wanted to believe God was instructing me. I knew something had pulled me to the ravine. And I knew there was no way I could have invented all of this in my mind. But, there was one thing that kept giving me some doubt—*would God really tell me to go down in that treacherous, deep ravine?* I didn't think so. It was enough to make me question my sanity.

CHAPTER TWENTY-THREE

For well over seven long hours, the nine of us had searched diligently for my red stag. We covered over twelve miles of unforgiving brush land, and not one of us had spotted the lost stag. We were tired and hungry and ready to get back to the lodge.

"With a good hot meal and a little rest, we'll all be ready to get back out there this afternoon and find that red stag," Josh told each one of the helpers.

They all agreed with that.

I patted Josh on the shoulder. "Thanks for all the help, my friend."

"Don't you worry, brother, we're gonna find that monster this afternoon," Josh whispered to me.

"I know we will," I answered.

It's all in God's hands, I told myself.

As we drove away from the 52-Pasture, the question that was haunting all of us was, where in the world within this thick pasture were those massive, enormous antlers?

We all sat quiet while the ranch truck tires gripped the caliche road heading back toward the lodge. I kept reminding myself that being unable to find the stag was insignificant compared to what millions of others around the world were going through.

2:58 p.m. Our entire crew of nine sat down in the lodge dining room to a delicious lunch of brisket sandwiches, cream corn, and potato salad.

Before we finished, Josh reminded everyone that we would be loading up and departing for the 52-Pasture at 3:30 p.m. Everyone nodded they understood.

Josh and I finished our lunch quickly and then headed for the rocking chairs on the front porch. We still had fifteen minutes to rest before hitting the brush. We had just sat down when we heard the rotor blades of a helicopter in the distance—it was coming our way, flying low.

"That's what we need," Josh said.

"Yes, sir. A helicopter would do it," I said.

Josh leaned his head back and closed his eyes. He spoke in a soft voice, sounding like he was already drifting off to sleep.

"If we had a helicopter, we'd pretty much be guaranteed to find him," he mumbled.

I closed my eyes and leaned back in the rocking chair. I knew Josh was right.

3:20 p.m. Tommy came out of the ranch office and walked straight across the complex toward us. Tommy was a big man, and he stood towering over us in our rocking chairs.

"I've called off the search party for this evening. I've dissolved the group. I'm going to send them out on the ranch to do other things."

"No, no, please don't do that," I said as I jumped up from the rocking chair. "We still have all afternoon to search, and we need those extra eyes."

Josh was on his feet. "Look, Tommy, we're all set to leave and go back out to the 52-Pasture in just a few minutes. We need everyone in the group to cover all the ground we still need to go over."

Tommy held his hands above his head, waving us off.

"Please, can y'all just wait a second and listen?"

We held our tongues and listened.

"I just spoke to Mr. Randolph on the phone. He decided to hire a helicopter to fly you two guys around the 52-Pasture this afternoon to find the stag."

"Unbelievable," I said.

Josh grinned, "Was that the helicopter we heard a few minutes ago?"

"It sure is," Tommy said.

Josh looked over at me. "This changes everything. We're definitely going to find your stag now."

"Yes, sir, we sure are." I gave Josh a big thumbs-up.

The excitement I was feeling was oozing out of me.

"Thank you, God," I shouted. "And you too, Mr. Randolph."

And then the sky echoed with the sound of a whining engine and the chop of the rotor blades as the helicopter angled in over us, flared, and landed behind the big lodge. We could hear the loud whomp and whoosh as the bird set down, and then the engine wound down, and the main rotor humming slowed and idled until it shut down.

Tommy was trying to talk over the helicopter noise.

"Mr. Randolph has instructed the pilot to fly y'all around the entire 52-Pasture until dark. This should give y'all a chance to search every inch of that place."

"Yes, sir, it sure will," Josh said.

"And Mr. Randolph is paying the pilot and helicopter. So, don't worry about any cost Mr. Akins," Tommy said.

"Please tell him I said thank you and how much I appreciate his help."

"I will, but he already knows that."

"This is incredible. Like I said, this is exactly what we needed to find your stag," Josh said.

"This is unbelievable," I stated. "A real blessing."

My mind raced with good thoughts. I was extremely appreciative of what the ranch was doing, and I couldn't thank Mr. Randolph enough for all of his help. This was exciting to be able to search for the lost stag in a helicopter. Now it was just a matter of time, and we would find him. I was sure now this was why God had sent me here. This was what we needed, a can't-miss path to my red stag's location.

"Let's go get him," I said.

"Copy that, my brother." I could sense the excitement in his voice.

We hustled around the building as fast as we could, stopping briefly to look at the new, bright red helicopter. The beautiful machine was parked in the field about seventy-five yards from the lodge. The pilot was standing out away from the helicopter, waiting for Josh and me to approach.

He waved for us to lower our heads as the main rotor was still winding down, and the tail rotor continued to spin.

We met the pilot at the helicopter, shook hands, and then gave him a quick rundown of how we wanted to do the 52-Pasture flyover. After we climbed aboard, Josh sat up front next to the pilot while I sat in the rear where I had access to a view out either side.

The pilot removed all the doors to give us the most unobstructed view possible, not to mention the most exciting one. After we strapped in, the pilot positioned and adjusted our headsets and microphones so we would have in-flight communications.

The pilot did his preflight and run-up and, the next thing we knew, we were lifting off as he pulled up on the collective stick and rolled the cyclic to the right, sending us upward and laterally all in one smooth motion. He continued to move us forward and to gain altitude until we had a good overview of the place and could see the familiar country loom into view ahead of us.

3:35 p.m. Josh sat holding his binoculars between his legs and staring out the open doorway of the cabin. The sky was crystal clear, and the visibility was perfect. My heart was racing and my adrenaline pumping. I was enjoying and savoring this glorious ride. I was sure this was going to be a guaranteed victory. I was going to remember this ride for the rest of my life. This was going to be the celebrated day when we found my stag. I couldn't wait to get my hands around those massive antlers. I couldn't wait to show the world what God created.

When we were about a mile away from the pasture, the pilot's voice came over the headsets. "Tommy sent me the exact coordinates and location of the 52-Pasture. I've already mapped it out."

Josh and I were listening.

"I'm going to fly a low grid over the pasture. This should give y'all a much better opportunity to search for the lost animal."

"That's perfect," Josh replied.

"I'll fly low and slow, crisscrossing the terrain in a one-hundred-foot wide grid pattern. This should provide y'all optimum visibility."

"How low will you fly?" I asked.

"Just above the tree line. Fifty to sixty feet off the ground in most places. You should have a great view."

I smiled. "Perfect."

"Sounds good," Josh said. "The animal has been dead for almost two months."

"Okay." The pilot nodded his head.

"We're only looking for the stag's massive antlers."

"I understand." The pilot made a hard left toward the east.

Josh turned in his seat and gave me a thumbs-up.

"We'll find him soon, brother," he said.

We made it to the 52-Pasture in ten minutes. Josh and I knew we had a little less than two hours of daylight remaining to search the entire 5,200 acres. The pilot assured us he would definitely get the search done with time to spare.

He already had the pasture laid out in a north/south, east/west grid. There was no wasting time. The pilot started the search immediately. He took us over the mountains in the north, then flying south, crisscrossing the pasture in one-hundred-foot wide strips until the entire pasture had been thoroughly viewed. We looked under every bush and tree and cactus.

Then the pilot flew us on an east and west route, crisscrossing the pasture into one-hundred-foot wide strips until the entire pasture was fully observed. Josh and I looked under and around everything.

This pilot flew with precision. And, each time, he flew us slowly and methodically along the grid, consistently just above the tree line. Our eyes never stopped searching, our excitement was palpable, and we knew at any moment one of us was going to spot him.

Throughout the flight, the brush seemed to disappear and allow our eyes to see almost every inch on the ground. There was no area of the 52-Pasture we left unsearched. Josh joked that neither one of us had missed seeing a leaf or a twig. But I knew, even in this helicopter, there were a handful of places too thick for us to see everything.

In the time it took us to cover the 52-Pasture, we spotted nine dead red deer. We circled over them dropped to thirty feet each time for a conclusive view. The carcasses included six hinds and three stags. These animals, along with their skulls, skins, and antlers, were clearly visible. But still, no sight of my red stag.

The low flying helicopter was spooking the animals. They were constantly running and darting in every direction. We saw at least five hundred hinds and about one hundred fifty red stags running frantically through the trees below us.

It was like a scene out of an African documentary with lots of hogs, several axis, oryx, elk, and other species scrambling out of the brush. At the higher elevations, we saw aoudad, mouflon, and Corsican sheep.

The entire afternoon we flew grid patterns with remarkable consistency and precision. This pilot was my age. He was a real pro, an old Huey gunship pilot who honed his skills in Vietnam. Josh and I were highly impressed.

The pilot spun the helicopter around on a dime, maneuvering us from one end of the pasture to the other end with meticulous attention to detail. Sometimes we got so close to the ground, it seemed like we were brushing the tree-tops. Josh and I knew he was giving us a great opportunity to view about ninety-nine percent of everything below us. And, with each passing second, I was sure one of us would finally spot my lost stag. But, sadly, that was not the case for the first hour and fifteen minutes.

We were down to about twenty-five minutes of remaining flight time. We had already flown over the giant ravine during the crisscross grid search.

At my request, we flew another pass over the deep ravine. But this time, the pilot dropped down low, almost like we were setting down, cruising the ravine slowly at ten feet above it. We flew from south to north, searching meticulously and carefully. The inside of the canyon looked brutal.

Most of the time, it was impossible to see the floor, but even with the thick brush and foliage, there were several occasions when we saw snakes, rats, raccoons, and coyotes slithering and running on some shallow outer edges along the perimeter. We looked closely, trying to view with accuracy every single image and thing in this dangerous ravine. But still, there was no sighting of my lost stag.

For the majority of the ravine, the depth to the bottom was unseen and immeasurable. And staring out the helicopter to the right and left, the sheer face of the rock walls on each side looked severe and hopeless to climb or descend.

After fifteen minutes, we flew from one end to the other. Josh and I were fairly certain we had seen almost everything there was to see inside the chasm.

I asked the pilot to go back and fly us over the large rock where I had sat a few hours earlier and heard the voice tell me to go down into the ravine.

My heart and mind raced as we approached the rock. I thought for sure we would spot my red stag.

Josh asked me why I wanted to check out this specific place so carefully.

"I just have a good feeling about it," I said.

"Okay, let's look it over."

The pilot hovered ten feet above the big rock and then maneuvered the helicopter over that particular area of the ravine for more than two minutes. I strained my eyes, searching the area to see as much as possible from that advantaged perspective. We sat in the helicopter only a few feet above the rock ledge, looking intently at the jagged wall and straight down at the sharp rocks and brushy zone below us. The trees, high grass, cactus, and undergrowth were thick and impenetrable.

We were hanging out the sides of the helicopter now, scrutinizing the area even more closely. From what we could see, we scanned every inch of this entire area. My eyes went from the big rock to the rugged cliff, then along the sheer drop-off and as far below and to the floor as we were able to see.

Josh and I agreed, we could see at least 99 percent of this area reasonably well. And we agreed that had my red stag been there, we would have seen him. We searched hard and diligently, but there was absolutely no sight of a carcass or skull or a massive rack of antlers. We stared at each other and nodded. We were satisfied and convinced my lost stag was not there.

The pilot flew us around in a wide arc, giving us one final look at the lower central west area before he pulled the collective, and the helicopter climbed to an altitude of two hundred feet.

5:40 p.m. The sun was beginning to set in the far distance. The pilot gave us a nod of his head to the west, and then he turned the helicopter, and we began flying rapidly toward the last remaining sunlight in the sky. We could see the lodge lights flickering in the distance. I must admit, I was stunned we had not found my red stag. This was not the way I had envisioned this helicopter ride was going to end. Where was the jubilant celebration? Where were the photos of me holding those massive antlers? This is why I thought God had sent me here. The failure to find my red stag was disappointing. I felt lost and confused.

We listened to the rhythm of the rotor and the whining of the engine in silence as the pilot covered the ground fast on the return flight to the lodge. Everything seemed to pass below us in a blur.

Josh turned toward me. He knew I was disappointed.

"We gave it our best shot, my friend."

His words rang inside my headphones. I didn't respond.

"I don't know what else we could have done," Josh said.

"We did everything we could possibly do," I said into the mic.

We both shook our heads at each other. I supposed Josh was shaking his head in frustration, and I was shaking my head in disbelief.

I sat quietly in the back of the helicopter. We were flying toward the western horizon at a fast clip. The clouds were beginning to stack on top of each other. The clouds were red and orange. The rays of sunlight began turning the tops of the clouds into beautiful yellow streaks.

My mind was churning like the main rotor above me. I didn't quite understand the meaning behind all of this sudden failure in my life. I disliked it. In fact, I hated it.

I couldn't comprehend the reason for so much disappointment and frustration. In the past, when I was in control, I would have jumped on this without God's help. I would have immediately begun clawing my way through this problem, trying to fix it. Then, after a while, if there was no quick fix, my determination, never-quit attitude, and my physical and mental strength would have pushed me onward. I would have eventually found a way to correct the setback, returning my life to normal until the next problem arose.

But that was my old life, and I had made an effort three weeks earlier to change my ways. God was helping me now with my problems. God was in my corner, ready to lead me and fix things. Sure, I was very disappointed that we had not found my stag, but this setback was in God's hands now. I trusted Him.

I knew Josh and I could not have searched any harder or better for the lost stag. We both felt if the red stag was anywhere in that 52-Pasture, we should have spotted him from the helicopter. Neither one of us wanted to admit it, but we both knew there was nothing more we could do to find him. We both thought the magnificent stag was lost for the ages.

5:51 p.m. The pilot flared in and set the helicopter down behind the lodge. I was still in disbelief that, after the entire afternoon of flying and looking, Josh and I never once saw my red stag. It was unimaginable. I knew now this was the end. This helicopter search was the final straw, the last chapter of our story about the unforgettable search to find my red stag. I had to accept the clear fact; my stag was gone forever.

There was no doubt in my mind that Josh also believed this was the curtain call in our grueling effort to find the stag.

Somehow, someway, God was giving me the strength and peace to accept this misfortune.

CHAPTER
TWENTY-FOUR

After we landed and unloaded the helicopter, I raced around to the other side and shook hands with the pilot, thanking him for his superb flying skills and for his tremendous effort in trying to help us locate the lost stag. In my opinion, he was the best helicopter pilot I had ever flown with. His ability to give us a bird's eye view of every inch of the 52-Pasture made me wonder how in the world we had missed finding the lost stag.

"Sorry I didn't find your stag for you," he said.

I smiled back at him. "Don't be sorry. You did an unbelievable job flying us around today."

"Thank you, sir. I love flying."

"Well, you're the best I've ever seen. Josh and I appreciate your hard work today."

"My pleasure, sir. Good luck to you in finding your stag."

The pilot waved at me, and then he walked over to Josh, who had already retrieved the four doors to reinstall on the helicopter. The pilot was in a rush now. He quickly attached the doors and was scrambling to get his helicopter back into the air. He had twenty minutes before total darkness, barely enough light to get him back to Uvalde.

When the rotors spun up to speed, Josh stood next to me. We held onto our caps and watched the helicopter lift off straight up and then tip forward and accelerate off into the distance and disappear into the waning light.

Josh turned to me. "We did our best, my brother. We left it all out there on the field."

"Yes, we did," I said.

"I'm really sorry we didn't find him," Josh said.

"Me too, Josh. Me too."

We stood there a long time, watching the sky. The bright clouds of red, orange, and yellow fading together now.

"I put finding the stag in God's hands," I said.

Josh looked at me with a questioning expression.

"I asked God to help us find him. That's all I can do now."

Josh was quiet. In all of our years in hunting together, we had never talked about God. This was all new territory.

"There must be a good reason why we didn't find the stag today."

The words surprised me as much as they did him.

Josh just stared at me. "There's no good reason, brother."

"I guess what I'm saying, a lot of times, we blame ourselves for our failures that aren't really our fault."

"Yes, sir. I do that sometimes. I blame myself and get so frustrated and angry that I can't see straight," Josh said.

I looked over at Josh. Our eyes locked.

"I would think, brother, that losing your enormous, potential world record stag would be absolutely killing you," Josh said.

"It was killing me. I was consumed by it. It was all I could think about. It was making me miserable and eating a hole through me. I just couldn't worry about losing my stag anymore. To keep my sanity, I had to put it all in God's hands."

Josh was mystified. This wasn't the old Marty he knew.

"Look, Josh, I'm still greatly disappointed. Okay?"

He nodded at me.

I reached over and patted him on the back. "But we did our very best to find him today. Didn't we?"

"Yes, we did."

"We walked over twelve miles searching diligently through that horrible, brutal brush, and we flew the entire 52-Pasture in a helicopter and saw everything. Right?"

"You're right."

"So, do I need to keep punishing myself for not finding the stag? Do I need to let this failure drive me crazy? Do I need to let losing the stag ruin my life?"

Josh was staring at me. His eyes never blinked as he stood listening.

"I mean, what else can I do more than to ask God to help us find him. That's all I can do. Guys like you and me have to learn to accept God's answer."

He was still listening.

"I'm not going to let this setback ruin our evening."

Josh was frowning.

"I mean, sure, it hurts me deeply not to find my stag. I wanted worse than anything to show him to the world and put my hands around those antlers today. But my life has changed for the better now. I've learned to put things like this in God's hands that aren't in my control. I've learned to move forward with God's help and guidance."

Josh nodded slightly like he finally got what I was saying.

"I want you to know I'm very grateful to you and to Mr. Randolph and Tommy for all of your help today. And I really appreciate everything you and the ranch employees have done for me."

Josh moved his head up and down. "It was our pleasure, my friend."

"And I'm especially thankful for our friendship."

"Copy that, brother."

"You know Josh, we've shared some wonderful memories together these past several years, including this lost stag hunt."

"Yes, sir, we've had some great hunts and lasting memories," Josh smiled. "I honestly believe the lost stag hunt will go down as one of my all-time favorite hunting stories."

"You're right about that. But mostly, the lost stag hunt is about a man who thought he was in complete control of everything in his life but found out he was wrong. It's about a man who finally asked God to help him, and that changed his life."

He smiled slightly.

I smiled back at him. "You know Josh; we don't always have to win to be victorious."

I had no idea where those words came from. Josh looked befuddled. Then he shook his head slightly before letting out a laugh.

"Honestly, brother, that really doesn't sound like you."

"I told you, I've changed. God is in control of my life now."

Josh looked me straight in the eyes. "You may have put this in God's hands, and you may think you have changed, but I know you, and I know that to you, winning is everything," he stated.

"You're right," I answered.

"Not finding your stag isn't winning."

"That's exactly what I'm saying," I replied. I stepped toward Josh. "I'm saying if we put our trust in God, then accepting a bad result in the beginning can make us victorious in the end."

Josh frowned at me. "You've lost me on this one, brother. I still can't believe you're not mad."

"I told you, I've changed."

After a few moments of silence, he said loudly. "Come on, let's go eat."

"Sounds good to me," I answered. "I'll meet you around 6:30 in the dining room."

"Copy that."

We both turned and started walking toward the lodge.

Josh looked over at me. "Let's get cleaned up and have a lot of fun tonight at dinner," he said. "Let's party."

"I like it," I replied. "No need to cry over spilled milk."

Josh smiled. "Copy that a hundred times." After a couple of more steps, he gave me a thumb's up. "See you soon, brother."

I walked to my room, knowing that somewhere deep inside me, something monumental had changed. After a disappointing day like today, the man I once knew would have been very upset, frustrated, and angry, at least until somehow, someway he could have fixed the problem.

No doubt, this expensive hunt and the lost red stag were a real nightmare for me. But now, by some new means, none of that seemed important. For sure, I was different. I wasn't giving those crazy ideas a second thought. Now, all I could think of was that God had brought me back here to this place for a good reason. Maybe not finding the red stag was a test. Maybe it would make me a better person. I strongly believed God had a good plan for me.

One thing was crystal clear to me. God was in control. He was the daily healer of my mind, my spirit, and my soul. My faith and trust, and belief in Him that He would eventually make things right were all that mattered now. I was satisfied with whatever answer God gave me.

The lodge was jumping and buzzing when I entered the building on my way to my room. The place was packed with mostly men but also a handful of women who sat around the trophy room waiting for dinner to be served.

I headed past them straight to my room. I felt as good as I could about the day. We had done our very best to find the lost animal. There was no debate about that. We had walked almost eight hours and over twelve miles. As a group, we had made a heroic search through that hellish place and somehow made it back, totally spent and beat up. And, during the entire time we conducted the helicopter air search of the

52-Pasture, I truly believed, at any moment, we would spot the lost stag. And now, walking to my room, as odd as it may sound, I still had a strong faith and trust that one day God would eventually show me my lost stag.

I sat on the edge of the bed, slowly removing my clothes. My pants were partially torn and ripped from the miles of walking and searching through that wicked and unforgiving brush. Luckily, my shirt had been protected by my heavy coat. I threw my pants away in the garbage exactly like I had done seven weeks earlier. I took some Advil, then sat motionless for a while. Then I went into the bathroom, shaved, and took a long, hot shower. Returning to the bedroom, I laid naked on my bed for several long minutes staring up at the ceiling, waiting for the Advil to kick in.

My legs, arms, neck, and complete torso were covered with red whelps, cuts and scratches, and deep bruises. The muscles throughout my entire body ached with relentless pain. I was keenly aware of this kind of physical abuse and pain. I had experienced it after every football game I played, especially in college, running the wishbone. I closed my eyes, trying to relax.

I can go home right now with no regrets, I thought. After all, we had gone through today, I was greatly disappointed, but I felt satisfied with all of it—even the idea that my stag was gone forever. I knew now, with God's help, I could face any situation. I knew with God's help I could move on. I stood up and began to put on my clothes. My legs and arms ached from the abuse, but I knew in my mind every step through that brutal brush was worth it. This was a journey that had brought me closer to God.

I exited the room with a clear conscience and a level head, and then headed quietly toward the large trophy room.

The trophy room is a grand and dramatic showpiece of the ranch's commitment to quality, filled with walls of world record mounts of every exotic species one could imagine. For a brief moment, I thought about my red stag. I knew he would have qualified for the wall himself and looked quite majestic.

But the stag was a fleeting thought. What stood out in my mind was the valuable lesson I had learned today. Those words which had come out of my mouth sounding as strange to me as they must have to Josh.

I said it to myself. *We don't always have to win to be victorious.*

I figured God gave me this valuable lesson to serve me well for the rest of my life.

6:35 p.m. I met Tommy and Josh at our table in the back corner of the dining room. The loud talking and laughing in the background from the dining hall and the trophy room were a stark contrast to our quiet table. Everyone was low keyed at first. We ate for several minutes before any conversation was started.

I finally broke the ice, "Hey Tommy, thanks for all the help today. I really appreciated you and all the ranch employees."

"No problem." Tommy looked at me. "We were glad to try to help you."

"Please tell all the helpers today I said thanks."

"I'll do it." Then Tommy waited for a moment. "So, how was the helicopter ride today?" he asked.

"Unsuccessful," Josh said. "But that's not going to ruin our evening."

I turned toward Tommy. "The helicopter was a lot of help. The pilot did one heck of a job for us. He showed us the entire 52-Pasture in slow motion. I've never seen a pilot who could fly like him. He could maneuver that helicopter on a dime, and he put us in a position all day for us to see just about everything close up and crystal clear," I said.

Tommy leaned forward. "Well, I really thought one of you would find him with that helicopter."

"No such luck," Josh said.

Tommy looked over at me. "That's too bad."

"I was sure we would find him too," I said.

Josh nodded. "We did the best we could."

"You're right," I stated.

Tommy made it sound final. "There's nothing else we can do at this point."

7:35 p.m. I stood and pushed my chair under the table. Josh and Tommy were still debating the location of the lost stag and trying to finish up their meal.

"I'm finished eating, guys. I'm going out on the porch to get in a rocking chair and try to relax," I said.

They waved me off and said they would catch up with me later.

After about twenty minutes, Tommy and Josh came out from the lodge and found me at the fire pit in a rocker, thinking. They pulled up two more rockers and then sat down next to me.

The fire pit had become a favorite location for me. There was something calming and compelling about watching the flames and being able to look up at the stars and the big moon. The enormity of that endless Texas night sky had the appearance of a black velvet robe scattered with diamonds.

"Any of y'all want a cigar?" Tommy asked as he fired up an expensive Cohiba Maduro he had snatched from the ranch humidor.

Even though I considered the Maduro to be an excellent choice, I declined. Josh shook his head.

The three of us sat there with our feet up, enjoying the hot fire and casual conversation.

When the time seemed right to Tommy, he leaned forward and began to talk to me in a serious tone.

"I don't think there's anything else we can do here at the ranch to help you find your lost stag."

Josh chimed in. "I would have to agree with Tommy. We've already done everything we can possibly do here."

I knew they were right, and I understood their desire to put this to rest and move on with their business.

"I understand," I said.

"Unless, of course, you have any other ideas," Tommy said, but it was framed as a question.

"I'm not sure there's anything else to be done," I said.

Tommy continued to justify the ranch's position like he was a trial lawyer putting the finishing touches on a closing argument in a case. "Just think about it. We turned out an unusually large group of our ranch workers this morning for seven hours, covering over twelve miles. We've hit a brick wall looking for the stag."

Tommy paused and took a deep breath. "And, to top it off, we hired a helicopter for another two hours plus. The pilot meticulously flew you and Josh the entire 52-Pasture, checking every square inch of the place. I don't know what else we can do to help you find him."

Josh looked at me and nodded his head.

"I agree with you both," I replied.

They both look surprised but happy. They truly had done everything possible and were relieved to be off the hook on this one.

"So, you agree, there's absolutely nothing else we can do to help you find your stag?" Tommy asked.

"Yes. I agree. 100 percent."

"And it's not going to make you mad if we stop searching for your stag?"

"Not at all."

Josh leaned in towards me. "Look, my man, we appreciate you, and you know it. We just think we're wasting a lot of valuable time continuing the search. I hate to say it, but I believe he's just lost to the world forever."

"I understand that, Josh, and I think you're right."

That was it. It was a done deal. Tommy wanted to put a bow on it and call it good.

"You've been a great customer here at the ranch, and we don't want you to be upset. Mr. Randolph wants you happy—of course, we do too."

"I completely understand. This is a business. Don't worry. I'll be out of here in the morning," I said.

Tommy patted me on the shoulder.

"Okay then, why don't you just relax here tonight in the lodge, enjoy yourself with the other hunters, stay here in your room, and then we'll meet for breakfast at 7:00. You'll be back on the road to Austin by 8:00. How's that sound?"

"That's fine."

I had the feeling I was being delicately ushered out of the place. Josh sensed it as well. He sat down beside me.

"I'm really sorry, brother. Tommy needs your room for two new hunters tomorrow at noon."

"It's okay. I'm very satisfied with our walk and search this morning. There were a lot of boots on the ground, and that's what we needed to try to find him. Everyone did an excellent job. I know they all tried their best to find the stag."

Tommy was still close by. He stepped over to me. "We've always done our best to help you find him," he said, still posturing.

"Yes, you have."

Tommy saw his opportunity to close the deal, and he took it.

"Thank you, Mr. Akins. We appreciate your understanding of our situation here with the other hunters coming in tomorrow."

"I'll see y'all at 7:00 for breakfast and be on my way right after."

Tommy shook my right hand, and Josh put his arm around me.

"My brother, I'm so sorry we couldn't find him."

It was an empty feeling for me but a mutual relief on many levels for all of us to be done with it. We stood and headed for our rooms.

The lodge sounded like it was packed. The atmosphere had a party mood to it, with music blaring and people celebrating. I noticed several hunters and their guides filter out onto the porch while a handful of them headed toward the fire pit where I sat. I welcomed them, speaking to a few of them about their upcoming morning hunts. I felt like an old veteran with glorious stories to tell of past hunts. They pulled their chairs in close and listened. Later, several of the hunters asked me questions about hunting in different pastures on the ranch.

From the sound of it, every pasture except for one was going to be filled with hunters in the morning. I thought it was strange that the 52-Pasture was going to be empty. I speculated that Tommy and Josh had intentionally not booked it for Friday in anticipation we would still be searching it for my stag.

I had hunted every pasture on this ranch at one time or another. I knew most of these young men and women didn't have a clue as to what they were getting themselves into. For the hunters who were there to spot-and-stalk, I offered my advice on how to negotiate the brush and rocky cliffs.

They all thanked me for my suggestions and were grateful for the advantage my insights would give them in terms of knowing the terrain and where not to go.

I wished them all good luck. I felt like most of them would need it. I left the fire pit, entered the trophy room, and approached the bar, where I picked up a cold bottle of water. I stood alone at the bar looking around the room. Everyone looked happy.

All I could think about was going home tomorrow morning empty-handed. No photos. Nothing to show the world of God's beautiful red stag. And that was okay. I didn't like it, but I accepted that result. I knew God was looking out for me. He had a plan for me. I knew I was a changed man. My mind was at peace, and I was happy.

But there still remained something in me that wanted to continue the search. I recalled something John Lennon had once said, "The more I see, the less I know for sure."

I could identify with that. The more we searched, the less convinced I was that we knew any more than when we started. All I knew for sure was my stag was out there somewhere waiting for me.

10:10 p.m. I stood at the bar for a few more minutes talking to a small crowd of people, amazed at how alone I felt among so many, all buzzing and laughing, having fun, and enjoying life.

10:25 p.m. I was back in my room packing. I knew it was going to be cold tomorrow. I laid out a nice pair of black slacks and a new white, long-sleeved Adidas dress shirt on the extra bed. I also had my black sport coat ready. My plan was to wear this outfit home tomorrow morning.

10:50 p.m. I crawled into bed. I thanked God for all He had done for me today and for His help and guidance in looking for my stag. I told Him how much I appreciated His taking control of my life. I was calm and satisfied with whatever God had planned for me. I firmly believed that with God in my corner, eventually, a setback would be rewarded with a gain, that a failure would be superseded with a victory.

I could hear the laughter and music in the distant background.

Goodnight God. Goodnight my family. Goodnight everybody. I closed my eyes and went to sleep.

CHAPTER TWENTY-FIVE

6:15 a.m. December 13, 2019. When I awoke, my entire body ached from the physical punishment the preceding day. But I wasn't about to let the pain affect my good attitude. I looked out the window at the cool, crisp morning and marveled at this magical place where so many different species of animals were playing and chasing each other in all directions in the complex.

I was moving slowly, but I was happy. My faith and trust in God were steadfast. Today was Friday the 13th. I remembered my father was born on May 13th. To me, thirteen was a fantastic number. This day had a good feel to it. And, even though we had not found my trophy red stag, I was in high spirits. I felt strong mentally and physically. I knew God was in my corner. He was with me all the time. I had nothing to worry about. I would go home today with good thoughts.

I looked out the window. I could feel it in my bones; this was going to be a glorious day.

I'll drive home slowly this morning and savor every minute of being in this beautiful, mountainous southwest Texas brush country, I thought. *No place like Texas.*

I took a hot shower to get my sore muscles and body moving. Later, I started putting on my nice black slacks, then slipped into my new long-sleeved, white Adidas dress shirt. I pulled my black cashmere sport coat from the closet and put it on. I checked out my appearance in the mirror. Everything looked and fit perfectly. As my wife always said to me, I looked like a million bucks.

I was soon all packed and had my bags sitting by the door. I sat on the bed for five minutes, talking to God and thanking Him for my many blessings.

6:58 a.m. I stood up and walked to the door. It was time for me to meet Josh and Tommy for breakfast before heading back to Austin.

When I put my hand on the doorknob, it wouldn't turn. *The lock must be stuck or broken*, I thought. I tried to muscle the door open, but nothing happened. As I bent down to examine the lock, the deep voice spoke loud and clear.

"Put on your hunting shirt. You will take photos with the stag today."

I stood very still and silent.

"Go back to the rock. Go down in the ravine."

The voice was clearly talking to me again. I knew exactly the place I needed to go.

"Yes, sir, I hear you, God," I said.

I reached down, grabbed my suitcase, and then turned away from the door and walked back to the bed. I opened my suitcase, took out a pair of worn blue jeans and my long sleeve camouflage shirt. I changed clothes, grabbed my camouflage hunting cap and high boots, put them on, and then walked back to the door. This time when I tried the doorknob, the door opened easily. Suddenly, I was out the door hustling down the hall.

7:05 a.m. I smiled. For the first time since I had shot the red stag, I truly believed in my heart I would find him this morning. I believed God was talking to me, and I trusted His words. I believed God had brought me back here for this moment.

I entered the trophy room. When I stepped into the dining room, only two hunters were there. The dining room was empty. Most of the hunters were already out in the brush hunting. I saw Josh and Tommy at our back table. I headed straight to them.

I could see, as I got closer, they were wondering why I was wearing camouflage, especially since I was supposed to be leaving for Austin this morning. Josh stood up and shook my hand when I arrived at the table.

"So, what's up with the camo this morning, my man?" Josh asked me.

I looked at Josh and then at Tommy. "I have a slight change of plans this morning."

"I need your room no later than noon today," Tommy said. "No exceptions."

"No problem. I'll get everything out of there and put it in my truck after we eat breakfast."

"Okay, good. So, what's up?" Tommy asked.

"Yes, what's your change of plans, brother?"

I looked over at Josh. "I want you to take me to the 52-Pasture this morning after we're done with breakfast."

"I thought we were finished in the 52. I thought we were done looking for your stag," Josh answered.

"We don't have time for any of this," Tommy said. He sounded frustrated.

"We are finished, Tommy. I just have one more place I want to look."

"Where's that?" Josh asked.

"It's in the middle to south, central west, over by the deep ravine."

"That area has already been searched a hundred times," Tommy said. He was clearly upset and impatient.

"He's right. That central west area has been walked over and searched many, many times, probably more times than any other area in the past seven weeks. Also, we flew that area for twenty minutes yesterday. The pilot hovered over it, and we saw every inch of that place. Your stag's not there, my friend," Josh said.

"I believe he is. And I intend to go back to look for him for one last hour before I leave this ranch," I said.

Neither Tommy nor Josh liked the idea.

"We don't have time to take you to the 52," Tommy stated. He was getting angry.

"Then I'll take myself."

"What makes you so sure that you believe your stag is there?" Josh asked.

"Because God told me," I said.

Josh and Tommy's jaws dropped. They looked at me like I was crazy.

"Do what?" Tommy asked.

"God told you what?" Josh asked me in disbelief.

I looked at both of them.

"I know it sounds crazy and probably unbelievable, but yes, I'm telling both of you that I believe God has told me where I'll find my red stag."

Tommy was still looking at me like I was insane. Josh looked at me and then over at Tommy.

"Tommy, let me take him."

"What?" Tommy shook his head with an emphatic *no*. "This is absolutely crazy."

Then, Josh leaned over to Tommy and whispered something.

"Absolutely not," Tommy answered. "No, no, no."

Staring at me, I could see Josh was conflicted. He didn't know what to do.

I stepped toward Tommy. "Come on. It's just for a couple of hours. Give me one more chance to find my stag."

Tommy shook his head no.

Staring at me for several seconds, Josh turned and made his case. "Look, Tommy, for several weeks now, I've needed to go repair a couple of water troughs in that 52-Pasture. No hunters are in the 52 today. I'll need to take two ranch hands with me to fix the troughs. I can drop Mr. Akins off in the central west along the main road, take an hour or so to get the water troughs fixed and working, and then come back by where I dropped him off and get Mr. Akins back here to the lodge so we can get him on his way by noon," he said.

At this point, I was sure Tommy would agree to almost anything just to get me out of his hair. He stared at Josh while he thought it over. He looked over at me.

"And this is going to be the last time you look for your lost stag on this ranch?"

"Yes, sir. This is my last go at it."

"I really feel like this is a waste of time," Tommy replied indignantly. He sat back in his chair, thinking.

After a few long seconds, Tommy nodded his head at me. "Okay then, fine. This is your last chance, and that's it. Go with Josh and get back here fast."

"Thank you," I said.

Tommy turned to Josh. "Take Pacho and Roberto," he stated firmly. "They're out there waiting for me by my truck."

7:33 a.m. We were finished eating. I stood first. Tommy and Josh followed suit.

"We'll all be back here by 10:30," Josh told Tommy.

"Then get it done and get back here. We need to get this behind us. I need those boys on those big tractors all day today."

"I understand," Josh replied. "We'll be back soon."

Tommy was clearly upset and unhappy. He exited the lodge quickly.

I walked straight to my room, retrieved my things, and loaded everything into my pickup truck. I waited for Josh in front of the lodge. A few minutes later, he showed up with the two ranch hands.

7:40 a.m. We were on our way to the 52 with Josh driving so fast, the caliche roads could barely hold the vehicle.

It was a wild ride, but we were soon at the iron gate. We waited on Pacho to open the gate and then close and lock it back. Two miles after we entered the big 52-Pasture, I began to watch for the right location. I knew it was in the middle of the southern end of the central west. As we got closer, I suddenly recognized the spot.

"Let me out right here."

Josh jammed on the brakes, and the truck skidded to a stop.

"This is it."

I swung open my door and jumped out. Josh checked his watch.

"8:26 a.m. I'll pick you up right here at 9:45," he said.

"No problem." I winked at him. "Thanks for your help this morning."

"What help?" He smiled. "The water troughs really do need fixing."

I smiled back at him. "I know I'm going to find him this morning. God told me exactly where he is."

Josh nodded at me as I closed the truck door. I could tell he didn't know what to think about what was going on. I was guessing he was almost convinced I had lost my mind.

As I walked around the back of the vehicle, I looked at the two ranch hands sitting in the bed of the pick-up truck. Pacho and Roberto stared back at me. I stopped for a moment and smiled at them. They smiled back. "I know you both helped me look for my lost red stag yesterday," I said.

They both nodded. "Yes, sir," they answered.

"I appreciated your help."

"Thank you, sir."

I looked them in the eyes. "I believe God has told me where my red stag is located," I said to them. "I'm going to find him this morning," I added.

They both stared back at me, but neither one said a word.

I smiled at both of them. I could see it in their eyes. *Este gringo está muy loco.* And I can't say I blamed them.

I waved at Josh and the two ranch hands before quickly turning toward the brush.

"Good luck to you, my brother. Remember to be here at 9:45 a.m. for me to pick you up," Josh yelled out the truck window.

I gave him a thumb's up.

"Don't be late."

I glanced back toward him. "I'll be back here waiting," I said.

His expression took a serious turn. "You be very careful," he yelled. "This is a huge pasture. Don't get lost."

"I'll be all right."

My eyes turned to the game trail. And as I quickened my pace toward the brush, I heard the vehicle start driving away, heading north. I never looked back.

I kept walking until there was no further sound from the truck. I was now officially all alone, and ahead lay the treacherous ravine.

I thought about the helicopter search from the evening before. I thought about how we had carefully searched the area below the big rock. I thought about how we were completely convinced my lost stag was not down there.

As I began moving my way through the ruthless brush, heading to the heavily used game trail to my right, for a slight moment, I questioned what I was doing.

I questioned whether or not I was making this all up. I questioned my sanity. I prayed.

CHAPTER TWENTY-SIX

The ravine was approximately a mile away, through the thick brush down a long sinuous trail, and then across a small clearing. I walked as swiftly as possible, entering the long game trail, then after several minutes, I took another narrow trail through the thick brush that led me straight west for a quarter of a mile. I was getting closer to the ravine now.

While I walked, I recalled the first time I hunted the 52-Pasture and Josh's strict warning about never going down into the deep ravine.

"It's way too dangerous. Nobody goes down in that death hole. It's like committing suicide," Josh had said. "Not even the Indians went down in there. It's called 'no man's land' for a reason."

His warnings were now ringing in my ears.

I still had another two hundred yards to the rock.

I maneuvered slowly through the brush, taking my time, wanting to hurry but knowing not to rush it.

8:57 a.m. I was at the big rock now. Forty-eight minutes left to search—it wasn't much time, and I began to feel the pressure.

On this ranch, my friends Mr. Randolph, Josh, and Tommy were the bosses. I was obligated to follow their exact instructions or risk losing my right to ever come back to this ranch. I understood they had legal and safety reasons for this and that, because of those reasons, their words were final.

But, because I felt I was being driven by something much larger than that, I intentionally had not told them where I was going this morning—they would have vetoed it. I knew, without any doubt, they would absolutely prohibit me from going down into that treacherous ravine where I was headed.

I also knew the omission of my destination this morning was not an act of dishonesty or disrespect to my friends. This was not about them. This was between God and me. By this time, I was now sure that all of this was God's way to help make me a better person. This was a test of my belief and trust in Him. It was never about the hunt or the stag—it was all about me putting my life in God's hands. It was my opportunity to experience the Lord like I never had before.

I sat down for a brief moment on the rock, more to build up my courage than to rest. Every instinct I had told me not to go down into that great abyss.

I believed and trusted what God had told me more than I feared what the formidable ravine had in store for me.

After that last message in my room, I removed all doubts about whether or not it was actually God talking to me. I was positive it was God. I knew exactly what He instructed me to do.

But deep inside my gut, I couldn't imagine God telling me to go down there.

For all I had heard and seen of this dangerous place, it did occur to me that—no offense to God, but what if it was just my mind playing tricks on me? After all, it wasn't like I knew how God's voice actually sounded.

I stood and walked to the edge of the ravine, looking down into the jaws of that intimidating place; it wouldn't be far-fetched to imagine the possibility it was the devil himself sending me down there. But, in my heart, I knew better. I knew my stag was down there, and I knew it was God who answered my prayer, and I knew it was God who took His time to point me in the right direction, more so with my life than the stag, but with the stag as well. When I decided this was God's way of testing my faith and trust, I sat down on the edge of the cliff and looked down over the side.

My stomach knotted.

You can do this, I told myself. *Come on. You can do it. God is with you.*

9:05 a.m. I hesitated. And then, I clearly heard the voice. "Go down there."

I prayed and told God I heard Him, and I knew He was with me. I adjusted my cap, took a deep breath, sitting on the edge of the cliff, ready to slide off and take whatever consequences befell me. I hesitated, looked down one more time, tried to envision some sort of a plan of descent, but nothing made any sense. There was no easy way to do this. In fact, there appeared no way to do it at all.

"Heavenly Father, I don't think my body can handle this," I prayed.

"Go down there," the voice said.

"It's too steep and dangerous. It'll kill me."

"Your stag is there."

"What if I walk down to the shallow part of the ravine and come in there?"

"You will never find him," the voice boomed.

"Okay. Please keep me safe, dear God."

At this point, I realized what a physical and mental challenge this whole experience had been. It was an emotional roller coaster that left me feeling conflicted about so many things, from my faith to the underlying reasons I was unable to give up on what must have appeared to everyone else to be an exercise in futility. I had been angry and, at times, depressed—but mostly, I was just upset and frustrated by the circumstances of the lost stag. As I prayed for the strength to continue, I began to understand that not knowing what had become of the stag haunted me and would continue to haunt me forever if we didn't find him. The more I thought about it, the more I knew that I needed God to help me and to be in my life every day.

And along the journey, I realized my life needed to change. Because now I knew it wasn't about the lost stag at all; it was about me putting my trust and faith in the Lord each day.

"With your help, God, I'm going to do this," I said out loud. I was ready now. I reached down and gripped a gnarly root with my left hand, hung my boots over the edge, and then slid off the cliff.

Everything gave way beneath my feet. I held onto the root, dangling over the cliff by one hand, scrambling to get a toe hold with my boots. I was barely able to hang on with one hand against the gravitational pull of my 215-pound body trying to drag me down.

With my feet thrashing the sheer cliff wall, I reached over with my right hand and got a finger hold on a narrow rock sliver. It was just enough to regain my balance and to give me time to jam the toe of my right boot into a crack. That allowed me to distribute some of the weight from my hands to the rock.

I lowered myself one precious inch at a time, my hands and boots searching for any kind of finger hold or toe hold I could find. I'm not a professional mountaineer by any measure, but when I realized this had turned into a high-skill-level descent, I knew I was fighting for my life.

9:20 a.m. I had descended approximately twenty feet. I saw a small tree growing out of the wall to my left. It looked solid. I caught it tightly with my left hand and began to lower myself.

The weight was too much. The roots gave way. I released my grip. The stunted tree disappeared into the abyss below. My hand swung free. I was losing my balance, but then my left hand somehow managed to get a finger hold on a small crevice between the rocks that saved me.

I held on. Tried to catch my breath and relax. When I looked down, the ravine appeared to be a bottomless pit choked in the dark shadows with trees and brush. I had no idea of its depth. I was praying it wasn't one hundred feet.

I hung there contemplating what to do next. Since I was not a skilled rock climber, I could ill afford to climb down too far and not be able to get back up, and with no way to get to the bottom, I could end up stranded with nowhere to go.

The uncertainty of it all was unnerving. I estimated I had another twenty-five or thirty feet to go, but I had no real idea. I guessed I was almost halfway to the bottom, but I wasn't sure of that either.

I hung there for a couple of minutes—suspended in indecision. I looked up where I had been. It looked impossible to go back up. Then I looked down where I was going. It looked impossible to go down. My whole situation appeared hopeless. My breathing and heart rates were much faster than normal. I took a deep breath, let it out slowly, and tried to regain my composure as I weighed my options.

The only thing I knew to do was pray. And I did. I spoke to God, not really praying, but speaking to Him in my normal voice.

"God, I know you're here with me. I can feel your presence. I know you won't let anything happen to me." My words echoed through the deep canyon. "Give me strength, dear Lord, to finish this."

I gripped the sheer rock wall. My muscles ached and quivered. I could feel my arms and legs tighten into a knot of fatigued muscles. I stared straight down into the black hole below me, terrified.

As I hung there clinging to the wall, the full impact of my situation hit me. No one knew where I was. At first, it was just a passing thought. Now it was real.

I didn't tell Josh where I was going. If I fell and injured myself to the point I couldn't walk, I could die here. If I lost my grip and fell, I could lay crippled and dying with no one who knew where I was and no way to get out on my own. If I didn't bleed to death or starve, I had no way to defend myself against the coyotes. And, since I had been told several times to never go down into this treacherous ravine, it was certain no one would come to this place looking for me. When I realized my best outcome would be to die from the fall, I knew I was in serious trouble.

The clear irony of the red stag and me sharing the same fate, being lost to the world forever, was now a good possibility.

I closed my eyes, and I prayed. This time I wasn't just talking to God—I was praying for my life.

"Dear God, you have my full trust and faith and love. I know you have sent me here for a reason. Thank you for blessing me. I won't let you down."

I hung there for a long time. I guess hoping for God to answer me and give me some direction. When nothing happened, I said the 23 Psalm (KJV):

The Lord is my Shepard, I shall not want, You maketh me lie down in green pastures, You leadeth me beside the still waters, You restoreth my soul, You leadeth me in the paths of Righteousness for Your name's sake. Yea, though I walk through the valley of the shadow of death, I will fear no evil, for thou art with me, thy rod and thy staff they comfort me. Thou preparest a table before me in the presence of my enemies, thou anointest my head with oil, my cup runneth over. Surely goodness and mercy shall follow me all the days of my life and I shall dwell in the house of my Lord for ever and ever. Amen.

9:30 a.m. This time, I was looking for a miracle. I needed God's help to get me safely to the bottom. I opened my eyes. I felt stronger and at peace

My breathing relaxed. I looked down at the wall hoping God would fill my brain with a plan. My arms and hands hurt so bad they were beginning to get numb. My left boot was wedged into a wide crack in the wall. One thing was for certain—I was not going to quit.

I inched my right boot down, found a fragile foothold, and then tested it with more weight until I moved down five more feet.

I groped with one hand and then the other and then did the same with both feet until, inch by inch, I began to make the descent. Progress was slow and uncertain. I went down another five feet. It was taking forever. My wrists and hands were cramping and losing strength.

But, what worried me most were my knees and ankles. Wracked with football injuries and the natural effects of an aging body that had been put through the wringer, I wasn't sure how much more they could take.

Forty feet off to my left and ten feet below me, the tops of several large tree limbs rested against the wall—my way down if I could only reach them. But there was no way. I continued working my way down, inching from one toe hold to one finger hold at a time.

9:35 a.m. Finally, I could see the tall grass and the tops of the prickly brush about ten feet below me. I took another deep breath. I had scaled down the wall fifteen more feet.

Now I was holding on to the wall with all my strength. I had climbed down the wall more than thirty-five feet. I looked around to find anything to help me lower myself down the wall. I saw nothing. There were no roots or jagged rocks or crevices for my fingers—nothing to support my boots. I clung to the wall. I needed to rest. My hands, knees, and body trembled. I knew I couldn't hold on much longer.

"Please help me, God," I shouted.

For a brief moment, I felt a burst of strength. I held on tight. I could only estimate the depth to the floor because it was still not fully visible. I guessed twelve to fifteen feet to the bottom.

If I jumped from where I was, I would likely break a bone or, at the least, sprain an ankle. If I landed wrong, I would surely blow out both of my knees or possibly land on something laying unseen on the floor that might impale me and cause serious injury or death. It wasn't a risk I could afford to take.

It was imperative I find a way to descend the wall a little more to get within a safer height if I fell or had to drop.

I was physically losing my grip and my toe hold. I was running out of options. I struggled to hold on. I pressed my body against the wall to keep from falling. I knew this was it. My strength was going fast.

"Please help me, God," I yelled out. This time I prepared myself for the worst.

And then I felt my fingers losing their grip at the same time my boot slipped from its foothold. I was going to fall. I pushed away from the wall with my right hand as best I could and then began plummeting downward. When I felt my feet contact the brush, I felt my knees twist, but they had not yet buckled. The impact with the brush bounced me off a rock. I tried to tuck and roll but ended up head first in a nest of cactus with thorns piercing my head and shoulders before the momentum carried me to my left against a vicious pile of deadfall.

When I finally came to rest, I was stretched out against a broken limb beneath a mesquite tree with its thorns impaled into my back.

I lay on my side, waiting for the pain to catch up with the injuries. My knees felt like they had been pounded with a sledgehammer. I looked down at my legs, dreading the thought of the sight of a bone, but there was no compound fracture and no blood, so I attempted to stand. My knees now buckled under the weight. I crawled to a big rotten log and pulled myself into a sitting position, and then took a deep breath. The high grass was lying over me. I looked back up at the cliff and the long drop. All in all, I was lucky.

I was down in the deep ravine and still alive.

I tried to stand. My knees throbbed and wanted to buckle. I hesitated for a minute, then tried again as I began to feel stronger, and then rose to my feet.

Here I was, in the depths of no man's land, looking up at the sheer rock walls that gave the place its name.

As ominous a place as this was, I felt God's presence as I took my first step through the brush. I immediately noticed the random water puddles. My eyes searched for snakes. I arbitrarily chose a direction, navigated slowly around a stand of mountain laurels, and investigated everything that looked promising in those first five steps.

Nothing.

I knew Josh would be waiting for me on the road in a couple of minutes. I was running out of time. I took two steps to my right and stopped. My eyes scoured the brush for ten seconds. I thought I saw something out of the corner of my eye. Nothing.

Finally, I turned my head two inches to the right and peered into the high weeds and shadowed brush. I looked, adjusted my position slightly, and barely saw what I thought were the crowns of a pair of antlers. They were less than ten feet in front of me but well-hidden in a persimmon grove. I moved in closer. From this angle, the antlers looked massive. But, I had been disappointed before.

When I was on top of the antlers, I reached down into the persimmon grove, got a firm grip on them, and began pulling them out of the tangled undergrowth that concealed them. All I could see was a section of the antlers and a portion of the skull. If the rest of the carcass was buried here, I couldn't see it.

My heart raced as I pulled on the antlers. *Was this really my stag?* I would soon find out. I wrestled with the antlers until my arms were exhausted but, when I had them freed and stepped back to look at them, I saw the signature large drop tine coming off the right beam.

It was him. This was my red stag.

9:45 a.m. Friday, December 13, 2019. The skull and enormous antlers were now resting firmly and solidly in my hands.

I dropped to my knees. I felt a weight had lifted from my shoulders.

Tears filled my eyes. I was overcome with gratitude.

"Thank you for this miracle, dear God," I shouted. "Thank you for your divine intervention and for this miracle."

"Your belief and trust have delivered you," the voice said.

"Thank you, God," I answered back.

I was overjoyed and electrified by what had occurred. I was jubilant and thrilled and excited; all rolled into one. I wanted to celebrate this miracle forever. I wanted to sing high praises to God forever. I wanted everyone in the world to know about this wonderful miracle.

"Glory be to God in the highest," I shouted. "Glory be to God in the highest."

The lesson I had learned the day before came back to me. *You don't always have to win to be victorious.* I had trusted in God the day before, accepting a bad result with the hope of being victorious in the end.

Now I knew why God had brought me back to this ranch. He had fulfilled my dreams. He had taken control of my life. He had changed my life with this red stag hunt. He tested my faith beyond anything I could ever begin to understand. He humbled me, He gave me peace of mind, and then He gave me strength. I knew it wasn't about the stag at all—it was about the fulfillment of a need I didn't even know I had. I needed God's guidance every day.

I had prayed about holding these massive antlers for eight weeks, experienced emotional highs and lows like I had never before known them. Now, I rolled over on the ground, draping these antlers over me like a blanket. I knew none of this would have happened without this miracle from God. None of this would have happened without His direct intervention.

I looked at the antlers and I saw them as a symbol from God to remind me and the world of His never-ending presence, and help, and hope, and love for us all.

CHAPTER
TWENTY-SEVEN

When I missed the 9:45 deadline to meet Josh, I tried to call him but had no signal on my cell phone in that deep ravine. Soon after that, Josh and the two ranch hands came looking for me. They drove around honking and shouting for fifteen minutes. When they didn't get a response from me, they were in a panic.

They then parked the truck and set out on foot to try to locate me. I couldn't hear any of this at the time, but I knew they would come looking when I didn't show up at the truck on time. When I finally did hear them calling for me, it was a faint, barely discernable sound coming from a long way off. I shouted out several times, but my voice was lost in the thick undergrowth deep in that chasm where no sound traveled.

I was still overwhelmed with the joy of sitting in the ravine, enjoying this magical moment holding those beautiful, massive antlers in my hands.

In searching for the lost red stag, my situation indicated nothing was ever going to improve or change. The facts suggested my path was going to be a permanent failure. My frustration and anxiety, and sometimes anger had risen to a maximum. I found at this particular time was when God amazed me. He showed up at the very last moment when the odds against me were at their greatest. He turned everything around when the obstacles lying in front of me appeared to be insurmountable. I learned that relying solely on my own determination and abilities and strength was not enough to make things work out for the best. I found that when I came to a dead-end, when it appeared that nothing was going right, and, at the very last moment, when everything looked bleak and impossible, that is when God showed up and did the impossible. He performed a miracle. He changed my life.

Josh and the two men knew the general area where I had gone that morning. They would naturally come in this direction and split up, I calculated. But I knew they would never consider the idea that I was down in the ravine. After all, no one ever went in there.

But the fact that I could faintly hear their voices getting slowly closer reassured me they were going in the right direction and would soon be close enough to hear me. I knew it was just a matter of minutes.

But, something seemed wrong. I no longer heard their shouts, and it seemed like it had been a lot longer than I expected for them to cover the distance I knew they had to travel to get close to the ravine.

Because the ravine was "no man's land," I decided to pray for God's help in guiding them to me.

And then, I heard Pacho's voice coming a little closer now.

"Mr. Akins, where are you? Can you hear me?"

I shouted back, but my muffled voice seemed to die in the ravine. There was no response. They were still too far away. I waited for them to get closer. After what I considered enough time for them to be within range, I shouted up toward the rim.

"I've found my red stag," I shouted. "I've found my stag."

No one answered me, but I could hear them talking about a hundred yards above me.

"Where are you, Mr. Akins?" Roberto shouted.

They've heard me. I was elated.

"I'm in the ravine. I've found my stag," I hollered. "I've found my stag."

I could hear Roberto yelling across the ravine to Josh.

"We can hear him over here," he screamed across the divide.

"Where is he?" Josh yelled back. "Is he hurt?"

"No. I'm in the ravine. I've found my stag," I shouted out. "I'm down here in the ravine."

"I heard him again," Roberto yelled.

"Where is he?"

"We don't know. We can't tell where he is," Pacho yelled.

"What's he saying?" Josh shouted back.

I could tell Pacho and Roberto were walking southwest and getting closer to the edge of the ravine.

"I think he's in the ravine," Pacho hollered.

"What? No way."

I could tell Josh was coming toward the ravine, heading directly in my direction. He was still at least seventy-five yards away from the edge of the ravine.

"Where are you?" Josh shouted.

"I'm down here in the ravine," I yelled. "I've found my stag."

Josh was still unable to hear me.

"Are you sure he's in the ravine?" Josh shouted to the ranch hands.

"Yes, sir."

Pacho and Roberto were now standing near the edge of the ravine, peering down into the gorge.

"He's down in there somewhere."

Josh's voice was very close now.

"Why on earth is he in that ravine?"

"I've found my red stag."

"I think he's saying he found his red stag," Roberto shouted across the ravine to Josh.

"He did what?"

"He found his red stag."

"No way," Josh shouted.

"I found my red stag, Josh," I yelled out. "I found my stag."

"Unbelievable," Josh hollered. I could hear the excitement in his voice. "That's incredible."

From where I sat in this deep gulch, I could see the sheer cliffs on each side of me. I was now looking straight up at the top of the cliff toward the east side. I could clearly see Pacho and Roberto. They were looking down into this perilous ravine trying to locate me. I waved at them, but they didn't see me.

I laid the heavy antlers down and moved a few feet to my left. I waved. Finally, they could barely see me. They waved back at me and pointed.

"We can see him," Pacho yelled to Josh.

"Where is he?" Josh hollered back from the west edge of the ravine, looking down, trying to locate my position.

Pacho and Roberto leaned over the edge.

"He's all covered up by the brush. He's got the antlers," Roberto hollered.

"This is crazy. This is truly amazing," Josh shouted. He was still leaning over the west edge of the ravine, looking down and searching for me. He looked back across the ravine at the two ranch hands.

"Where is he?"

They pointed down into the thick, impenetrable brush at the bottom of the ravine.

I was waving at Josh. When he saw me, he waved back.

"What are you doing down there? I told you never to go in there."

"I found him, Josh," I yelled. "God showed me where the lost red stag was, and I found him."

I tried to lift up the antlers so he could see them, but they were too heavy.

"I just can't believe this," he yelled out.

"It's truly unbelievable, isn't it?" I hollered.

I could see he was shocked. And I could see the emotion in his eyes.

"I can't believe you found your stag," his voice cracked. "This is truly amazing."

"It's a miracle," I yelled up to him. "A real miracle."

"Yes, it is." Josh stared down at me. "Yes, it is," he roared.

"No one back at the lodge is going to ever believe this," he shouted.

"I need some help to get this big boy out of here. These antlers weigh a ton," I shouted, looking down at the monster rack. "I can barely move them."

They all looked over the edge from where they stood.

"There's no way any of us can get down there from here," Josh hollered.

"I did it," I yelled back.

"And you're one crazy dude, my brother."

I laughed, "Just come get me out of here."

"Copy that," Josh shouted down to me.

He looked across the ravine at Pacho and Roberto. Josh was gesturing toward the northwest.

"Let's head back to the truck. We'll go down in the ravine from the shallow end," he yelled. He was still pointing to the north when Pacho and Roberto turned and began walking.

And then Josh looked back down at me.

"We're coming to help you, brother. We'll be coming in from the north end," he shouted.

The two ranch hands had already started north. Josh was still looking down at me.

"It's going to take us a little while to get back here to you, at least an hour or more. Don't go anywhere."

I laughed. "No problem, brother. I'll be here waiting on y'all, holding on to my red stag." I gave him a big grin.

He smiled back at me. "You sit tight. We'll be back down there with you in a little while."

Josh turned to the north, waved, and then disappeared.

It was a long hike for them to reconnect with the shallow end of the ravine. Josh said an hour. It would take all of that and more to negotiate access through the uncut brush. I was content to wait. My faith and trust in God had rewarded me. I had a lot to think about and a lot to be thankful for, not the least of which was the opportunity to finally see these spectacular antlers up close and to actually be touching them. As far as I was concerned, sitting here deep inside this ravine, just me with my red stag, was a once-in-a-lifetime moment.

After an hour and a half of hard work, Josh and the two ranch hands, hacking their way with machetes, finally broke through to my position.

11:48 a.m. I stood up and smiled when I saw them coming. Josh rushed toward me like a bear and threw his arms around me. He told me he had already called Tommy and Mr. Randolph and told them the good news.

"Everyone is going crazy. Everybody wants to see the stag. The whole ranch is busting with excitement. They're ready to have a celebration at the lodge. It's going to be an amazing party and celebration. No one can believe you found your monster stag. It just doesn't seem real to any of us. It's unbelievable," he said.

"It is a miracle. It's nothing short of a miracle from God," I said.

Pacho and Roberto stood quietly, admiring the massive, thick, giant antlers. Josh reached over and shook my hand.

"I still can't believe this," he said.

"I told you all that God told me where the stag was."

"Yes, you did."

We were both beyond excited. Finding the lost stag was something out of a dream. This was an extraordinary event. There are no words to adequately describe the moment.

And then the reality of our circumstances set in. We still had to get these enormous antlers out of here.

The weight of the antlers alone would have been a serious enough challenge but, when you added in size and the cumbersomeness of them, it was clear this was going to be tough. We struggled just to clear them from the brush and pick them up. It was decided that Pacho and Roberto would alternate carrying the antlers on their backs while Josh and I, on the way out, would hack a wider path with the machetes. As exhausting and difficult as it was to extricate ourselves from the grip of that inhospitable place they called "no man's land," it turned out to be the favorite journey of my life. We waded through the vines and thorns and brush, with Josh and me reliving every detail of the hunt that got us here. We laughed loudly and enjoyed telling the greatest hunting story of our lives. We knew this was a moment and an experience we shared that would be seared into our memories forever. This was a life-changing adventure, and we both knew it. When we exited the ravine at the shallow end, Josh pointed to a rock in the clearing where the sun shone on it, and the tall grass framed it like a Norman Rockwell painting.

"Set the skull and antlers on that rock," he told Pacho, who was carrying it.

We watched as Pacho and Roberto placed the stunning rack, so the sun cut across the surface of it and lit it in an artistic light.

"Perfect. We need to get some pictures of you with the stag," Josh said.

I was more than happy to do that. Josh took photos from several different angles while I was still trying to catch up with the reality of it all. By all measures, I should have been in my truck close to pulling into my driveway in Austin right now, but here I was.

All I could think about was God telling me in my room this morning to put on my hunting shirt because I would be taking photos with my red stag today.

They say God works in mysterious ways. Amen to that—this experience is an undeniable testimony that God does indeed work in mysterious ways.

I knew God had blessed me.

After he finished taking pictures of me and the stag, Josh stuck his finger in my face.

"I thought I told you never to go down in that wicked ravine," he growled angrily.

I was shocked.

His expression was so serious. He looked really mad at me.

I stared straight into his eyes. I smiled at him, but he still looked angry.

"I'm telling you, no one has ever gone down into that deep ravine," Josh shouted at me. "Not even the Indians." He kept frowning and pointing his finger at me for several more seconds. "You could have easily killed yourself."

I didn't say a word.

He was fuming and looked irritated.

Then, a big smile lit up Josh's face. I grinned back at him. Josh let out a big laugh. The jokester had his fun. I could see he was kidding me.

"Yes, sir, I do remember you telling me to never go down in that ravine," I replied to Josh. "But, you were overruled when God Almighty told me otherwise."

We both laughed.

Josh put his arm around me as we walked toward the truck. "Well, brother, honestly, what you did was really stupid, dangerous, and dumb," he said.

I looked over at him. "I only did what God told me."

We laughed again.

"You're one lucky, crazy dude!" He smiled at me. "I still can't believe God showed you where the red stag was," he added.

I nodded. "Believe in miracles, brother!"

"Copy that."

Then we shook hands and made our way the final two hundred yards to the truck carrying the antlers like the prize they were.

Josh and I watched as Roberto and Pacho lifted the enormous rack carefully and placed it gently in the bed of the pickup truck. It was obvious these two men were honored and extremely grateful to have participated in touching and carrying the stag's antlers.

And, after they had secured the antlers in the back of the pickup, the two men kneeled and prayed. And then, they rose, crossed themselves, and kissed their fingers—they knew they had just witnessed something sacred. I was moved by their reverence and innocent acknowledgment of what they had been so much a part of. Both of them turned to me, their eyes filled with reverence and deep respect.

"Mr. Akins, these antlers are holy and sacred," Roberto said.

"They have been blessed by our divine God," Pacho stated.

These two statements were touching and profound. Another moment to this hunt I will never forget. My throat tightened.

"Amen," I said to them. "Amen."

May the glory of God and the blessings of heaven always be with us, I thought. I truly held God's intervention as a sign of faith, hope, and love for all of us.

Twelve days later, on Christmas day, reflecting back on it, I knew the four of us had participated in something we are sure was a miracle from God. Words fall short, and the intensity of it pales in the face of what we experienced out there that day. But, after all we had witnessed and been through, when we sat in that truck pulling away from the deep ravine, four men shared a mutual realization that, for all the troubles we are experiencing in our world today, one thing gives us hope—God is alive and well.

———

"I will prepare and someday my chance will come. That some achieve great success, is proof to all that others can achieve it as well."

ABRAHAM LINCOLN

———

"The time is always right, to do what is right. The ultimate measure of a man is not where he stands in moments of comfort and convenience, but where he stands at times of challenge and controversy."

MARTIN LUTHER KING, JR.

———

"What you think and what you believe is who you are."

HEAD COACH RAY AKINS

———

"The harder you work, the luckier you become."

HEAD COACH DARRELL K. ROYAL

———

"There is one God looking down on us all. We are all Children of one God."

GERONIMO, APACHE WAR CHIEF

———————

"Frustration, depression, fear, anxiety, stress, anger, failure, obstacles, or limitations will never keep us from our destiny.

In Romans it says, "What shall we say to these things? If God is for us, who can be against us?" God closes doors that no man can open, and He opens doors that no man can shut. Only God controls those situations, opportunities, and victories that lay in our path. And when the time comes, I believe our God, through His divine powers, will close and open every door in our destiny."

MARTY AKINS
12.25.2019